Praise for *Nobody's Horses*

"*Nobody's Horses* are everybody's horses. Protect them. This book comes from the heart of a veterinarian who gave an oath, and meant it."

—Michael Ackerman, DVM,
Manager, Lextron Animal Health, Inc.

"*Nobody's Horses* is a wonderful story that reveals the author's care and concern for the horses in every chapter, and also reveals elements of the wild horse programs to which few have been privy. Dr. Höglund shows through history and contemporary drama the events of the wild horse capture and the horses' intimate ties to human lives."

—Nancy Kate Diehl, MS, VMD

A four-year-old stallion calls to his harem.
Photo by Don Höglund and White Sands Missile Range.

NOBODY'S HORSES

*The Dramatic Rescue
of the
Wild Herd of White Sands*

DON HÖGLUND

FREE PRESS
New York   London   Toronto   Sydney

*f*P

FREE PRESS
A Division of Simon & Schuster, Inc.
1230 Avenue of the Americas
New York, NY 10020

Copyright © 2006 by Don Höglund, DVM

FREE PRESS and colophon are trademarks
of Simon & Schuster, Inc.

For information regarding special discounts for bulk purchases,
please contact Simon & Schuster Special Sales at
1-800-456-6798 or business@simonandschuster.com

Designed by Kyoko Watanabe

Manufactured in the United States of America

10   9   8   7   6   5   4   3   2   1

Library of Congress Cataloging-in-Publication Data
is available

ISBN-13: 978-0-7432-9088-3
ISBN-10: 0-7432-9088-7

For Salt Creek Sam, Jimmy Brown, and Friends

CONTENTS

PART III

The Light of Midnight

In wildness is the preservation of the World.

—HENRY DAVID THOREAU

INTRODUCTION

When they desperately needed an advocate, nearly two thousand wild horses on the White Sands Missile Range in New Mexico didn't belong to anyone. They were trapped on a two-million-acre tract of unforgiving desert and mountain, their lives strangely entwined with the history of the Wild West and of the military installation and its top-secret weapons testing.

When scores of the horses died in the summer of 1994, the Army made it clear that they were not in the horse business. Management in the wild was not a viable option for the horses on White Sands. Unable to fund a large-scale sanctuary off-range that would maintain the horses, the commanders of White Sands planned to round them up and remove them.

Although roundups are traumatic ventures that disrupt family groups, rescue was the only timely resolution of the horses' problems. Thousands of taxpayers wanted to adopt those that could be trained and self-supporting sanctuaries would welcome the remaining three hundred wild horses. With the good and productive assistance of concerned wild horse protection groups, the U.S. Army, and a team of wranglers and biologists, we began the dramatic rescue of the wild herds of White Sands.

PROLOGUE

I was not ready for a surprise on the morning after our first capture of White Sands wild horses. The roundup had taken the better part of a day, plus three helicopters, six ATVs, and one dozen men, but we had corralled more than one hundred starving horses. It was supposed to get easier after that adrenaline-pumping ordeal. But when I returned to the corral, I found a surprise waiting for me on the other side of the gate: a tiny sorrel foal, just hours old, alone and bleating for his mother. Two-thirds legs, knock-kneed, and wide-eyed, he was deeply distressed.

As I approached, the baby turned his face and ears toward me, willing to ask even a two-legged stranger for help. His face was beautiful, delicate with a white blaze down his nose, and long eyelashes out of all proportion with the rest of his features. He mouthed his lips and gums in subordination as foals do and then quieted as I neared him.

I stepped inside the fence to examine him up close as he sniffed me curiously. By the look of his ruffed coat and the dried sweat caked on his sides, he'd probably searched through the night for his mother before coming to the barrier in desperation. Severely dehydrated, he stood still while I looked him over. His umbilical cord had broken off recently just an inch from his gaunt belly. I bent down and put my nose to his mouth, trying to discern if he had nursed at all before ending up here alone, but he did not smell of mare's milk, and he nuzzled my ear hopefully. I looked more closely at his eyes. They were opaque. The colt was blind.

I spread both arms wide, knelt down, and wrapped one arm around the abandoned baby's neck and the other around his rear, then lifted and carried him to a small, separate enclosure where he'd be safe from the frequent scuffles and commotion in the herd. I hurried to my veterinary truck to retrieve a bottle, a blanket, water, and a supply of mare's milk.

I'd planned to serve as a cowboy, a veterinarian, a leader, a laborer, and a negotiator on this job rescuing wild horses. Now, it appeared that I was going to be a nanny, too.

PART I

---◆---

Out West

"You become responsible, forever,
for what you have tamed."

—Antoine de Saint-Exupéry

Chapter 1

Outlaws Upon Outlaws

Years before the rescue of the wild herd of White Sands, I was working under federal contract in New Mexico, watching a beautiful iron-red colt run in a round corral made of eight-foot dirt walls. His hooves stabbed the earth and propelled him to full stride in his effort to get away from where I stood in the middle. Rail-thin, but with powerful hindquarters and wide-set shoulders, he stretched thirteen hands and framed seven hundred pounds of taut muscle. He flared his nostrils and sucked the crisp / clean / pure / high mountain air. I balanced on one foot, turning clockwise in the center as the wild-eyed mustang circled the perimeter, always twenty feet from my nose. Terrified at his lack of options, ears rotating like radar dishes, he was a force to be respected.

Until three days before, this young horse had never been confined. He'd had full run of much of the state of Nevada, living on public lands and sharing the wide Western sky and open desert with his own herd and upwards of twenty-five thousand other wild horses. In his two years of age he'd most likely never seen a fence he couldn't jump or a human he couldn't get away from. After being caught northwest of Elko during a federally mandated capture, he had survived a twenty-two-hour ride in the back of an eighteen-wheeler lowboy crammed cheek-by-jowl with his herdmates. All of them had been run through a narrow chute where they were given medical treatments. He had been freeze-branded, vaccinated, and made to swallow a nasty-tasting de-worming medicine. After all that, the colt was let loose in the middle of my corral.

He was desperate to be free again, but no matter where he moved he could get no more than twenty feet from me. The high walls allowed no sightlines to the outside; he could run only in dizzying circles or stop dead in his tracks. But still there was the unnerving presence of a man in the space with him. That problem was more than his brain could comfortably process.

Perched on a catwalk above the walls were more than thirty men. They were a rough-looking crew. All of them wore blue jeans and T-shirts, though some had cut the sleeves off their shirts or rolled them up to expose tattoos on muscular biceps tanned from long days in the sun. They represented nearly every ethnicity, from a slight, wiry Mexican named Angel, to Bubba, a square-jawed, muscle-bound Anglo biker from the Mississippi lowlands. Some of the guys wore sweat-stained straw hats; others had bandannas around their foreheads. Already at midmorning on this fall day, the men were sweaty from the glaring New Mexico heat, and dirty from the fine dust kicked up by the horse.

At some point in the training, the horse must
stand tied. This mustang is not quite ready.
Courtesy of George Ancona.

Some of the men sat attentively. A few leaned back and looked indifferent, but all eyes were on that horse and his futile attempts to run as far and as fast as his legs would carry him. This was a group that knew how it felt to be forced into confinement. With the exception of one man, a guard who kept a watchful eye not on the mustang but on the crowd, my audience was a group of inmates of the New Mexico Correctional Facility at Santa Fe.

As the mustang circled the ring forty, then fifty times, I spoke in a low, even voice, explaining the importance of staying calm when faced with a panicked horse. I kept my words few—silence was best—to avoid agitating the mustang further. Both the men and the horse listened closely. They always did. The men wanted to learn, and horses are prey animals that watch and listen to everything. Just as a bull will dip the horn he intends to gore with, a horse's eyes tell you where he wants to go, I explained. There's a fine line between controlling a horse and damaging his spirit by dominating him. The solid round corral offers control; the circling the colt was doing was subtly bending his will to flee. The rudeness of using a rope tied hard and fast would have pulled him up short. That's domination, and it can ruin a horse's character and can also give him a debilitating neck injury. At some point the horse must learn to yield to the constraint of a halter or reins, but in the beginning a trainer simply has to create a safe environment for gentling. He has to let the horse find the path of least resistance.

I'd helped establish the National Wild Horse Prison Inmate Program at three facilities in New Mexico at the start of 1987, and I'd been a part of the actual training and health program for over two years. Working with horses had proved to be a very effective way of reaching the convicted felons. Most of them didn't give a damn about people, but they were fascinated by horses and wanted to learn how to tame the wildness. Some were initially fearful, some inclined to be heavy-handed, but most were able to unearth reserves of patience and empathy with which they'd otherwise lost touch in prison, and sometimes long before, as they learned to gentle and train the powerful, instinct-driven horses. They learned to civilize animals that had been yanked from their lives in the wild after one year or twenty years of free roaming so they could live peacefully in a barn and paddock. Though I didn't particularly like how the men came to be inmates, we were all in agreement that the horses that came into these corrals were worth our attention and time. Outlaws have a natural kinship with other outlaws.

The inmates were trainers because they'd asked to be. The job of gentling the horses wasn't a chore like picking up litter on the highway, spending hours in the prison laundry, or being assigned to assemble furniture, which their peers did day in and day out. They signed up for this duty and then waited their turn to be chosen to work with the horses. Only inmates with a clean behavior record and those nearing the end of their sentences were permitted in the program; none was considered a flight risk. They had a great deal of responsibility—and also much autonomy—compared to those in many other prison work programs.

Each of us in the program was willing to risk bodily harm, which came frequently and in many forms in this work, and to sacrifice his time and energy to help the horses. Inmates who found their way into the program who were not willing to sacrifice themselves were quickly reassigned. That was rare, and cuts, scrapes, bruises, and even the occasional broken bone endured while working with the wild horses were worn with pride.

The mustangs were slated to be put up for adoption after training, and potential adopters would choose animals that appeared accustomed to people. Some inmates were allowed to attend nearby adoptions, such as the state fair in Albuquerque twenty minutes north of one training center at Los Lunas. They took great pride when their horses readily took to halter, led well, and even better, if the horse allowed a rider. When one of their horses was adopted, the men walked tall and worked with confidence. They seemed most gratified when they heard the new adopter call the horse by his inmate-given name: *The Kid, Streak, Blaze, Bonnie, Clyde,* and *Outlaw.*

The colt I had in the ring would be a challenge, though, I thought as I watched him gallop, his mouth frothing and nostrils flaring. Horses in this frame of mind, desperately trying to escape, generally do not find homes.

"All horses move away from the greatest pressure, unless they're taught otherwise," I explained quietly, as the mustang began to slow to a canter. He was certainly not tired—I'd seen horses like this run full-out for ten miles without tiring—but he was getting weary of making this effort and going nowhere. I took a small step to the left, and the colt stopped in his tracks, raising a cloud of dust that drifted over the men's heads. The horse weaved in place, shifting his balance from leg to leg. His muscles trembled, his veins engorged, and his eyes moved back and forth repetitively, a horizontal nystagmus we veterinarians call it. The low atmospheric pressure of the Santa Fe 7,200-foot altitude and his panicked circling had caused him to breathe rapidly, a sign that could mean he was dizzy, so I sent him running the opposite direction a few revolutions to unwind his middle ear. I stopped him again.

"He has an ear and an eye glued on me, watching for signals," I continued, and then took one step backward. The inmates leaned in, waiting, curious to see how the horse would respond, looking back and forth from the horse to me. They held their breath, although a few wouldn't have minded seeing the colt come charging at me. The mustang turned his head to face me and plant both eyes on me, gauging the distance between us. Then he leaned forward. The crew on the catwalk muttered among themselves, eyeing the horse and assessing his demeanor. I hoped they tucked my instruction into their mental inventory of training tools: Take a small step back and wait for the horse to move in. They'd be able to use it later, and they wanted to know as much as they could before each took his own turn standing in the middle of a corral with a wild horse.

"Once the trainer steps back, the greatest pressure on the horse is from the solid wall," I continued. "The horse steps away from it, and inadvertently toward the trainer. Since he can't pass through or over a properly built wall, and because it's his inherent behavior to move, he comes toward you. That's the beginning of getting the animal to understand that it's safe to be near you. This way he thinks moving is his idea, and for it to work, you have to be reliable, consistent, and fair." The horse sighed, and a number of inmates nodded in agreement. "One signal from you means only one thing. Don't gesture to go and whoa at the same time." Giving conflicting signals is a sign of a poor trainer. Quiet, slow, sure movements provide a better connection between trainers and a new recruit.

"Make the wrong thing hard and the right thing easy." I was talking to them just as much as I was talking to the horse. "If he does what you want, don't continue to stimulate him." I listened to the men mutter among themselves, "Running makes him dizzy. Standing quiet is easy, for everyone."

A few in this group of inmates were new today, but I singled out an experienced one I knew to join me in the corral without getting himself killed. "Jimmy, come down here and work this horse," I said.

Jimmy Begay was at times my biggest complication in this program, and at other times my greatest asset. Jimmy had perfected passive aggression, was reflexively opinionated, but he understood the horses intuitively. I'd made the mistake of greeting his group on his first day in the training facility with a curt "buenos dias," and he'd

Jimmy and his new recruit slowly develop a trust.
Courtesy of George Ancona.

drawn himself to his full height and squared off, looked me in the eye to reply icily, "I am Navajo. I don't speak Spanish." Jimmy's face was lean and angular, with prominent cheekbones and deep-set eyes and the long straight nose of his ancestors. The Navajo Nation, the Diné Bikéyah, or Navajoland, covers more than twenty-seven thousand square miles of unparalleled beauty in Utah, Arizona, and New Mexico and maps more land than ten of the fifty states in America. Jimmy was from the nearby Farmington area in the northwest corner of New Mexico.

With his remark, Jimmy had defied me and conveyed a measure of disdain for his fellow inmates, who were mostly Mexican, and had instantly isolated himself from everyone. Resentful and suspicious, Jimmy distrusted his fellow inmates almost as much as he distrusted me. Yet guarded as he was with people, Jimmy had an ease and agility in working with horses. I glanced up at him on the scaffold where he stood preparing to drop down into the corral at the farthest point. Keeping both eyes on the agitated mustang, he gracefully and quietly leaped down, planting his feet and absorbing the shock of the jump by bending his knees and squatting slightly forward. Slowly he straightened and came alongside me as I took another step back. I was taller and heavier than he was, and wearing boots and a cowboy hat made my six-foot-two frame seem even bigger, but nothing, certainly not size or authority, intimidated Begay. He faked a sidelong glance in my direction and waited for me to move out of his way. I stepped back and he moved forward. The horse watched anxiously, shifting his weight on his front hooves, ready to break back into a full gallop at any second.

I eased through the canted, solid corral gate and let the inmate take over the ring. Lean and muscular, Jimmy was about five-foot-eight, and his rod-straight posture gave him an imposing presence. His black hair in a long braid down his back, a bandanna tied around his head, he moved with precision and dignity, never showing any fear. Many of the other inmates approached a wild horse in the ring with the manner of a doomed gladiator. Not everyone liked Jimmy, but they all respected his fearlessness.

Jimmy had more God-given talent for working with horses than anyone I'd ever met to that date. I had gentled more horses than I could count, but from the first time I saw this inmate step into a corral, I watched closely to see what I could learn from him. Jimmy stood silently in the middle of the ring, breathing evenly, assessing the quivering horse without making eye contact or a sound, looking as though he had all the time in the world. Truth be told, the men gathered around that catwalk had nothing but time, but they were impatient all the same.

The biggest problem the inmates had in training horses was that they moved too fast. Quick movement provokes a horse's powerful instinct to run. Its primary defense is its speed, and horses can run as far and as fast as necessary to avoid any perceived danger. It had taken a team of twenty men, two helicopters, a handful of four-wheel drive trucks, and a painstakingly constructed camouflaged enclosure to capture this mustang with others in his herd. As long as he was intent on running in circles, we would make no progress in training him. Making him stop demanded patience and stillness. Jimmy had both.

Jimmy stood quietly, his muscles loose, his breathing slow. Many inmates made the mistake of holding their breath in corrals with wild horses. In the wild, when a creature holds its breath, there's usually a good reason, like the presence of a predator. So, naturally, when a mustang finds himself trapped in a ring with a creature that's too afraid to breathe, he panics, anticipating a crisis he's sure will ensue.

But Jimmy's horse was listening and watching, snorting and stomping the hot dirt, sending up swirls of dust. An inmate started to speak and Jimmy raised one finger behind him in the direction of the voice, a signal to stop. For a moment, the men were quiet again. I wished they'd shut up that easily for me. The colt cocked one hind leg, looked down and sniffed the dirt, breathing heavily, waiting. Then he launched off to the right, racing around the ring again for a couple minutes. Jimmy calmly circled with him, facing the horse, giving no signal. After twenty revolutions, the inmate

stepped hard to the right, and the horse pulled up as though someone had pulled his emergency brake. Jimmy took a step back and
the colt turned to plant both eyes on him. Then Jimmy retreated to
the far wall, leaned one leg against the adobe, and relaxed even
more. The mustang, relieved at this new safe distance, took a step
toward the middle of the corral, breathed deep, and sighed. Jimmy
sighed with him. The horse's ears shot forward, eyes calmed a bit,
he liked that sigh and preferred the space. The tension eased a little, both inside and outside of the ring.

"I still see the whites of his eyes," Jimmy commented in a low
monotone, keeping his own eyes focused on the horse's movement.
"He knows I'm not some stupid paleface that's gonna hurt him."
Even though Jimmy had learned a lot from me in this program, he
often straddled the line between engaging and baiting me when we
worked together.

"Nah, he's just worried you might try to steal him," deadpanned
another inmate, a chiseled, wiry, swaggering man named Julian, a
blue-eyed direct descendant of the Conquistadors. He often made
a point of reminding us that the mustangs were descended from
horses his people brought to North America, and that the *Natives*
were famous for their facility at stealing the coveted horse stock of
the Spaniards.

"He'd be better off with me," another Native-American man in
the group responded soberly, glaring my way. "My people don't
slaughter good horses."

I had never slaughtered a horse in my life, but this type of comment was thrown my way periodically. Some Native-American
inmates liked to remind me of an incident so etched in their cultural history that it had been elevated to legend. Not surprisingly,
it had been glossed over in my education, as it was not a proud
moment in American history. In short, in 1874, Ranald Mackenzie,
commander of the U.S. Cavalry, tracked a group of Comanche to
a secret camp in Palo Duro Canyon in west Texas. After a battle, the
outnumbered Comanche warriors retreated, leaving behind some
fourteen hundred of their horses, thinking they'd likely be herded

away as spoils of war. Yet, what followed was an abomination: The commander ordered his men to seize and then slaughter the horses. Mackenzie's own men strenuously objected, but over the course of eight hours, more than a thousand horses were shot and left in the desert to rot. It was a heinous tactical move meant to bend the spirit of the Comanche with the message that the cavalry had a capacity for brutality, an act that no one could easily forget, not the men who returned to find the grisly scene, nor those who had carried it out.

A hundred and fifteen years later in New Mexico, the crew who trained horses with me was inclined to compare the government captors of the wild mustangs with Commander Mackenzie and company. In their minds, the solution to the crises of overpopulated wild horses at Palo Duro, and to the captured horses at the correctional facility, and to their own imprisonment was about the same: They should all be left free. The prospect of setting the horses loose came up almost every time we got an especially wild one inside a corral. The inmates debated endlessly about whether a mustang could clear that eight-foot wall and find his way to freedom. Maybe he'd back all the way up to the far wall and approach from just the perfect angle and with just the right velocity. The inmates loved the idea of a great escape. Julian spoke for all of them: "We should just turn him loose. Man, just watch him run right out of this piece of hell. I bet he'd find his way back home in less than a week."

Generally a man of few words, Begay couldn't resist this line of thought. "Yeah, break him out instead of break him in," he replied, his tone soft, his gaze glued to the horse. "How'd you like that?" he asked the wary colt.

"This horse don't belong here," he muttered as he worked his way closer to the animal, at angles, never directly and never staring the horse in the eye. Jimmy closed the distance from yards to feet. He glared over at me and asked, "Why didn't you leave him alone?" as if I'd captured the mustang myself.

"Freedom, yes," I said, "but right now we're trying to save their lives." That was the bottom line at the time. The politics surrounding wild horses governed the law: The law said the government could catch them. Whether the inmates or I liked it, the horses had been captured. Our job was to gentle them, and ultimately to keep them from a slaughterhouse. I pointed for Jimmy to concentrate on the animal.

"So he'll end up in somebody's backyard." Begay knew that adoption was the best option available to the horses that came to this facility, but he regarded potential adopters with suspicion. The inmates often had the opportunity to talk with adopters and told them about each horse's training and temperament, but Jimmy also asked as many questions as he could get away with to find out what kind of life his horses had ahead of them. How much land would the horse have? How much riding? Begay would always try to impress on the adopter that each horse needed plenty of space and freedom.

"Hey, Jimmy," Angel spoke up, leaning over the corral. "You think you're gonna' ride that one tomorrow? I think this might be the one to break your back."

I could tolerate a certain amount of taunting and mocking—two of the main forms of communication the inmates used with each other—but now there was a man in the corral with a skittish, untested seven-hundred-pound horse, and it wasn't the time for it.

"Stop talking and concentrate on that horse, or I'll put another man in there," I ordered. Jimmy stepped from the wall toward the horse, stopping in the center again. The horse's head flew up, watching and waiting and quivering like an exposed nerve. With his arms hanging naturally and his mouth closed, Begay took two steps to the right, and the horse started a slow trot left. It was exactly the way this process was supposed to happen—a slow-growing trust between the horse and the trainer as the horse learns that he can read the man's actions. Begay had spent more than a year in my program, and even when I gave him the worst possible horse to train, that horse turned out the best. His work ethic was second to none.

I turned to the group on the catwalk. "No matter what you intend to teach the horse during the lesson, watch his head, his eyes, and his mouth. He'll tell you what he's thinking. A low head is relaxed, a high head and he's looking for an exit. A smooth, oval-shaped upper eyelid is good. An inverted angle at the front is concern. Chewing is good. A chin smashed to the jaw is fright. Eventually, when you can cover both of his eyes at the same time with your hands and his head stays low, you're trusted."

The men acted as if they knew it all, but I knew they were processing the information. "Keep your hands to yourself, but once he has acknowledged you, never let your horse walk away from you. You control him, and then step away."

The colt slowed his trot and again turned his head to eye Begay. "There are a hundred ways to gentle a horse," I said. "Some are safer than others. Some are more effective, others are quicker. Try them all and choose what works best for the individual horse. But remember, horses watch everything, and they think about it. Their feelings—and they do have feelings—follow their thoughts, which are simple and mechanical and they get them from moment-to-moment memory. Fear and pain produce flight. All of it drives their emotions." I pointed at the cautious colt. "What you do to him may be kind ten times in a row, but he'll remember the one time you lied." I looked around at the men and they nodded. "Whatever you do, do not make the mistake of hitting him in the head. Regaining the trust you lose is near impossible."

The colt swiveled his ears toward Begay, who took a step backward and to the left. The horse stopped in his tracks, then quickly pivoted to face the man. This dead stop might have looked unremarkable, but it held great significance for the horse—this was the moment when the animal began to make decisions and not simply to use its instinctive flight response. This was the moment I lived for. Horse and trainer were beginning to understand each other, a connection had developed.

The horse breathed heavily and Begay took another step backward, away from him. The colt's nostrils flared and he watched Begay with both eyes. This was the second just before training begins in earnest, the moment where the horse waits for a clue to react to. Begay took another step back and the colt leaned forward.

Begay backed up another step. The colt stepped forward, toward Begay. Now the colt was beginning to learn that he was safe near his trainer, who would give him only as much pressure as he needed to make the next move—the move Begay *wanted* him to make. The colt sighed deeply and smelled the air. I saw Begay sigh with him.

"Let's let him have the rest of the day off," Begay said. I agreed. The inmates broke into groups of three and moved to the other corrals, mocking me all the way. In each of six walled pens, another wild mustang waited for training. There was a lot of work to be done, and I spent the next several hours walking along the catwalks of each corral, instructing, correcting, and observing the inmates with their horses.

I had a crew of select inmates, and those who showed the most responsible nature were candidates for the health-care crew. Being chosen for the veterinary crew carried with it an honored title, and Julian chose each man for the team. Julian was the majordomo—the leader of the vet team, the highest position on the inmate horse training crew.

For foal care, none was better than Bubba, a gentle, three-hundred-pound Hell's Angel who had a special touch for the babies. Sick babies were his domain, and when humanly possible he brought them back from near-death circumstances. I admired him for it. His love for the horses made him as good as he was. Once I watched him save a palomino foal that was a candidate for euthanasia just by sitting by its side for days on end, breathing energy into it.

New Mexico's Inmate Horse Training Program was created after officials in the state government were embarrassed by the bad publicity that followed reports of a high number of prisoners who'd been beaten and killed in prison in the 1980s. Bill Richardson, congressman for New Mexico at the time, and a man of his word who had great compassion for mustangs and other animals, instigated federal funding through the Bureau of Land Management for a large-scale inmate wild horse training program similar to one that had worked well at a prison in Colorado: a hands-on, inmate-labor plan to train wild mustangs and make them adoptable. Back then

Colorado trained fifty horses per year, and we trained hundreds per year in the three New Mexico facilities Richardson helped set up: the Los Lunas medium-security prison, Santa Fe penitentiary, and the facility outside Las Cruces in the southern part of the state.

The name *mustang* came from the Spanish word *mesteño*, meaning "stray" or "ownerless." The captured horses we trained were probably not really true Spanish Barb mustangs, but horses with some mustang blood blended with ranch horse stock. That made them feral animals by some definitions, wild by argument, and native to North America as defined by their molecular biology. As many as fifty thousand wild horses still roamed the continental United States in 1988, down from about two million at the turn of the century, with the majority in Nevada, Wyoming, California, and Utah. And though small populations in places like Assateague Island in Maryland still live relatively comfortable lives and attract tourists, the vast Western herds have a mixed reputation. To some people the horses will always be a symbol of American freedom and strength—beautiful, powerful horses running and grazing unowned and unfettered. To some landowners, however, they are nuisance animals. To the cattle industry, they're a waste of valuable public grazing land and an environmental disaster waiting to happen. I've never understood why wild horses are considered the cause of environmental damage when range cattle outnumber them one hundred to one, and I've voiced that quandary to Congress and inmates alike.

The government's solution to all these concerns is to cull the herds—capture some horses periodically and remove them to keep the wild populations at sustainable levels. But once they had captured the animals, the Bureau of Land Management faced the problem of what to do with them. The mustangs received some protection under the Wild Free-Roaming Horses and Burros Act of 1971, which back then contained a provision forbidding the government or adopters from selling horses for slaughter. But, without gentling, many wild horses are not suitable for adoption.

Coupling prison inmates in need of meaningful work with horses that need gentling was a healthy antidote for me after an extended period I'd spent in an equine practice that catered to quarter horses, thoroughbreds, and racehorses. The wild mustangs suffered few of the genetic ailments that are so common in custom-bred, domesticated stock: ultra-small hooves compressed by the weight of the horse, lack of stamina, and sameness of color. Lethal inbreeding and natural evolutionary mutations compounded problems like hyperkalemic periodic paralysis (HYPP), a muscle condition in one popular quarter horse line that causes debilitating weakness. Most of these defects had come from generation after generation of related horses being selectively bred by people more concerned with appearance and color than with health and functional athleticism.

I became disillusioned with my first private veterinary practice after a client requested performance-enhancing drugs for his racehorses. I refused, but a couple of my colleagues surrendered their ethics and supplied the drugs. Greed had gotten to them. I had needed income as badly as anyone else in the practice but I wasn't willing to administer the stimulants. So instead I moved on, practiced with Dr. Michael Callahan, consulted for the government and private companies on matters as varied as the capture of the mustangs, equine pharmaceuticals, and the control of animal-borne diseases. I even helped produce a popular Wild West show at Disney Paris.

The prison training program for each mustang—or the forced-friendship program, as we called it—started in the round corral. It usually took three to four months to complete. I preferred to exit the round corral as soon as the horse would acknowledge the trainer and stand quietly. I would only return to it if a horse rejected advanced training and needed a reminder of basic obedience. A horse will reject any given lesson three to ten times before accepting it, and he's not above forgetting that he once knew anything.

During his tenure in the forced-friendship program, each animal had to learn to accept a lot of unfamiliar activity, from wearing a halter to being tied to a fence. The animal needed to stand quietly when approached by a person and allow his feet to be picked up and inspected without resistance. Trust does not come easy to any wild animal, and we all had reasonable expectation on any day that we could be bitten, kicked, or trampled. I was as susceptible to injury as the next guy, though a lifetime around horses made me a little wiser than most in avoiding the dangers. It was not uncommon to watch an inmate being chased out of a corral by a horse, or attached to the end of long rope and dragged behind a mustang running at a full gallop. It was also not uncommon for an inmate to pour affection on his animal. Bubba wept over his foals at times, and I think that his compassion helped to heal both him and his horses. The program is definitely not for every inmate, but those who did succeed in it never shied away from a hard day's work, or even from getting black and blue. In many cases, both suited them perfectly well.

The men themselves were often temperamental. They had learned to be angry. Gentling a beast that was much bigger and wilder than they were taught them how to react to violence without using it. The horses never forgot a wrongdoing, so the men had to temper themselves. They had to learn to be quiet and patient, and very few came naturally to those qualities. They had to find a way to earn and keep the trust of the horses. And of course, they were expected to apply those lessons in the human world, as well. As each partnership between man and horse ended, it was clear that horses were not the only ones who had been changed by the process. Inmates who were part of the wild horse program had one-tenth the recidivism rate of those who did not participate—did not often come back to prison after being released.

In the early days of the New Mexico prison horse training program, my driving route to and from the Las Cruces facility often took me along the outer perimeter of the White Sands Missile Range. Thousands of magnificent horses lived on that range, kept inside with fences that had been put up only to keep out people. The highly secret range was home to government weapons development and testing, from bullets to lasers and drones to the space shuttle. It was also where the first atomic bomb was tested. Those tight borders encased a big part of the history of the Old West, too. What I didn't know then, driving to my oversight job at the mustang prison program, was that I'd soon be spending most of my time on that missile range, trying to solve a deadly mystery and save a large and far-flung band of wild horses.

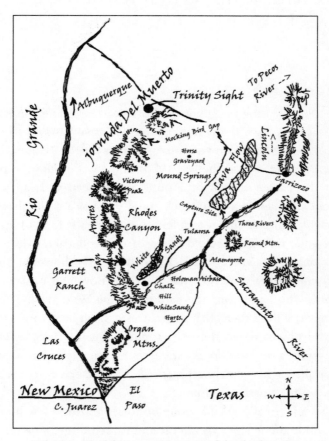

The Jornada del Muerto (Journey of the dead man),
a part of the Camino Real, was a shortcut across the
desert, but has no water for more than a hundred miles.
Art by Ben Höglund.

Chapter 2

Standing Outside the Fire

The first time I ever saw the horses on the White Sands Missile Range, I was just passing by, driving south through New Mexico on veterinary business for the National Wild Horse Program. It was the late 1980s, and I was as close to flying down the barren stretch of Route 54 between Carrizozo and Tularosa as a man in a Ford truck could get. For a while that road runs right alongside the eastern fences of the nearly four-thousand-square-mile missile range. I'd heard of the legendary wild horses that populated it. Many were descended from the horses of Sheriff Pat Garrett, Billy the Kid, and other cowboys and outlaws and denizens who had braved the hard life in the Wild West. The fact that they still lived there, that their ancestors had been onsite when the government tested the first atomic bomb in 1945, endowed them with a reputation of strength and independence—even immortality—that was almost mystical. I would crane my neck as I drove, hoping to catch a glimpse.

The day I finally spied a group of horses grazing a few hundred yards inside the fence, I veered off and parked to get a better look with binoculars. They were magnificent. The sole stallion was easily seventeen hands high and seventeen hundred pounds heavy—thick-bodied, with rippling muscles and an air of superiority that was hard to argue with. He was light gray, with a yellow-tinged mane and tail, feathering at the ankles, and he strutted around his

Pat Garrett, known as the unluckiest man alive.
Courtesy of the Museum of New Mexico (MNM/DCA).

mares with a wary eye in my direction, ready to whisk them all away in a second if I decided to come closer. There were six mares, two gray like the stallion and four in a variety of chestnut shades, some with white markings, and two foals contentedly sticking close to their mothers. I could almost see the ghosts of the outlaws, Indians, and town in the distance.

It should have been a bucolic scene—this land had barely changed from two hundred, even four hundred, years ago—except that there was a taut, five-foot, five-strand barbed-wire fence between those horses and me, which extended for more than 250 miles around the missile range. Within ten yards of where I stood, signs declared PROPERTY OF THE UNITED STATES GOVERNMENT, DAN-GER (with PELIGRO beneath), and smaller, vertical rectangles emblazoned with CAUTION: HIGH RADIATION AREA. There was also a NO STANDING sign hanging on the fence.

Any tranquillity in the appearance of these horses was deceptive. They made their home on one of the most desolate, unforgiving stretches of desert in the United States, which was also one of the most mysterious, secret, high-security tracts of land in the country. White Sands was dedicated to advancing and perfecting implements of war. Flying missiles, unexplained explosions, and even unexploded munitions on the ground were facts of life. Two MPs in a drab-green Humvee rolled up just inside the fence and stared at me. They looked from me to the horses and back, then curtly waved me on. Rattled, I dropped the glasses, shifted the truck into gear, and rolled back onto the highway, staring back at them in my rearview mirror.

The image of those horses and the strange, unpredictable, hard-scrabble life they must be living inside that barbed wire stayed on my mind for miles. I could conjure them, powerful and peaceful on the wrong side of the fence, for years after. And every time I remembered those regal creatures, I muttered to myself as I had motoring down the highway: *That's a hell of a hard life for a horse.*

White Sands Missile Range has two million fenced-in acres that are different from any other landscape in the Southwest, even its most desolate corners. A very small part is rolling pastureland, but most is treacherous, inhospitable desert. Much of the range is covered with pure white gypsum sand that ripples and moves as if sculpted by ocean currents, surging and collapsing in vast dunes, a no man's land, punctuated here and there by the occasional soaptree yucca, one of the only plants that can withstand constant burial by the shifting sands. At sunset, the sky over the dunes is sensual, a colossal cornflower-blue dome arching over flaming orange clouds that set the mountains on fire. Below it all, bone-white sands press forward with the prevailing winds.

Other foliage on the range looks deceptively delicate. There are dusty green mesquite forests festooned with billions of two-inch thorns that can pierce a person through to the heart. Large thatches of cacti with their blooms and fruit in spring are striking to the eye, but dangerous to the body. Miles of scrubland and sagebrush survive the hard winters and the scorching dry summers. Shimmering mirages of heat have tricked thirsty travelers for thousands of years into seeing oases. Every plant and animal lives in subsistence mode until the rains come in the fall.

The moonscape of fine gypsum gives way to the ruddy cliffs cradling the Tularosa Basin in the distance. Barren rock formations and valleys peak and fall at the edges of the range. About forty miles to the east, the scarlet Sangre de Cristo mountain chain rises out of the sand and strikes out for Colorado. Among them are the Sacramento Mountains, or Rainbow Range as cowboy-poet Eugene Manlove Rhodes called them, on the Atlantic side of the missile range and the San Andres Mountains on the west. Winds whip across the alkali flats in the basin and create the luminous dunes of sand in middle. A hard, black lava flow snakes slowly from northeast in the Tularosa to southwest—the Malpais badlands, as the area is known in the territory. The serpentine mass, twenty-five miles of unforgiving obsidian, is jagged and dangerous—more than one person has been cut to shreds after slipping on it. The whole basin stretches one hundred miles long and forty miles wide, with a sky so clear that the eye could probably see through to the Rio Grande River on the western side if the San Andres weren't in the way.

Rhodes penned this incomparable description of the Tularosa Basin, in which "the explorer's eye leaped out over a bottomless gulf to a glimpse of shining leagues midway of the desert greatness—an ever widening triangle that rose against the peaceful west to long foothill reaches, to a misty mountain parapet, far-beckoning, whispering of secrets, things dreamed of, unseen, beyond the framed and slender arc of vision. A land of enchantment and mystery, decked with strong barbaric colors, blue and red and yellow, brown and green and gray; whose changing ebb and flow, by some potent sorcery of atmosphere, distance and angle, altered daily, hourly; deepening, fading, combining into new and fantastic lines and shapes to melt again as swiftly to others yet more bewildering."

Early history of the range is as colorful as its landscape. From about 700 to just after 1300 A.D., the Jornada Mogollon natives cultivated fields along the range's few creeks. Countless boulders on the range are inscribed with their petroglyphs, rudimentary drawings of symbols and figures. There are actually about one hundred thousand known prehistoric drawings in this desert, some dating as far back as twelve thousand years, well before the Mogollon people lived there—and there are also fossil footprints of mammoths and other extinct species of the Ice Age. Little is known about the Mogollon, who disappeared from the land; some believe that drought forced them north.

In 1598, Conquistador Don Juan de Oñate camped on the western border of what is today White Sands Missile Range. His route comprised the north end of El Camino Real de Tierra Adentro, the Royal Road of the Interior Lands. In the next decades, many Spaniards veered east, away from the Rio Grande, to attempt a shortcut in the eighteen-hundred-mile road from Santa Fe back to Mexico City. In 1680 that desert route over ninety harsh, unforgiving miles of hell achieved the name of Jornada del Muerto, "journey of the dead man." The Jornada became the feared north fraction of El Camino Real, the King's Road. There, Pueblo Indians revolted against Spanish rule, killing almost six hundred of the two thousand frail, ailing, famished expatriates. The invaders were not the first to know the reality of the dreaded route, however, and it was not exclusively a Spanish trail. In the centuries before Columbus had come ashore Tierra Nueva, "the new land," with his six small horses, this desert route had been used by Pueblo Indians for trade, connecting the robust Rio Grande pueblos with the immense civilization of the Casas Grandes in central Mexico. Later, Cochise, Geronimo, Victorio, and other Apaches braved the Jornada and raided Mexican caravans from its protected enclaves.

The Spanish reintroduced horses to North America along the Camino. Their mounts were genetically identical to ancestors that had evolved in North America millions of years earlier but gone extinct. Cattle and sheep also first plodded into the Western Hemisphere along trails like the Jornada. Christianity, European customs, metallurgy, the wheel, even written language first entered the territory by trails such as the dead man's walk. El Camino Real affected the course of American history more than any other trail. Historically, it is the most significant of all trails of the Old West, more so than the Santa Fe Trail or the Oregon Trail. And through all that time, virtually nothing has changed. Expansive, empty, it is a seemingly lifeless valley with no water, nothing to eat, and no wood for fire. Even today, as one keen observer wrote of the Jonses, that living in the region of the Jornada (the camino is habitable) is "a study in the science of doing without."

After the Mogollon and until around 1600, the Apache reigned supreme in the area now known as White Sands range. When the Spanish Conquistadors explored the land, they captured the Apache for the slave trade. The Apache certainly didn't give up without a fight, and later, in the middle 1800s, engaged the U.S. Cavalry in bloody battles over land. They were forced west by the Buffalo Soldiers of the Ninth U.S. Cavalry, a group of African-Americans who protected the settlers, miners, and migrating travelers. Ranchers began to move in to the area, setting up to fulfill the demand for meat in New Mexico. Their success attracted a notorious crowd: Billy the Kid and Black Jack Ketchum, infamous outlaw train robbers, were known to have spent years on ranches around the springs on White Sands. Sheriff Pat Garrett, who had the distinction of capturing and killing Billy the Kid, ranched horses in the area. After the sheriff's assassination near Chalk Hill by a shot to the back of the head, his horses were left to roam on what is today missile range property.

Eugene Manlove Rhodes, the cowboy bard of the turn of the century who captured life in the Wild West for future generations with his writing, also had a ranch on White Sands. He is buried there in a cemetery a few hundred yards inside the Military Range Gate. Rhodes Canyon, a gorge through the San Andres, is named for him, a tribute to his importance to the

Eugene Manlove Rhodes,
"Bard of the West."
*Courtesy of the Museum of New Mexico
(MNM/DCA).*

area and its history. Rhodes was a prolific writer, and imbued his poems and stories with a romantic view of the West that makes him a cowboy's cowboy and author, the real thing. *The Saturday Evening Post* and other periodicals popularized his work, establishing him as one of the first of the great Western writers. His epic poem *The Hired Man on Horseback* and his memoir of the same title paint the classic portrait of the true cowboy, a man of passion and principle, a rugged individual who aroused an American literary and cultural tradition.

The White Sands range inspired poetry, but it was also the scene of the brutal nineteenth-century killing of attorney, colonel, and businessman, Albert Fountain, and his eight-year-old son, Henry. The accused, rancher Oliver Lee, also a famed cattle rustler, and a ranch-hand, Jim Gililland, hid out near Rhodes's ranch.

Among these infamous men who contributed to the lore of the West was Charles Goodnight, the inventor of the chuck wagon (the cowboy's portable kitchen), and one of the wealthiest cattle ranchers in the West. He was said to be the one who first crossed buffalo with cattle, producing the "cattalo." The remnants of his JA Ranch, which once supported a hundred thousand head of cattle, is in Palo Duro Canyon, Texas, today, still a working ranch, but a fraction of the original size. Goodnight's business partner, Oliver

Loving, was also an important cattleman in the area, and the Goodnight-Loving Trail is a cattle trail named after the duo. The trail stretches from Texas through New Mexico just east of White Sands, with branches

Jim Gililland, ca. 1900.
Courtesy of the Museum of New Mexico (MNM/DCA).

extending into Colorado; it is part of the backdrop for many books and classic feature films, such as Larry McMurtry's *Lonesome Dove*.

The U.S. military chose White Sands as a base of operations around 1942. It was the perfect place to test destructive weapons because of its minimal habitation, minimal traffic, low visibility, and location far enough inland to ensure it was defensible. The missile range fully encompasses the White Sands National Monument and the San Andres National Wildlife Refuge—both ecologically delicate areas now situated inside one of the largest military facilities in the United States.

In a move that is contested by local residents to this day, the government exercised its "right of eminent domain" and moved the ranchers living on the range. They "asked" the ranchers to leave, ninety-seven families in all, using patriotism as the prod. The land was for the war effort, the government said, and made the ranchers feel that they couldn't argue. A few ranches on the perimeters were permitted to stay, with the caveat that they would clear out for a weapon testing every time the government ordered it, which could happen as often as a few times a week, but most ranchers were offered condemned-land prices for their homes.

According to White Sands officials, nearly every type of deployable ordnance developed in America since 1945, along with many others created on foreign turf, has been tested on the missile range. One of the defining moments of modern history, the detonation of the world's first atomic bomb on July 16, 1945, occurred at White Sands. That particular experiment generated heat four times the temperature inside the sun, melted the sand in its immediate vicinity to glass (an artificial mineral now known as Trinityite), and was visible as far as 250 miles away. It took place prior to White Sands' development of an environmental affairs department to limit significant damage to the land, its ancient cultural remains, and the creatures it supported.

Many ranch horses, including the equine stock of the famous frontiersmen, had to be abandoned on the range. As the government moved families off the range and helped them find temporary

or permanent homes nearby, the ranchers easily gathered and mar-
keted their cattle, but had to leave behind the notoriously crafty
horses. The ranchers had been told they would get their land back,
that the government was taking a temporary lease, and they figured
when that happened they would also retrieve their horses. To this
day, none of the land has been returned to the ranchers.

Instead, over the course of the 1940s and 50s, more land was
appropriated for the missile range. With top-secret research and
weapons development taking place in the desert, the Army soon
put up fences, trapping the horses that had once relied on their
instincts (or inherent behaviors) to ensure their basic needs. Now
effectively property of the government, but left to fend for themselves, the horses survived, carrying on in spite of limited forage and
water, and in spite of bullets and bombs exploding all around them.
Between 1945 and 1989, more than thirty-eight thousand missiles
were fired on the White Sands Missile Range, enough firepower to
ruin half of Europe. But the wild horses were of hardy working
stock. They could travel twenty-five miles a day to find forage and
water. In wet years, when forage was plentiful, the desert plain burst
with flowering cactus, yucca, and the ocotillo plant. Gold and lilac
wildflowers spring up among patches of pink and emerald carpet-
ing the desert floor and the horses shaded themselves and foraged
in the dense mesquite forests. It wasn't the perfect landscape for a
grazing animal, but the horses adapted.

By the 1980s, the horse population on the range was broken up
into four herds, each ruled over by powerful stallions. The Eugene
Manlove Rhodes herd in the gorge was reddish-chestnut in color
with flaxen manes and tails, and full white blazes and pasterns (the
area above the hooves). Two herds with bays and browns were probably descendants of Sheriff Pat Garrett's horses, and in the north
were grays that had hailed from west Texas. On the whole, many
looked like draft horses, big working animals with feathering on
their fetlocks, like Clydesdales, but some had the strong, sinewy look
of racehorse lines from the 1920s. All of their giant hooves were polished to a high shine, buffed by running through the gypsum sand.

Over decades, the lore of the horses, their strength and perseverance, grew. Neighboring communities, including the nearby Native-American reservations, and even the prisons where I worked, regarded the horses with awe. Many admirers even suggested that phantoms of the great horses that had populated the Old West lived among the herds. Some of the ghost horses were believed to be from the slaughtered fifteen hundred Comanche horses in Palo Duro Canyon, just 360 miles from White Sands, a tragedy that had made the desert hallowed ground for both Native Americans and cavalrymen.

White Sands is a unique combination of fragile environments and destructive activity. More than four hundred animal species populate the range, including bighorn sheep, mule deer, elk, oryx, mountain lions, coyotes, and three different kinds of rattlesnake. Within its very sparse water system, the range also hosts the White Sands pupfish, a threatened species believed to be as old as the North American continent and not found in any other place on earth.

No one knows more about the ecosystems on White Sands Missile Range than wildlife biologist Patrick Morrow. In 1989, Morrow came to work at the White Sands Missile Range as a civilian employee. He was twenty six years old, well-educated with a master's degree in wildlife biology, the son of a trusted medical doctor in Springer, New Mexico. Eager to do worthwhile work, he would ply his craft in one of the most complicated environmental situations imaginable. When he arrived, there were already well over a thousand horses roaming the range.

Morrow's primary duty was to review upcoming activities on the range and determine whether they complied with federal and state laws, including the conservation regulations, endangered species restrictions, the Clean Water Act, and eventually the Clean Air Act. He was charged with understanding the animal populations and their conditions on the range, and with anticipating any threats to their well-being that might be brought about by the twice-weekly, or more, missile exercises taking place on the range.

Morrow had the same reaction to the White Sands horses that most of the military staffers held: He saw them as charismatic emblems of the range and the Old West. As he gathered information and began the process of counting the animals, a task that had to be conducted from the safety of the air in a helicopter, Morrow started to worry. Reviewing earlier studies of all the animal populations, and counting and assessing the horses, he realized that their growing population could pose big problems on the range in the not-too-distant future.

When good annual rainfall led to good forage, the horse population on White Sands increased by scores every year, and the Army culled the herds to keep the numbers down and to keep the horses out of harm's way. The military would round up about a hundred head a year and auction them off to the highest bidder. In 1989, animal rights groups caught wind of the annual horse harvest at White Sands and cried foul because some buyers were selling the horses for slaughter. They declared a tourism boycott of New Mexico, which caught fire with the news media fanning the flames. Tourism was the state's second leading source of revenue, just behind the Defense Department projects, like the weapons testing at White Sands. Governor Garrey Carruthers was concerned about this bad press and his director of the State Tourism Department called me. We met to discuss a solution for the problem with the White Sands horse auction scheduled for that year, 1989.

Though the bands of horses on White Sands Missile Range probably had mustang blood streaming through their veins, they didn't fall under the Wild Free-Roaming Horses and Burros Act of 1971, because White Sands is Army-owned territory. So, the horses were not protected by any state or federal law. Declared feral by state law, the White Sands herds legally could have been rounded up and slaughtered if the military had chosen that way of dealing with them. The Army certainly wasn't in the horse business, but because environmental conditions promoted herd growth, there were just too many horses on White Sands.

Once I understood the facts, I suggested working as an intermediary between the New Mexico Correctional System and the U.S. Army to help capture the White Sands horses, remove them from the missile range, and bring them into the prison training program. It seemed like a logical course of action, a win-win-win for the state, the Army, and the horses. I sent letters to Dr. Steve England, the secretary for the state livestock board, who was then considered the legal guardian of the wild White Sands horses, and I spoke with the range's commander. Each considered my solution not only possible, but palatable. Nonetheless, for reasons not divulged to me, no deal was struck, and the one hundred horses captured and penned at White Sands were turned loose again onto the already overpopulated missile range.

Disappointed, I turned back myself to a solo practice I had started in Santa Fe. Then I had the opportunity to work with internationally famous horse trainer Mario Luraschi in Santa Fe and in France. I turned over the reins of the practice to my partner, Dr. Michael Callahan, and trained stunt horses, full time.

Luraschi horses have appeared in film classics such as *The Black Stallion—PBS, The Bear, Joan of Arc, Excalibur, Napoleon, The French Revolution,* and dozens of other well-known epics. Incredibly gifted, Luraschi learned from the great Bernard, trainer of the movie horses in *Ben Hur,* a story written by a former New Mexico governor, Lew Wallace. I studied with Mario for five years and learned firsthand how he worked his horses—the European way. His training method, built on five-thousand years of learning to deal with the horse from the horse's perspective, is a tradition that has not yet been honed in North America. Cowboys like me have a mere two hundred years of equine experience to draw from. Until recently, the Western equestrian tradition focused on the domination of the animal instead of treating it as a companion and workmate, a relationship built from sound horsemanship and trust. Yet I was able to give some of my own gifts to Mario: the use of the lariat, cattle-and-horse logic, and patience, particularly the patience he needed to teach a cowboy to relearn what he thinks he already knows.

While I was casting and training horses for live shows in Las

Vegas and Paris, the situation with the wild horses at White Sands was becoming dire. As Patrick Morrow surveyed the herds and observed them through late 1993 and early 1994, he saw that they were becoming increasingly emaciated without enough water or vegetation. Yet even as the animals began to suffer the visible effects of a long drought, their population continued to grow. By the summer of 1994 more than fifteen hundred horses were eking out an existence on the range, with new foals born daily and demanding more nutrition than their mares could provide.

On a July day in 1994, while making a routine survey of the range in an Army helicopter, Morrow spied a scene that he still describes as an "Oh, God" moment. From the air, he and the pilot discovered a mass of dead and dying horses in and around muddy watering hole—no water, just mud—at Mound Springs. The White Sands horses were being brutally culled by starvation and a paltry water supply.

Morrow called together his colleagues, who, along with a handful of range riders, civilian cowboys employed by the range to help keep fences mended and trespassers of all kinds out, met at the scene and stared in awe and anger and disgust at the gruesome horse graveyard. The horses who were dying had no chance of survival, and their circumstances seem to beg the mercy of euthanasia. The biologists, trained to respect wildlife, and the cowboys, raised to value and respect the horse above all animals, were unprepared to handle the nightmare.

As they tried to ease the agony of the dying horses, the workers also had to contend with nearly twenty foals who ambled among the dead, wailing desperately for their mothers. The lead range rider, Les Gililland, a cowboy who had lived on or near White Sands all his life, took charge of the foals and began transporting them one by one to the relative safety of pens miles away on the range. Soldiers stationed at the facility did what they could, stunned that the rugged horses they'd admired for years from afar, horses that many had speculated ran with ghosts, were mortal after all.

All told, 122 horses died at the watering hole over a forty-eight-hour period that July. Even people acutely aware of the horses' harsh circumstances had trouble understanding how so many horses could have expired at the same time from gradual starvation and dehydration. Almost immediately, rumors began among insiders about other causes that might have contributed to the horrific event.

The sudden die-off might have stayed an internal matter on the military installation, but a disgruntled range rider, incensed at the painful deaths of all those majestic, historic animals—trapped, thirsty, and hungry—within the White Sands fences, called an animal rights watch group that same day. *The Dallas Morning News* got wind of the story, and within twenty four hours the rest of the world became aware of the terrible fate of the 122 horses. Appalled Americans and other people around the globe and media representatives swarmed into the area looking for photographs and any inside scoop on whether that many horses truly could have died of malnutrition, or if something more sinister—something befitting a military installation—had killed them.

Now, with the very public die-off, animal rights groups from across the country had stepped up with the vigilance of the 1989 horse auction boycott and were watching intently to determine if further calls for tourism boycotts were in order. Some of the groups, including the Society for the Protection of Wild Horses and Burros and the Humane Society of the United States, sent their own representatives to New Mexico to ensure that the surviving horses were dealt with in a manner they found acceptable. Within days, the matter of the horses not only became a high-priority matter for Patrick Morrow, but a top agenda item for the most important government offices in the state as well. The governor, the lieutenant governor, the general in command of the missile range, the head of the state livestock board, the district manager for the Bureau of Land Management, a senator from New Mexico, and at least one state congressman were all directly involved in a task force to decide the fate of the rest of the White Sands horses.

I was in Denver, Colorado, having just finished a Wild West

show, when I picked up an early morning copy of *USA Today*. I was horrified by what I read and saw, and felt a profound sense of regret. I'd admired those horses from outside the missile range fences more times than I could count, knowing that they had to struggle mightily just to survive. They were from strong stock, and they had bred offspring that were even stronger, but there's no such thing as a native desert horse. Horses need water, and if these animals hadn't been confined by the government's need to keep its weapons testing secret, they would have dispersed to live where there was plenty of water and vegetation to keep them alive.

After that first pang of regret, I became furious, sharing the range riders' outrage. How dare the government trap these horses inside the missile range? These horses and their ancestors had belonged to honest ranchers and some of the greatest and most notorious men in the history of the American West. I, too, began to wonder what had really happened to the horses to make them die en masse. I remembered that thousands of unfortunate sheep that had been grazing downwind of the government's nerve gas experiments in Utah had died years before and that the military had denied responsibility for decades, even though it paid the owners market value for their dead animals. I couldn't help wondering if something similar might have happened to the horses on the missile range. A picture of a healthy foal in the newspaper, a nursing baby, made me more suspicious. Why wasn't he dead along with the adults?

Back on White Sands, the range riders, under the direction of the wildlife biologists, were trying to keep the rest of the horses alive. This was no simple task, as the drought continued with no sign of change.

"It was bad before the die-off," a range rider told me later. "In the days leading up to the die-off, the spring had almost completely dried up. It was just a trickle of water that made mud, and the horses had created wide, worn ditches in the land to get to it. There wasn't enough, and there was no food for them near that little mud hole. It was just too barren."

Even after the die-off, horses were unwilling to seek water away from the only place they had ever found it. The range riders brought it out to them in massive vats on trucks, but the dehydrated, suspicious, and sickly horses had never been fed or watered by humans, and it was a long shot to think that they'd drink the water brought to them. The water they were used to was heavily saline, and the water in the troughs was sweet and fresh. Some weakened White Sands horses did choose to take the water and survived. But even in the face of death, some didn't trust the water.

"When a nine-hundred-pound wild horse is so weak you can push him out of your way so you can get to the watering trough, it's just disgusting," one disheartened worker told Morrow after the troughs were set into place.

Next, the powers-that-be had to decide what to feed the starving horses, but some didn't want them fed at all, arguing that it would upset the ecological balance of the range. Eventually, they weighed the costs and practicality of starting to feed the horses and having them come to rely on it, and they decided not to offer any food.

Task force meetings began in late summer to redefine the ownership of the horses. The Wild Free-Roaming Horses and Burros Act of 1971 would have defined them as "living symbols of the historic and pioneer spirit of the West," and sheltered them from "capture, branding, harassment, or death," and also governed the manner in which they could be moved and adopted when absolutely necessary. But because they resided on land owned by the Department of Defense, they were exempt from that protection. Even though the horses' ancestors had once been the property of private citizen ranchers who had populated the range before the government acquired it, they no longer belonged to any single individual. If they had been defined as feral, they would not have been protected by any law and could have been shot on sight. After much debate, Tom Udall, then attorney general of New Mexico, and his team declared that the horses, under common law, belonged both to the "people of the state in their collective sovereign capacity," meaning that they could pass legislation regulating their treatment, as well as to the United States government by way of the Defense Department.

The consensus of the meetings was that the horses could not stay on White Sands and continue to starve and suffer. Despite the good intentions of the task force, it was difficult to determine who would pay for the removal of the horses and who would be liable if anything went wrong. Through the months of meetings from August to December of 1994, the horses continued to suffer from the drought as the debate continued about who would take ownership of them after they were captured. What would happen if they were moved, if they crossed state lines, if they died in transit, if foals were born while they were in temporary quarters? At what point would they cease to be "wild" horses.

The horses had a temporary reprieve when the seasonal rains arrived in late September. In December, the task force disbanded with no resolution. Frustrated, Brig. Gen. Jerry Laws, the action-oriented commander of White Sands Missile Range, took matters into his own hands and accepted responsibility for whatever might happen with the horses. He ordered that the horses leave the range one way or another. Representative Joe Skeen set about securing funding from the taxpayers, but he wasn't helped by Arizona Senator John McCain calling the proposed funding "pork barrel politics." General Laws, an Oklahoma native and a man who cared for horses, declared that White Sands Missile Range was not in the horse business, called his field environmental directorate and ordered a go. I came to call it "Operation: Desert Horse Rescue."

Up until General Laws's public decision, I had been staying out of the fracas, since my efforts back in 1989 to get the horses off the range and to safety had been turned down. This grated on me every time I heard more news about the die-off from the national media or friends in New Mexico. The Army had been right all along and the state of New Mexico weak and indecisive. I was also due to go to Nevada soon to help with the National Wild Horse and Burro program. But then a colleague of mine, a veterinarian in New Mexico and fellow admirer of the horses on White Sands, called to tell me that the rescue plan was in the works and that auctions were also being planned to sell off the captives. He feared that many horses would be hurt, lost, or even killed if the rescue was poorly planned and executed, and that more would die at slaughter if they were sold at uncontrolled auctions. Others might wind up being abused at rodeos.

My friend convinced me to place a call to Patrick Morrow to ask if he would like to see my 1989 plans for moving the horses off the range. After we hung up, Patrick investigated my background and learned that I had also helped to move herds of wild horses from Wyoming and Nevada to the New Mexico prisons, and had taught the inmates to train them. Faced with the enormous task of supervising the capture, veterinary care, and relocation of more than eighteen hundred horses, and having no prior experience with any of those tasks, Patrick liked what he learned about my old detailed plan and called me back a few days later.

"We'd like you to come out here, take a look, and make some recommendations," Patrick explained. He and his workers had been overwhelmed by the desperate condition of the living horses and the dead animals, and they were still plagued by media demands to see the site of the Mound Springs die-off. They'd done what they could to clean up the scene so it wasn't as much of a shock, but no one wanted to escort the media out to the site. "Nobody wants to get out in front of the cameras in this disaster, but someone needs to do what's right for these herds. We don't want another hundred horses to turn up dead tomorrow." The remaining horses needed help, and soon.

I knew we could figure out a good way to round up the horses, but an auction was a bad idea and I told Patrick so. I suggested adopting out the horses to people who could handle a spirited horse's needs and who wanted to care for a part of our national history. Whether the horse was intended as a companion, or merely adopted as a pasture ornament, a once-wild horse needed special care and handling, and I urged Patrick to convey that message to the public. He should not allow any owner to adopt more than a couple of animals, and the adopters should have to sign a statement that they could and would protect their charges. He needed to make people agree to keep the horse for one year, so that the owner would have put enough money into the animal that selling it to slaughter wouldn't pay.

We spoke of the liabilities in the adoption operation. People might adopt a horse, take him home, and then the horse might get loose and hurt somebody or kill himself. Then the adopter would come back with an ambulance chaser who would say that Patrick Morrow and his Army had let the horse lover have a dangerous, testosterone-loaded animal. The stallions needed neutering—"brain surgery" I called it—to avoid a lot of those problems. Then we could take them to Oklahoma, to a wild horse sanctuary used by the Department of the Interior horse program north of Tulsa, where they'd be safe until they were healthy enough to be adopted to good homes.

As we talked, I was staring at a heartbreaking photo in the *El Paso Times* of healthy nursing foals trying to pull the last few drops of mares' milk from their emaciated, dead mothers. After I hung up the phone, promising to consider a visit to White Sands, I paced, tormented by thoughts of baby horses wandering hungry and confused. The pictures of the horses' agonizing deaths pounded in my head. Those horses had suffered—there was bright crimson froth around their mouths and their carcasses were skin and bones. I blasted out the door and sped twenty minutes by car up the eastern foothills to Boulder, Colorado. There I walked the familiar hills into the low mountains overlooking my homeland. Winded, I suddenly realized that I couldn't go any higher. I had wandered to the highest peak I could reach, exactly the kind of thing Eugene Rhodes did when his brain wouldn't stop rolling—roamed until the road ran out and then sat down to take it all in. Rhodes wrote that, when people like himself, Will Rogers, Pat Garrett, and Will James, *"got wind of an adventure roundabout they went for a look-see. Whereas most of us, at any hint of adventure, lock the door and telephone the police."* Real

Westerners would have bagged the fear and gotten involved at White Sands no matter the danger, but here I was, frightened of the risks in taking part in the operation, trying to protect my own safety and comfort.

I sat at the highest point I could climb to on Flat Iron Peak and looked south to Denver. I traced the railway track as it exited the tunnel in the rocky hills and curved south. I followed the train in my mind to southern New Mexico, a place I'd once loved. Hell, I still loved it. I could see the wild horses on that vast missile range. I remembered them from the great tales by Frank Dobie. I believed in them, in their storied past and in the value of their unique legacy. The wild horses on White Sands Missile Range were trapped, dying, and they needed help.

I thought of the oath I'd taken when I became a veterinarian: *Being admitted to the profession of veterinary medicine, I solemnly swear to use my scientific knowledge and skills for the benefit of society through the protection of animal health, the relief of animal suffering, the conservation of livestock resources, the promotion of public health and the advancement of medical knowledge. I will practice my profession conscientiously, with dignity, and in keeping with the principles of veterinary medical ethics. I accept as a lifelong obligation the continual improvement of my professional knowledge and competence.* When I took that oath, I meant it.

Dizzy, perhaps from the high mountain air, I felt the chill of winter return. I did not want a life not tried, but merely survived. I yearned to be doing something worthwhile, as I felt I had in the mustang prison program. I'd made a difference there and I just could not countenance hanging back in warmth and safety while those horses died. Saving them might lead me to my purpose here on earth. I couldn't stand outside the fire any longer.

My hands trembled. I was going back to New Mexico, to Rhodes's home country and Pat Garrett's old ranch land. I was going to go have my own look-see.

Chapter 3

Secrecy and Security

Security at White Sands Missile Range is a matter of strict priority. Patrick Morrow, his fellow wildlife biologist Dr. Brian Locke, and I began our journey at a large, well-fortified guard shack where MPs patrolled with pistols at their sides. The two biologists knew the routine. They escorted me inside a security building where I was politely asked for my driver's license and proof that the truck I'd driven down from Colorado had valid insurance. I was photographed, questioned, and directed to wait while a background check was performed. I was even asked if I was up to date on my federal income taxes. The guards also talked to Patrick out of my earshot.

Before being allowed to enter the range, I was required to sign a waiver limiting the government's responsibility for my well-being. Among other stipulations, it stated that, "I fully understand that there are many areas of White Sands Missile Range that are contaminated by unexploded munitions, for example, mines, ammunitions, and bombs" and continued that "other serious dangers exist on White Sands, which may include, but are not limited to, missile and rocket launch hazards and debris, rough terrain (both natural and man made), wild animals, poisonous snakes, insects, dangerous weather, abandoned or lost equipment, power lines, and other man-made structures." The document required a promise that I would not approach or touch anything man-made on the range, and that

I understood that many of the unexploded munitions were "delib-
erately designed to blend in with the terrain," and that "their presence may not be immediately obvious to the casual observer." After
a long, worrisome wait, the three of us were cleared to proceed.

Patrick slid into the driver's seat of a government-issue truck
while I sat nervously behind him. Jet-black hair jutted out from
under his crumpled ball cap and he toyed with his bushy, black
mustache while he filled out some paperwork. I didn't want to
seem like a novice, so I didn't ask about anything, but being inside
the place known as the most secret military installation in the world
made me pretty paranoid. I wondered if I'd ever be allowed out
once we went inside. Dr. Locke slouched unconcerned in the passenger seat.

We backed out of the security building parking lot and crept
toward the patrolled headquarters entrance with its NO CAMERAS
signs. The old WWII barracks and buildings beyond the front gates
bustled with civilian and military personnel. Behind them were two
million acres of missile range that were closed to almost everyone
who worked at the edges of the facility as well as the adjacent Holloman Air Force Base, fifty miles east of headquarters, and Fort Bliss
on the southern end of the range. A huge sign reading WHITE SANDS
MISSILE RANGE glared down at the vehicles. Guards in pressed uni-

The "Missile Museum" at the White Sands Missile Range.
Courtesy of White Sands Missile Range.

forms smiled, hands clasped behind their erect backs as they peered through dark sunglasses at the driver and passengers and looked for proper identification, waving each in when satisfied. I held my new photo badge up close to the window, feeling the same apprehension I had felt years earlier whenever I entered a prison wild horse facility. I prayed that I wouldn't look at the wrong thing or say something offensive, or ask an incriminating question or commit some punishable indiscretion. The peach fuzz on the back of my neck stood up straight when I spotted the many rockets planted in front of the missile range museum. There were fifty different missiles, poised for launch. I looked hard to see if they were set in concrete. The whole of the missile range was surrounded by jagged mountains, which meant an escape required a jaunt uphill, where the perpetrator would make an easy target for any of five thousand sharpshooters who lived here, all of whom looked like they could pop someone as part of a day's work.

There were forty eight Stealth aircraft hidden underground at Holloman, but one ripped across the sky as we entered the range, rattling my teeth. It was fast, tiny, and oddly shaped. I was perspiring, hoping to calm down before I had to shake hands with anyone. I fingered the six-month-old newspaper photo hidden in my jacket pocket of the baby horse trying to nurse from its dead mother. I wondered if I should just chew it up and swallow it.

Inside the fence, the missile range seemed even more ominous than from outside. Small groups of MPs led scientists in guarded caravans. GIs marched or ran in formation, their dog tags bouncing to a familiar cadence—left-right, left-right chant. I wondered if I had somehow just enlisted. The sky was so blue it stung my eyes, and the sunlight reflecting off the white sand had a brilliance that gave everything a surreal hue. Shadows seemed miles long, and at every corner, the White Sands Missile Range presented some new sight that amazed and awed.

Patrick needed to pick up some maps at his office in the environmental directorate, so I sat outside to wait on a wood-and-iron park bench. The buildings were much older than I expected, surprising for a modern missile range, a top-secret enclave in the U.S. military complex. I had expected brand-new buildings, super-duper gadgets everywhere, and all the business-world amenities, but the 1940s, drab green, barrackslike, prefab offices spoke of a bare-bones, make-do command decorated by prickly-pear cactus and yucca plants. The nearby elm trees and bushes didn't look so healthy to me, either, without their leaves, which concerned me until I remembered it was December.

Back in the long Suburban, I subdued my paranoia as we passed back out the main gate, past the waving guards, crossed Highway 70, and pulled up to another guard station. After explaining our mission, we signed another host of lines, initialing everything from top to bottom on the page, and were allowed to head north at fifty-five miles per hour along one of two paved roads that divide the range for one hundred miles, north to south. We passed a handful of military vehicles along the route, including tanks parked near our entry point. After a mile or two, a tiny sign indicating SMALL MISSILE RANGE pointed off to the left. The thickly graveled road, rutted by heavy trucks, elevated a smooth five miles west toward some buildings tucked against the San Andres Mountains. Boulders and pine trees hid all but the glistening roof of the double-fenced facility.

We encountered only one other moving vehicle on our seventy-mile drive—a Humvee carrying four heavily armed, stone-faced MPs. Several miles in, the sight of two side-by-side buildings gave me chills—the remains of a barely recognizable adobe house with an old-fashioned tractor alongside, and a large, 1950s-era multi-vehicle garage. Its walls had broken down and the roof had collapsed. Rows of large bullet holes streaked through it—clearly it had been strafed from the sky with precision. The second building was also leveled in several places, apparently by missiles. It was the tractor, more than anything, however, that put me on edge. It didn't look as though it had just been struck—even by a bomb. Its shape was strangely distorted, the metal melted at angles that were not tractorlike, a sign of great heat. I hated to think the government could be testing metal-melting bombs out here, in proximity to towns, schools, and pregnant women. Each abandoned building, homestead, and overturned vehicle made me want to point and ask questions, but I kept mum.

Mirages mirrored and disappeared on the road in front of us and coyotes skulked through the mesquite. I didn't see a rattlesnake but then, it was winter, which is when they hibernate. The first southern miles featured mostly low vegetation and salt grass with no trees except on the hillsides. Vast prickly-pear patches grew here and there, an army of short, green gremlins on a deadly march, their large pear-shaped pads studded with long, menacing thorns. Each brandished a dusty, dark-green fruit pod that looked like a grenade. Thirty miles north, the alkali-stained white sand gave way to green, ten-foot-tall mesquite trees that had developed jade-colored bean sprouts from the recent rains. About as nutritious as average alfalfa, they were a good source of protein for the remaining horses. I was glad to see them.

As the wheels hummed along the faded black macadam road, Patrick and Brian mumbled to each other about salt water and pupfish, little birds and bighorn sheep, talking shop about Category 01 fish, the phylum *Chordata,* subphylum *vertebrata* stuff. More than just horses' lives depended on the resolution of the herds' plight: We passed places where the horses had obviously overgrazed grasses and destroyed low shrubs and bushes. Suddenly Patrick sat upright, grabbed the steering wheel with both hands, and turned abruptly right, sending the Suburban east along another old paved road. I slammed up against the door and Patrick looked back through the rearview mirror. The commotion must have jogged Patrick's memory and reminded him that he had another passenger and a mission more important than merely providing transportation. As we rolled past a two-foot-tall pile of horse manure he began to give me a quick summary of the distribution of horses on the range. Much of the information was not new to me, but it helped ease my growing anxiety and injected a sense of normalcy as I viewed the decidedly abnormal sights.

"There are four main herds out here," he began. "They all live on the northern half of the range. That's about six hundred thousand acres. We refer to the herds by the place they use as their primary water source: Mound Springs in the middle north, Malpais Springs south-central and sort of easterly, Salt Creek over on the west side where we just passed through, and the Oscura Range in the way northeast. We have different varieties of horses out here. There are recognizable mustangs but no real Spanish Barb tiger stripes. Thoroughbred blood is here, quarter horses, draft horses, no paints or Appaloosas, and as many blends as you can imagine. The herds are generally a mix, but they seem to know to steer clear of each other's watering hole." Patrick stopped and tipped the brim of his hat at some sage grouse and said he thought he saw through the brush a whitetail buck looking to sneak across the range road. Occasionally a modern fighter aircraft would streak across the basin at what seemed a hundred feet up from the top of the trees and he would point and just bark a name matter-of-fact like, "Warthog," or "F-16," or "F-117A," and "B2" for the stealthy ones. He'd thumb south and spit out, "Holloman," or jab north and east to "Cannon Air Force Base." Then quick as that he'd go on about the critters, since these marvelous air battleships were everyday to him. "The horses involved in the die-off are the Mound Springs herd. They are in somewhat better shape now because we had some rain this fall, but many are still not good."

Abruptly, Dr. Locke shouted something that sounded like "Armageddon" and Patrick hit the brakes, again jarring me out of my half-listening, desert-mesmerized daydream. He pulled willy-nilly off the paved road and headed off briefly into the jutting dunes and mesquite brush forest. Dr. Locke looked like Indiana Jones spotting the Temple of Doom, and has kept shouting, "Armageddon," and urging Patrick to step on it. I braced with my arms on the roof and my legs planted on the metal floor as we hurtled left and right, up and down, through the roughest ride I'd known. I thought at any minute that we'd be swallowed by some long-forgotten bomb-gouged hole or hit a rocket that had neglected to explode.

"There," Dr. Locke screeched again. Patrick slammed the brakes, spun the wheel, and the vehicle drifted to a slow-motion stop sideways in the loose sand. They both popped the doors open, hopped out, and ran hard-south on foot while pointing and gesturing wildly at something downrange. I flipped my seat belt loose, missed my first step on secret soil, and landed on palms and knees in the cool gypsum. My Western hat rolled on the brim for several feet and then toppled over on its silver crown. In stunned silence, I knelt there afraid for my life without a clue why, as dust swirled around me like a little desert devil. Off in the distance I could just make out Dr. Locke still shouting about Armageddon. I couldn't understand.

About ten minutes later they returned, running just as hard as when they'd left. Patrick, though more portly than when he had been a young track star, still showed signs of his former 440 ability. Dr. Locke, arms pumping like a jackhammer, was back a few paces but holding his own. Patrick yelled something unintelligible in my general direction and pointed for me to get back in the truck—fast. I grabbed my hat, practically levitating into the truck as both men struggled around their open doors, smashed back into their seats, and slammed the doors tight. Patrick hit the ignition, crammed the gear into reverse, and raced the engine as we backed thirty yards where just as suddenly he stopped and we sank a few inches in the sand. I couldn't see a thing for two full minutes until the dust settled around the vehicle. Both runners breathed heavily, and Patrick looked over at an exhausted Dr. Locke. "Think he stopped?"

Brian shrugged.

I sat there dumbfounded, when out of the dust eddies in front of us emerged a 450-pound male antelope with several females and calves. His two horns stood thirty-two inches straight up, and angled from his hard skull. With a sense of who he was, the bull stood guard as the harem drifted back into the dense green and brown. Patrick looked into his rearview mirror at my pale-white face and smiled. "Pissed-off oryx bull," he grumbled.

"No sense of humor," Dr. Locke followed.

The only true antelope in North America, ninety-three of these African animals—bulls, females, and calves—were introduced to White Sands in 1969 by the New Mexico Department of Fish and Game to entice hunters to visit the area for annual hunts, and they are still considered game today. As many as three thousand of these animals roam the missile range along with the wild horses, and they thrive in the terrain. Very aggressive, they consider this land their own.

Patrick said, "The African oryx doesn't contribute to the water problems on the range. They have a kidneylike organ in their nose tissue that conserves the water they get from plants."

"Okay," I said. "But Armageddon?" Both men looked at me and each other and a long silence followed. Wrinkling his forehead, Dr. Locke finally looked back at me and said, "Aplomado falcon."

I mulled that over for a minute and then he cleared his throat with a dusty cough and continued, "We saw a big bird back there, before the oryx happened along, an Aplomado falcon. It used to be common along the southern gulf coast of Texas and Mexico. Used to be all over the Southwest. Disappeared as a breeding species during the first half of this century as a result of the combined effects

An oryx, an animal with a humorless flair for the dramatic.
Courtesy of Patrick Morrow, WSMR.

of habitat loss, human persecution, and pesticides. Prior to releases by the Peregrine Fund, the last recorded nest within the United States was west of here a hundred miles in Deming, New Mexico, in 1952." I could tell the scientist loved his find.

"I was born in 1952," I said in a lame attempt to be a part of all of this. Neither man said a word, but Patrick's coal-black eyes flicked at me in the mirror. Dr. Locke flipped open a worn, official-looking notebook and recorded the sighting in a kind of shorthand. I don't think he included my comment.

Our first scheduled stop was the site of the die-off at Mound Springs. The spring itself had been enclosed in a fence made of metal pipe. The top was some six feet high, and it had several middle rails that prohibited larger animals from getting in. It enclosed several hundred feet around the water source to keep the springs themselves from being damaged. Surrounded by tall greenish-yellow willows and other desert plants in what's called the riparian zone, the calcium carbonate spring bubbled up through the deep limestone layers of earth below. Sedimentary marine organism deposits had formed the layers millions of years before, and the flow of water up through the porous calcite had carried minerals with it to create mounds around the springs. Normally, the water pooled in a quarter-acre, salty but clear pond about two feet deep within the fence. A channel had been built from the main pool to a smaller pool just outside the fence where animals could drink. But in the drought, all of the water had dried up. And all around the outside of the fence, clear evidence of the terrible deaths remained.

More than four months had passed, but the scene was still hard to look at. It reminded me of an elephant graveyard I had seen in the Serengeti, in east Africa. Sun-bleached hides and long leg bones lay on the barren White Sands landscape. No living thing stirred near them. Not even ants. I wondered why, and I mulled the lack of prints of coyote and other predators. Why had the prairie wolves not taken the bones for the marrow? A hoof with ratty brown hair jutted out of the ground in one spot and in another a mandible with a molar missing lay glued to the mud near the now-replenished spring. It was an eerie, sorrowful place, and we didn't stay long. Whatever secrets might have been there in July, the military no doubt had done a thorough job of removing them before I came along. The lack of predators and insects stirred my veterinary mind, which started to list possible causes of the deaths. I didn't like the inventory of diseases or toxins that would ward off carnivores or bugs, even six months later, that I came up with.

As we were making our way back to the truck, I mustered the courage to show the men the wrinkled picture from the *El Paso Times* that I carried with me and asked why the baby horse standing over his dead, emaciated mare's carcass was so healthy. They looked at each other then back at me as if they had been asked that same question a million times. Dr. Locke turned and walked away, back to the truck, and Patrick answered in a low, practiced tone. "Doc," he said as if he were a politician writing his own press release. "You know why and I know why. Why talk about it?" Then he, too, turned away, neither sheepish nor smug, and hopped into the truck where Dr. Locke sat biting his thumbnail and writing something in a book that he closed abruptly when I got close. Dr. Locke apparently had a safe distance, and I'd just crossed it.

We were all silent as we drove fifteen miles south down the long, straight desert road where we encountered our first small band of White Sands horses of the day. There were eight altogether, mostly tall brown mares with white blazes and not a single white mark on any other part. Each mare had a yearling at her side, but no new foals. An enormous, lone gray stallion with a fire-yellow mane and tail, easily two hands taller than the others in his group and almost twice as wide, presided over his family. They were very lean but had bloated bellies that could be blamed on the heavy salt content of the water they drank as it mixed with forage high in indigestible fiber and low in protein. Their bellies were not pendulous as they are in starving, anemic human children, but resembled antique bathtubs slung from a bony vertebral column, neck and head bolted on one end and a fly-swatter stapled to the other. The yearlings were as healthy as could be. Patrick watched me as I scrutinized the younger animals.

The horses eyed our vehicle as we approached from several hundred yards off, standing attentive on a small, treeless rise about one hundred yards in from the paved road. They had been feeding on the low salt grass there but didn't take flight as soon as they saw us. Apparently they were accustomed to seeing some traffic on the range and would feed as long as their distance from activity on the road was comfortable. If a two-footer were to step out of a car, they'd be gone in a flash. When we had neared to about a hundred yards, the stallion nudged the mare closest to him and took off at a high-tailed gallop. The other horses stood for a second, looked at us again, and then wheeled and raced behind him. Patrick stopped in the road, and we watched them glide effortlessly across the gleaming white sand toward the mountains miles to the west, followed by billowing clouds of dust bursting skyward. I looked away for just a second, the sun stinging my eyes, and when I looked back they were gone, dust and all, absorbed into the great whiteness all around them.

Crafty old mare leads the escape.
Photo by White Sands Missile Range and Don Höglund.

The huge, flea-bitten, gray stallion with a mane like a forest fire and hooves trimmed perfectly by the sand occupied my mind as we drove. A few more minutes' drive south, we were deep into the heart of the north-central range. We turned onto a narrowing dirt road heading east and approached the southern tip of a rare geological formation of obsidian embedded in the earth. Snaking west and south from its birthplace in the Sacramento Mountains, twenty miles across as its widest, the black, slick, sharp obsidian walls rose twenty-feet high out of the light sands. The volcanic stone was less than one million years old, not yet dulled by age, weather, or wind. As the western end of the magma had flowed and slowed, it had cooled into a five-acre bubble that created a blind canyon—a natural enclosure for holding horses. I marveled at this geological wonder and the practical solution it presented us.

Patrick sighed, slowed the truck to a roll, turned onto a hard-packed sandy lane that snaked between high brush on one side and the lava flow on the other, and stopped in the middle of the road. Under other circumstances he might have pulled off, but White Sands had little traffic and strict guidelines that required vehicles not to stray from official routes, in part because of undetonated missiles and also to protect the unique cultural environment and plant life. Clearing his throat, Patrick glanced at Brian, then turned in his seat to watch my reaction as he said, "There's one thing we haven't talked about, but I think you'd better hear it before we get into the capture site. You'll be meeting Les Gililland. He picked this site, designed it, and is building the capture pens. You might have heard his family name—they're well known around here. Les is a range rider and the son of ranchers whose homestead still sits out here, rotting. His family was one of the ones pushed out by the government in the 1940s. He's kind of bitter about it, and to say the least, Les is . . ." Patrick thought for a moment, "Les is cantankerous." Dr. Locke smiled, nodded slowly, and pursed his lips. He held his thumb and forefinger an inch apart indicating, "just a little bit." I got it.

"I think it's fair to say Les thinks of this land—and of those horses—as at least partly his own. He spends more time out here than anyone else, and he can be trusted implicitly to look out for their interests. Besides, there are probably descendants of the Gililland horses out here."

Brian Locke chimed in, "Les is an excellent caretaker and the workers here respect him, but he may give you some trouble. The last thing he wants to see in this world is those horses taken off this range—and right after that he's going to hate the thought of them

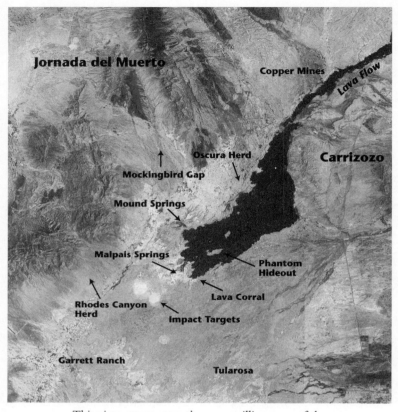

This view covers more than one million acres of the
northern part of the missile range.
Courtesy of Terrametrics, Inc.

taken by an outsider who has twelve years of higher education running the show."

Brian, with his Ph.D., apparently had some experience with Les.
From his downcast eyes, I could see that Les had given him problems. "I've never met a man I can't get a job done with," I
answered—feeling as if I were in a job interview. I'd worked with
all kinds of men, from CEOs in three-piece suits to ten-million-
dollar-a-picture actors who wore whatever the hell they pleased, to

prisoners in stripes, some of them killers and pure sociopaths. I figured that if I could work with all of them and still accomplish something, I could work with Les. I had come to this place with too many reservations to list. But now I was also going to have to placate a cowboy who hated authority.

Patrick hesitated, looked at me hard and long, and, apparently satisfied that I'd at least heard the warning, put the vehicle back in gear and eased us in through the big front gates covered with drab-green tank camouflage netting. We sat at the entrance for a moment and talked about the holding pens that we could see being built straight in front of us by range riders and some construction cowboys. If nothing else was certain, all of them seemed to have accepted that the horses would have to be captured, contained, and moved off the range.

I had to accept that the Army had started building the capture pens and the processing chutes before I got there to advise them, but now I could see that the pens were constructed all wrong. One big cowboy with arms like tree trunks and fingers like branches was slamming a sledge hammer on the top of a center post that was sinking obediently into the hard-packed sand, a good two inches at

The processing chutes at the White Sands Missile Range Lava Corrals.
Courtesy of White Sands Missile Range.

a whack. From the corner of his eye, he watched every move we made. That had to be Les Gililland.

We pulled up to the construction site and stepped out into the winter sun. It was short-sleeve weather in the desert and I was sweating under my sports coat. Patrick signaled to the rail driver, who fixed his eyes on me before he dropped the sledge. Appearing irritated at the interruption, he strode toward us through the sand with authority. He was a strong six-foot-three and looked about ten years older than the early forties he had to be, ruggedly handsome, some would say, with light-blue eyes and leathery tanned skin. He was broad faced, with wide-set eyes, a gap between his front teeth, and a defiant smile that could easily be taken as a sneer. He held a cigarette in the corner of his mouth as if it had been there for most of his life. The all-American cowboy. As Patrick introduced us, I stepped forward to shake his hand. His grip was like a vise and he knew he'd hurt my hand when he squeezed, but no one else did. I've sized up many men over a handshake, including some who were never to be colleagues or friends, but none—even the inmates—had exuded hostility as clearly as Les Gililland. Obviously he had known that I was coming, and he wanted no part of my advice. I was in for a rough start.

We were of similar build, although he was an inch taller and more angular, and I was broader. But both of us were lean and muscular from long days of working with horses and taking the inevitable lumps that come with that job. We were about the same age and weathered from the sun, but Les's face bore the deeper lines. My hair was just starting to turn gray at the temples, but his full head of short unruly hair had turned completely gray.

His workers closed ranks behind Les as he stepped back to size me up. I could feel the disrespect coming from him. I was office-clean while Les and his crew were dirty from the hours of hard work already behind them. In another setting, that would have been to my advantage, but out on the wilds of the military range, my pressed shirt worked against me. Thankfully my boots would tell any range-hand I was no novice to outdoor labor. There's nothing more pathetic in their eyes than a guy who shows up on in a new pair of four-hundred-dollar alligator boots and a Stetson that don't sit right. One of the worst criticisms a Southwesterner can level against a newcomer is that he is "all hat and no horses."

Les's blue eyes melted into dog-angry black, his lips tightened to thin threads, and he squared his shoulders. I'd have to watch my back with him. He turned to Patrick and began updating him on the status of the holding pens in growling, short statements that left no room for maybe. Pointing with his leathery chin for emphasis, he smoked but never touched the cigarette with his hand. It burned ember-red when he sucked and smoldered in between. Les didn't look at me or address me again until I asked a pointed question about the design problem I'd spotted in the construction— one that would be much harder to repair down the line than right now. Without looking at me, Les dismissed my comment with a quick, "these pens are fine," and continued talking with Patrick. But I stepped forward to explain, and Patrick interjected that I'd helped design and build the corrals at the prisons in Las Cruces and Santa Fe. When the crew realized I'd had a hand in gentling and adopting thousands of horses through that program, most granted me a small margin of credibility and were willing to talk and listen. After a forced, uncomfortable conversation, the crew stepped off one by one and set about making the change without Les's direction. A few of the workers seemed to let up on me right then—seeing that I at least knew something about building a reliable horse enclosure. Seething, Les breathed through gritted teeth and watched them.

Hanging back from the others, Les kept a wary eye on me, occasionally asking a question that seemed designed to trip me up. He spit out the burnt filter of his cigarette and lit another, replacing it in the crook of his mouth as he said that there was a potential problem with a blood test the horses required before they could leave the state of New Mexico and that if I couldn't solve the issue, the horses couldn't leave the missile range and we should just forget the whole idea of captures. It reminded me of exchanges I'd had with

Jimmy Begay and other prisoners about freeing the wild horses in the prison program. Many times he had told me that the fur looked better on the mink and that the horses deserved the freedom of the range.

Les's quiet assessment of me, and his few carefully worded challenges to my presence in his territory, made it clear that for as long as I was on the missile range, I'd have to keep my eye on him. He didn't want me there, and I didn't blame him. He'd spent most of his adult life feeling personally responsible for these horses, and now many were suffering and many had died and many were going to be shipped away. It was a problem he was afraid to entrust to anyone other than himself. The biggest resentment he had, I figured, was that the military didn't trust him enough to give him full authority over the rescue operation. I sensed that really got to him and hurt his feelings, and I felt sorry about adding to his bitterness. That is, until he insulted me again. Which only took about another thirty seconds.

That afternoon, the biologists and I left White Sands range from the nearby east gate. I felt overwhelmed by my hours of immersion in that dramatic landscape, by the majesty of those large horses running across the dunes, and by the horror of the horse die-off. Clearly they had suffered. They had foamed at the mouth, beaten their heads on the ground, broken their teeth, and died terrible, agonizing deaths. It looked to me that they had suffocated, and I could not think of any manner of death, except maybe fire, that would be worse than drowning in their own lung fluids, or even blood. My mind raced through the chemical weapons I had read were used in the Gulf War and might have been tested at White Sands. Doubtless the military had stores of nerve agents, anthrax, and other weapons of biological war, but I doubted the authorities would tell me if these had played any role in the torturous deaths of those horses.

It seemed implausible that the Mound Springs horses could all have died of starvation and dehydration in the same few days, but that was the official story. I had just enough understanding of chemical science to realize that if there were some other culprit, surely anything that could kill scores of half-ton animals, it could kill me, too. But whatever it was, it hadn't killed the nursing foals. It hadn't even made them sick. That fact burned in the center of my brain. The easiest way to protect myself would have been to head straight back to Colorado and forget the whole matter.

Chapter 4

Little Road Block,
Big Cottonwood Tree

Alamogordo, New Mexico, looks as if the whole community had slipped from the peaks of the mountains above it to lodge at the base in an awkward pileup. Handsome nonetheless, the village was low slung, low roofed, and the distance between its earthen structures and the cobbled avenue was the width of a screen door. The late afternoon sun cast an amber hue on the bundles of red chili peppers adorning the doors and windows of small curios shops. The delightful scent of pasolé, a stew of onions and browned pork, heavy with garlic and green chili, wafted from a small café. It was almost too perfectly quaint, and I found myself wondering if the place glowed at night.

Past the partitioned homes and street markets jutted a fifty-year-old, World War II military barracks, still active. Within a block, the pretty town suddenly morphed into a loud jam of vehicles centered around the liquor store. Pickups, loaded with GIs, crammed into stunted parking stalls while an occasional low-rider, teeming with local Hispanic youth, sneered and honked at the burr-heads. *Damned suicidal attitude,* I thought.

Patrick cranked the radio dial of his Suburban that we had picked up back at the main gate and the theme music of *Thunder Alley* bellowed inside my head as we cruised through the crowd. The uneven road made my teeth rattle to the loud music. Brian drummed his fingers on his cloak-and-dagger notebook and panted.

Patrick yelled over the music that he and his wife Shelly had just built a new home for themselves and their first baby, Clay, on the hillside south of town. Alamogordo (Spanish for big cottonwood tree") did not have the cultural flavor of villages in the northern reaches of the state, he explained. This once-Apache territory was calm enough on the surface, but it had no real middle class to stabilize it. "That's a recipe for trouble," Patrick said. At the top are the rich retirees and at the bottom the military and laborers, for whom two incomes means that their status improves from miserable to impoverished. As in so many Southwest towns, there is an open resentment of money flaunted, white authority, and the frequent roadblocks that go with the military presence. Sent by Roosevelt and Truman fifty years earlier, the military had stayed, and so had the bitterness it engendered. After all, what community likes occupation? I spotted rodeo grounds, with a nice fence around them, as the place where I'd won a cutting horse competition years earlier, and logged that into the column of good things to remember about Alamogordo. And possibly it would be a good place to hold a well-planned auction for wild horses.

We rounded west and the evening sun reflected from the bumpers of recreational vehicles lumbering south, heading for El Paso or Juarez, Mexico. Rays bounced off Patrick's two-sizes-too-small sunglasses and hit me straight on, contributing to a brewing migraine.

Patrick's charcoal sideburns boasted a Hispanic gene, his face round, strong, and tanned. His talk conveyed he had an excellent grasp of his employer's needs and of the environmental and cultural complications in the basin. And I admired my new biologist friend's way of handling conflict. I could learn from him. As he moved the day's toothpick from the corner of his weathered lips to his front teeth to bite it into mush even as he continued his dissertation on our surroundings, I realized that Patrick wanted to ask me something. He wasn't ready, though I could feel that his friendly talk was leading somewhere.

Brian Locke seemed annoyed, and I wondered if my standoff with Les had caused the guy's mood swing. I had done my best with a difficult man, but maybe I'd done wrong and would be heading home soon enough. The Suburban crawled behind a long line of cars, and Patrick sighed. Brian popped open his folder and ran his finger down the page. "Yep," he mumbled, "four o'clock sharp." He pointed to the head of the line while Patrick looked long and hard at his watch. I was stalled at my first military roadblock.

At the head of the line an old rancher stood in front of his faded army-green pickup, berating a pretty, young, female MP. The strain on his face reflected his pain. A few aged mama cows shifted in the rusted truck bed. He gestured out toward the desert and gave a toothless speech until, suddenly exhausted, he leaned back on the truck and scowled. The MP's hands pleaded for him to relax like the other people at the roadblock and motioned for him to get inside his truck. It looked like they had done this dance before.

The area known as the White Sands proving ground had been established in 1942 when the British were invited to practice bombing runs there to prepare to retaliate for Hitler's blitzkrieg attempt to bomb London out of existence. After Germany had surrendered, White Sands Missile Range evolved from proving ground to testing site for ground-based and aerial artillery, opening for business on July 9, 1945. The local ranchers had been patriotic, some vocal, all loyal, but the fact remained that the U.S. Army had "borrowed" more than two million acres of ranchland for a pittance. The military claimed, of course, that they had purchased the property fair and square, but some of the ranchers still demanded the return of their property, arguing that the Germans, Japanese, and others had had to return the spoils of war, so the U.S. Army should have to return their land, too. I understood the local resentment at the Army's practice of eminent domain. These lands of the American West meant more than money to the locals.

Brian interrupted my musings with a motion toward the center of the desert. A thin column of dust appeared about fifteen miles in as a screaming Stealth A-117 headed back to Holloman Air Base. The runway was broadside, five miles straight in front of us.

The guards stepped back, abruptly ending the roadblock. The cars began to roll around the old rancher's personal little roadblock. Patrick yelled in a high-pitched voice through the window to the old codger as we rolled past. *"Qué pasa, Señor?"* The rancher looked at the Suburban and its government tags in disgust. After about a mile Patrick looked at me in the rearview mirror and explained, "Les's kin. Tons of them around here. They're good people, just bitter."

That night, I sat in the delightful Pancho Villa bar in the Holiday Inn in Las Cruces and ordered a tall, double vodka and tonic—my second. Old photos of the Mexican revolutionary and his hombres on spirited horses decorated the stucco walls. The bandit mustangs struck fierce poses, their hooves flailing the air as if on attack. They looked identical in size, shape, and color to the horses I'd watched fade into the crimson escarpment of the San Andres Mountains earlier that day. I couldn't help but wonder if the gray stallion with the fiery yellow mane was related to Pancho's band. Each creature in this isolated corner of the West was linked to those of its kind that had come before.

The hotel sat across the main drag that fronted New Mexico State University. Being near a university always calmed me. The bustling library there had been a good friend to me years earlier when I had worked with wild horses and prison inmates. Here I was camped again in the same little college town, in the identical hotel, in the exact cozy bedroom with its comforting Kiva fireplace tucked neatly in the corner. It helped ease all my fears. In a few days, if I stayed, I would undertake the most dangerous task I'd ever faced. I needed an exit strategy, and kept hearing the lyrics "Slip out the back, Jack." I was second-guessing my abilities to live with the constant danger that working with wild horses presents, even though it had once been a way of life. I drummed the table and slammed my vodka-tonic between gulps.

At the end of the bar, a tall, heavy Native-American man with broken glasses and a weathered, angular face nodded to me. I liked the look of him. I raised my glass, and in a minute we were talking. He went by Maynard, and he had lived around Cloud Croft and Alamogordo all his life. A full-blooded Mescalero Apache, he was way-out-West these seventy miles from home in Las Cruces studying about Victorio, a famous Warm Springs Apache and evidently a relative of his. The library was a favorite place of Maynard's as well. Victorio had a peak named for him in the middle of the missile range and was the last of the real-life free Apaches of more than hundred years ago.

A retired teacher, Maynard was well-spoken and easy to listen to. His hair was naturally jet black and trapped under a classic red headband. His chocolate-hued face spoke of the wisdom of an ancient people. I marveled at his thick bifocals, which rested on the huge bump in the middle of his considerable nose and wondered if he knew that I knew that the right lens was gone. Like every other local for a hundred miles, my new friend knew all about the history of the White Sands horses, and about the fate of the 122 horses that had brought me there, and he liked to talk conspiracy. His talk eased me into my third vodka, a single this time. Maynard drank a strong lemon in water with a shot of Tabasco and chewed Red Man tobacco. He leafed out the tobacco from a little pack stuck in the inside pocket of his handcrafted vest, then wrapped the tobacco pouch around itself with a precision known only to a true aficionado. He chose his words only after thinking about them. I could tell he was a careful man. Refusing the peanuts in the small, colorful clay dish, he ordered a popcorn refill. He'd been eating maize for seventy years and liked it salty. Peanuts gave him gas.

"Those horses are a part of this place," his soft voice informed me, after I'd moved to a stool one away from his to talk easier. "They belong to all of us—to the descendants of the Spaniards who brought them, to the sons of the Comanche and some Apache who became great horsemen, to the ranchers who bred them and raised them and had to leave them behind on the missile range." Initially, he said, the natives had been quite surprised when they saw Spaniards mounted on those horses, but if a brave could master it, it looked like a better way to get around. "You could ride your lunch to work." Maynard smirked as tipped his glass for another short, lippy taste of spiced tobacco, and then winked at me.

"In the early 1940s, when everybody here was asked to depart to safer ground, the cattle were easy to catch and they didn't venture too far from the well house and the nightly grain fed them. The ranch horses were rangy," he added. I nodded, assuming that was slang for horses that liked to travel a bit.

"Who they don't belong to is those people who've been sitting around a table at the range for six months arguing about who is going to pay to get them off their land, how they're going to do it, and just how much they can stand to have the press poking around out there before it's too much," he said.

Maynard gave me a first-class seminar on Indian lore, phantom stallions on the missile range, ghost mines, and Apache customs. Then he asked, "So, I wonder, what do you have to do with it?"

I told him I wasn't sure about anything. If I did stay to help— and if they still wanted my help—Maynard and I agreed to meet again at Pancho's and perhaps later, over in Alamogordo, where Maynard was sure I'd be living at the Holiday Inn soon. That hotel was closer by eighty miles to the capture pens than the one we sat in that night. He said it was where he preferred to not-drink. Then he pushed the popcorn tray away. I wobbled a bit in my chair, pushed my half-full glass of ignorance with a touch of lemon and tonic out of arm's reach, stood on weak knees, and bid Maynard a fond *adios*. He frowned at me as if he didn't understand. I smiled.

In the morning, I met with Brian Locke for breakfast in the same bar-restaurant. He had never dealt with a mess like the one that greeted him at the missile range each morning. Brian asked if I could stay and help, but I'd seen half a dozen sights on the previous day that made me inclined to stay away from the White Sands Missile Range for the rest of my life.

"What do you see when you look at those horses?" Brian prodded. "Don't you see something worth saving, even if you have to get in there and get your hands dirty?" Brian was trying, I'd give him that.

I set down my menu and ordered coffee, black. "I see a piece of American history—and I see a part of it has already been destroyed. But the military and the state have plenty of veterinarians who can help you."

"You and I both know your experience is unique in this area, and we can't afford to botch it up. There's too much at stake—from the general's next star to this state's tourism, and how many of those horses will end up standing in line for slaughter next year."

Brian paused until the waiter had arranged the huevos rancheros he'd ordered us squarely in the center of our dilemma. "We're all willing to do this right. The Army, the governor—they want to do the right thing for these horses, but there are holes in the plan right now. You've forgotten more about wild horses than most of the people involved in this project will ever know, and we need some help."

I glanced out the window, then at the table, and considered everything. I felt something along the lines of guilt. My real job here would be more like bullfighting than healing, and with the world in attendance. And my objective was to keep the "bull" alive instead of killing him while he tried to pound me.

"You might remember your oath," Brian said.

I swear he'd read my mind. My veterinary oath, word for word, was coming back to me once again. I had sworn to aid in the relief of animal pain and suffering. I scoured my recall for any fine print suggesting that if it was too dangerous or if I didn't trust someone or disliked anybody, I could disregard the oath. No such release clause there. By the time I'd finished my coffee, Brian had shamed me into agreeing to help write the strategic plan that would start the rescue off properly and safely for everyone. When I looked up, I could have sworn I saw a glimmer of acceptance in old Pancho Villa's eyes. I'd help write the book on captures. After that, I'd probably hightail it to safer pastures.

Brian jarred more than our breakfast when he tossed a heavy stack of bound governmental-looking papers on the old cedar table, opened to the first page. Big bold letters glared at me: DRAFT ENVI-RONMENTAL ASSESSMENT FOR FERAL HORSE MANAGEMENT, U.S. ARMY. It had the smell of a classified document and as always happens, if you touch a federal document, you are inducted. When I helped with the prison program, that "helping a little" grew to long-term involvement. Once you took hold of something even tentatively, they jerked you in before you could let go.

Brian flipped over the cover and put it squarely into my open hand. In large red letters, the page read: RESTRICTED USE ONLY. Pancho winked.

I needed a risk assessment, and I'd just gotten one. The 142 pages would help me formulate our strategy for removing the horses from White Sands. My first step was to make sure we had someplace safe to take the horses off-range once they were caught. Few will welcome eighteen hundred wild horses, some of which also carried bellies full of baby horses, for an indeterminate period. My preference was for the ranch I knew in Oklahoma, but I needed to find out how many horses it could hold, and what taking them there would cost John Q.

"We already have a potential place in mind," Brian told me, and then outlined a plan that had been offered up by the head of a wild horse rescue group. She wanted all of the horses to go to a hundred-thousand-acre, unfenced ranch in Arizona to create a foal production brood farm that would generate a constant stream of revenue for her fledgling animal rights group. And while she wanted the military to fund the start-up in my mind, unfenced meant free to roam, and if I knew horses, those transplanted White Sands horses would simply roam home. I could see it clearly. The stallions would stop off at every ranch along their journey back to the desert, their original home, dry and waterless or not. It would be high spring-time then, and after breeding every mare they could find, tearing down every fence, and trampling the last remaining garden or eating the crops to stubs in the field, they'd strike out on the first major highway they found, cars and semis be damned. I shook my head at the thought. The White Sands horses would be back in New Mexico in a few weeks, though a few would have met a fate worse than starvation on the range. But I knew that the alternative we came up with would have to meet the scrutiny of the animal rights reps or they and the media would ruin careers over it.

That night I needed another dose of Maynard. I sat with my new mentor at Pancho's hotel bar again and talked horses. Maynard told stories that sounded real about white stallions on the staked plains of Texas and life in a white West. I told him I loved horses and how I had wanted to believe in these creatures who could survive without humans.

Referring to the Captain Mackenzie slaughter, Maynard said that the legend of the horses needed to live on, but we needed to learn from past failures. The parallels between the White Sands horses living among a modern army and the horses slaughtered at Palo Duro Canyon by a frontier army nearly 120 years earlier carried an eerie resonance. The old Mescalero Apache rested his thick arms on the rosewood bar and leaned into his dissertation on the spirit world and the connection between the People, as he called Native Americans, and the horse. "Mythology explains to the People everything that happened before people came up from the ground. The old medicine men chant about it and tell the stories about the business of life as a Mescalero, all of it symbolizing Apache belief."

I ordered a no-alcohol drink and he continued, his fingers rolling and twisting as if he were drawing his stories in the smoky air of the room, "Life is a process, a dance—an interpretation of the teaching of the mountain gods. Every growing thing, all of the elements of nature, the horses, are the bloodstream of life. In the beginning there was Yusn, the Creator of All, whom nobody knew very much about." Maynard touched my arm with his soft fingers, sending a hair-raising energy up to my shoulder, as he said, "Close to the People are the other mountain spirits, who lived inside the sacred mountains, the Sacramentos, you white men call them." The old man thumbed to the east and finished, "Sometimes the spirits reveal themselves to those in need of something, or the distressed. Sometimes the spirits call on people who can help."

Maynard was trying to get me to think of the horse problem as more than just a die-off. He wanted me to see a kind of spiritual journey of the horse and man together, the horse as the oldest member on earth and man as the newest. I thought of Midnight, a horse from the 1930s, that became the foundation sire of quarter horses since then. I'd collected photographs of Midnight over the years and both the first gray stallion I had ever seen on White Sands as well as the stallion I had seen the day before looked just like Midnight. They were gray turning to white, with husky bodies, brute shoulders, thick leg bones, foxlike ears, refined heads and the unusual, flame-yellow mane and tail. I also knew the form because I owned several of Midnight's offspring. "Midnight horses are out there, on that missile range," I blurted. "I saw two of them."

Maynard nodded with the assurance that only comes from knowing something is true. "Midnight's out there with seven others, standing guard. Apaches are very afraid of ghosts," he informed me. "The Apaches' unwritten Bible tells us that ghosts are found on the range. But the people believe that there is power in every piece of nature and that that force could be channeled for good or evil. The Mescalero has a deep understanding of these things."

Maynard passed the legend into me, instead of just at me. He wanted me to see that the gray stallions were being driven by a spirit. Although they had been slaughtered in Palo Duro, they had survived the atom bomb. He gave the U.S. Army credit that they'd refused to let history repeat itself. "The rescue is going to happen, with or without you," he concluded. "If you understand the calling and you know the way of it, you should get in touch with the feelings that go after good and stop the evil." Maynard shrugged and shoveled a load of popcorn into his mouth.

I pushed back my test-glass of Tabasco-spiked ice water, without tobacco, thanked my new mentor for the incentive to do the right thing, and dragged my feet to my lodging. My life would take a drastic turn when I awoke in four hours.

In my room overlooking the library at the university, I marveled at the flickering Christmas *farolitos,* the little lanterns that lined the roofs and walkways of every building and house. They reminded me of the life I'd loved in New Mexico. I called the good people at the BLM, the Bureau of Land Management, and left a message that I would not be heading for Palomino Valley, Nevada, and the National Wild Horse and Burro program. At forty-two years old, aging by the second, I'd been drafted.

The next morning, the biologists outfitted me with a desk at an environmental contractor's office in Las Cruces, gave me several computers, and promised any assistance I needed to lay out the strategy to get things moving forward. We were all acutely aware that if the captures didn't begin before the foaling season in early spring, the horses could suffer another die-off. With Dr. Brian Locke at my side much of the time, we worked through the next seventy-two hours, generating a plan for the removal, veterinary treatment, short-term accommodations, and long-term adoptions—slaughter-proof and rodeoproof—of the horses. The work felt more important than anything I'd ever done.

At daybreak on December 8, 1994, we finished a series of fact sheets describing the basis for the strategy to capture the animals, their medical and surgical needs, and transport requirements to the National Wild Horse Sanctuary in Bartlesville, Oklahoma, owned and operated by Tadpole Cattle Company, the horse holding place I'd proposed to Brian. With the package I submitted the paperwork including a letter from the leader of the International Society for the Protection of Mustangs and Burros declaring the Tadpole ranch the best place ever—for a wild horse to roam.

Immediately a hitch in the plan became apparent. Because the government wanted no ownership of the horses once they were confined at the missile range, the moment they were captured and fed they needed to be transferred from the care of the United States military to that of an independent agent. The Oklahoma ranch refused to accept ownership as well. So, we added a note to the final contract that a "private, knowledgeable entity" would act as an agent for the Army and accept responsibility for the horses from capture to adoption. Unadopted horses would remain the responsibility of that agent after the expiration of the agreement. I named a few agent candidates I felt were good and capable horsemen, but in the end, Patrick Morrow would have none of it, saying that the White Sands horse rescue needed someone who could chase five hundred flesh-and-blood ghosts at a full run toward the razor-sharp obsidian corral, turn them at the last moment, slow them to a trot, and capture them safely. I looked down to find that beneath the line where the agent had to sign the one-page letter agreement was my name. Nobody's horses, whether starved, injured, unborn, or unwanted, were about to become mine.

PART II

"Call Up All Your Cowboys."

—Eugene Manlove Rhodes, *Out West*

Chapter 5

Off to the Races

Wild horses behave wildly because it's their nature. Horses evolved as prey animals and nothing about that has changed. They prefer flight to fight, but as anyone who has ever cornered a scared mare knows, she will fight when pressured. Horses can strike with the front feet faster than the blink of an eye. A threatened mare will bite and kick and strike without equal. As equine veterinarians and people training or shoeing horses will attest, you might see a hind hoof just before you feel it, but the front legs will hit you before you ever see them coming, even if you are looking right at them. Most of the horse's fighting behavior is programmed in their genetic code, but throughout the eons, those who learned to avoid danger probably lived longer, and naturally passed their prey-animal instincts to more offspring. Some preternaturally aggressive oddballs do exist, and as cowboys who have dealt with wild mustangs know, one in ten thousand of those wild horses are man-eaters, nearly carnivores, and they will not be changed by any manner of gentling.

Each morning before working at the range, I ate a large stack of pancakes at the local diner. I had no way of knowing when I might eat next, and wasn't accustomed to brown-bagging it. By the time I remembered I had food stashed in the truck, it had melted, spoiled, or ripened beyond recognition. At four thirty in the morning, while it was still dark, I drove to the Missile Range guard shack on the eastern boundary of the range, and from there the fifteen miles north to the capture site. Each evening, I drove back after a hard day's work to the Holiday Inn in Alamogordo, my new home for the next eleven months, as my wise Apache friend had foreseen.

My primary contact at White Sands, Patrick Morrow, did everything possible to help ensure the success of our mission. My day-to-day partner in the hands-on work was Les Gililland. Les worked as hard as any man I have ever met, and he commanded the same kind of passion from his crew. He made a point of keeping his distance, always looking at me through squinted eyes, his head cocked to the side, searching my face for signs of emotion or weakness. Often he wouldn't speak to me for hours, even though we worked as a team, practically nose to nose. This made for some long, monotonous hours while we surveyed the horse herds on the six-hundred-thousand-acre northern territory by aircraft and truck. I guess that after years of watching state and federal government people talk and argue and debate and do nothing, in his view, to help the horses, he had good reason to be guarded. He still didn't peg me for a real cowboy. To him, I was just one of *them*.

As the person who knew the most about the range's horses, Les was invaluable in finding them. It was a big area to search, but Les knew it from corner post to corner post. Patrick's head would be on the chopping block if any miscalculations resulted in problems during the captures, so we counted and recounted the horses from afar, and the crews then helped me assess their health and readiness for capture.

After watching Les do his job, I finally decided that he was angry, not mean-spirited. Anger is a secondary emotion, and that concerned me, not for my well-being—but for the horses'. Horses are adept at reading body language and Les's anger could breed fear in the animals. I needed to do something about Les's surly disposition. I didn't think a beating would do it. I also didn't think I could get a beating done fairly. He was too big and too tough. I'd have to plan an assault on his attitude and sneak up on him.

Even with all the media attention and the involvement of officials from the top ranks of the military, state, and federal agencies, the horses on White Sands Missile Range continued to take a backseat to the range's primary function: weapons testing. The military as well as private weapons companies like Raytheon and Martin Marietta had had dates on the White Sands calendar for months in advance, sometimes years. The private companies paid the military for airspace and ground support, and these testing days were absolute. Any horse rescue operation had to be scheduled around them. The military could just as easily, and legally, have shot the remaining wild horses on the missile range, so we needed to get moving on the captures before the Army changed its mind.

The first order of business was safety training. All of us were schooled for a full day on security, how to avoid unspent munitions on the ground, what dangers to look for, and the absolute importance of not going where we shouldn't. The range was a dangerous place, even when bombs weren't being dropped.

To catch a wild horse, we had to use the horse's inherent behaviors to our advantage. Just as in the prison training programs, the horse should be made to think that the route she travels is her idea. I wasn't worried about that part of it. We just had to do it all before the major foal-dropping time in the middle of spring. It would be better to herd a pregnant mare slowly than to stress a newborn in the all-important days just after birth.

Each cowboy employed for the captures had to have unique horse talent, and every part of our large holding facility had to be camouflaged to blend in with the surrounding scenery. The smaller holding pens were constructed to help the team sort horses, so that stallions would be housed with stallions, and mares and nursing young together. Weaned animals up to two years could live together regardless of their sex.

All that the White Sands horses had needed in their wild lives was food and water and space to roam. They didn't need vaccines or wormer medications. They didn't need blood tests and brands or trailers or health certificates. They didn't need covered enclosures or water tanks or huge transport lowboy semis. But they would need all of these now. A modern horse capture faces problems that veteran cowboys like Eugene Rhodes or Pat Garrett or J. Frank Dobie didn't need to think about. Most vaccines and blood tests for such ailments as equine anemia hadn't even been invented back in their day. However, once these horses were captured they became *my* horses from nose to tail tip, and I was responsible for everything—health needs, vaccines, unborn foals. The liabilities were mine, all mine. It was all written in the laws regulating veterinary health care, and what was not there, was in the Army contract. And to transfer the horses one inch off the missile range, I needed signed health certificates and negative equine anemia blood tests recorded, animals de-wormed, stallions castrated, and all adults freeze-branded. I also needed a heaping dose of patience.

On the chilly, tense February morning of our first horse capture, I met my crew early at the Malpais lava flow. The team included three helicopter pilots, Patrick, six range riders, selected from the White Sands construction crew, trained on all-terrain vehicles, and led by Les, and another half dozen handlers on the ground who stood ready to close the gates when the horses entered the site—*if* the horses entered the site. We weren't really sure what the horses would do, but we had a lot of strategies. But a potential fly in the ointment was that the powers-that-be had agreed to allow the media to observe this event. There would be twenty-seven national news stations on site, five White Sands public relations people to handle them, and twenty MPs to help with crowd control. And it would be a huge crowd. I'd never conducted a clandestine horse roundup in front of an audience. I was as nervous as if I'd been selected to sing the national anthem at the Super Bowl.

I'd planned this day down to the minute. We arrived at the capture site while it was still dark, ahead of the media, and tucked our vehicles into crevices and behind corners of the lava flow where the horses wouldn't spot them as they ran past. I surveyed the location, trying one last time to anticipate anything that might ward off the herd.

The head of the Society for the Protection of Mustangs and Burros, and two of her supporters, would be among the observers perched on the lava flow. Seemingly confident that her concern for the well-being of the animals made her an expert in all things equine, she would undoubtedly have a video camera at the ready to document any potential flaws in our operation, and of course, her criticisms. If this operation didn't turn out flawlessly, she could become a real enemy as she still wanted the horses for herself, and was jockeying for that right. I'd do anything I could to stop her, but, if I messed up now, she might gain some ground in her appeals.

The pilots turned up right on time, in full flight gear, gloved, with helmets shining. All three brought the hard-earned expertise they'd gained in the Persian Gulf war, and they were as qualified to drop down and rescue troops in a foreign land as they were to chase wild horses across the heart of America. I felt both relieved and nervous when I saw them saunter over to our group. This was happening, and it was happening now. The part of the day's plan I'd entrusted to them might be the only part I didn't have to worry about. Or so I hoped.

According to our strategy, the horses would be herded by the helicopters. The loud ATVs on the ground would apply pressure along their flanks when needed, for bunching, and at the front for turning the herd. For this gathering, we would concentrate on horses that inhabited the land within five miles of the capture site, at Malpais Springs. My chopper would fly north for five miles, and the other two would go to their designated spots. We had drawn out a basic circle with a diameter of about ten miles as the day's working area. Some of the horses would travel up to fifteen miles from the point at which we spotted them, until they were safely inside the capture corrals. Because of the distance, injured horses, the big-bellied mares, and the newborn foals were of special concern. Any horse that looked like it couldn't make it would be culled from the herd by Les or one of his men on an ATV and would be captured by other means later, probably around a watering hole.

Some one hundred horses would move from the open desert up to the south-facing lava wall and pass unwittingly through the covered front gates. Once they were inside, they would arc right, past the recently built and camouflaged working chutes, then arc left and pass through a second set of well-disguised twelve-foot-by-six-foot-high livestock panels used as gates. As the captives thundered past the second opening and into the back lava-walled corral, I hoped they would feel that they'd escaped. The chasers, the choppers, and the ATVs would then back off and wait out of harm's way, as the gatekeeper shut all of the horses inside the back enclosure. As the horses followed the natural contour of the lava formation there, they would see the twenty-foot-high wall of lava one hundred yards in front of and safely encircling them. This large, naturally occurring corral was better than anything my crew and I could have constructed. With plenty of time to slow down and stop and with no humans present, the horses would swirl, calm, and rest. At least that was the idea.

In a wild horse capture, the system can adjust to one or maybe two surprises, but no more. If one old mare in the group got wind of a trap, or spotted an overanxious cameraman, saw the glint of a reflective lens, *or* the white flash of a light, nothing could get her through the green-covered gates. She'd scatter the herd like quail, and then we'd never be able to herd that same group back toward the lava site. Horses have a cast-iron memory.

It was a good plan, but with two busloads of journalists and camera crews due to arrive in a couple hours to document it, it had to be perfect. General Laws, the commander of White Sands, had been leaning on Patrick for weeks to make sure this went off without a hitch. Patrick reminded us that there was no room for error, and the job better get done and done right—today to assure that we all came out heroes at the end of it. The media wouldn't realize that we'd be gone for four hours before they saw the dust and fury of the horses arriving. It would be at least an hour after they spotted us before we pressed the herd up against the southeast side of the lava flow and turned them back west toward the capture flow gates, plenty of time to write some color for their papers and magazines.

Two pilots would fly Kiowa OH-58 reconnaissance helicopters, another piloted a Huey, each painted red and white with ARMY emblazoned on the sides. The choppers were about forty feet long, twelve feet high, and weighed about forty-five hundred pounds empty. I climbed into the left seat of the lead chopper, inspected my flight map, and reread my paperwork to settle my nerves. I studied the herds' locations and average band sizes and memorized the number of foals counted at the last flyover. As I buckled myself into the seat of the chopper, I was filled with fears about how many things could go wrong. Then I noticed that the doors had been removed from the helicopter, so I tugged at the seat belt and shoulder harnesses to make sure they were good and tight—right then I couldn't think of a worse place to fall out of a chopper than over White Sands Missile Range.

My pilot, a captain named Tom, climbed in and reviewed his flight plan. He checked and rechecked his instruments. I put on my headset and tested my connections to the other pilots, to Les, who would lead the team on the ground with the ATVs, and to the crew that would remain at the capture site. Tom turned to me, ready to remind me of my obligations as the passenger in his bird.

"You keep an eye out for dust devils and hawks, both for our chopper and the others," he said. The constantly shifting sand dunes on the missile range frequently offered up dust devils, swirling tornadoes that could rise as high as two hundred feet above the floor of the basin. They were a source of fascination on the ground, but in a chopper they meant danger. Each had the potential to catch a helicopter in its swirling air pattern and flip it.

"How often do the dust devils happen?" I asked, already surveying the landscape.

"Every day," Tom said. He had a good sense of humor.

The hawks and other birds of prey had a different, but equally threatening story. On hot afternoons on the Tularosa plain, they had a bad habit of soaring around the thermals. Birds had been known to crash straight through a chopper's windshield. If we spotted one, the counter-maneuver required the chopper to head straight up, then, usually, the bird would dive, averting the potential disaster.

Fifteen minutes later, with everyone in place and Les's ATV crew positioned on a low rise overlooking the nearby desert, the huge blades of the choppers began slowly to swing around, signaling the start of the rescue. The helicopter jostled up and down as we lifted into the air, tilted, and turned south from the lava flow. We crossed over the camouflaged, one-quarter-mile wing fence that Les had built as an aid for the final touchy minutes of the capture. All looked ready for the race.

The noise was deafening. Dust rose on all sides, grit blew in between my teeth. Shuddering and grumbling, the monstrous machine headed out into the desert morning.

In moments we were out of sight of each other's choppers and the dust clouds of our liftoff had dissipated. The pilots communicated frequently with each other and with the control tower. Because I needed to watch the overall operation, Tom directed our aircraft to about three thousand feet above the surface. The other two choppers were scouring the ground, one to the west and the other south of us. Our air was clear, and the perspective from high up created a familiar sense of control that I'd felt at my last wild horse chase. The picture of the desert gathering began to take form in my head and my false courage gave way to the real thing. My heart raced, but the can-do spirit of our mission took over.

The rugged volcanic peaks of the Sacramento Mountains rose up on the east where they punctuated the Sangre de Cristos chain running north into Colorado and created a natural barrier. The Organ Mountains, the west-side blockade, looked just like the pipes of their namesake and I imagined I heard the portentous opening of J. S. Bach's Toccata and Fugue in D minor—*the Dorian*. Just over the edge of that skyline rested Las Cruces and Pancho Villa.

As we bumped around above the sand, I spotted lines of dust streaming from the moving herds. Eighteen groups of horses were heading south, just as we wanted. But traveling with them were five groups of oryx. We wanted to avoid them because their aggressive, unfriendly attitude could play havoc with our rescue.

We didn't use binoculars in the air because they caused vertigo, so we strained our eyes scouring the topography for horses. Mound Springs, farther north and outside of our range for the day, had many horses gathered around it and I was glad to see a small sparkle of water at their watering hole. About 450 head had survived there, but they were still emaciated, just skin and bones and sinew. There was no vegetation for about four miles out from the spring, and the trails those horses used to get from water to forage were as straight as if they'd been drawn with a level and transit. The horses were all in dire need of food, but before the longer, more complicated drive, we first needed to remove the ones closest to the capture site. Today's horses would have interfered with a Mound Springs herd roundup, which was planned next. Also, the experience we'd get from today's tactics would help us decide the rate of speed and optimal number of Mound Springs horses that our team could safely handle. We might also be able to capture other herds around their water source and not have to chase them at all. Our job was to save lives and relieve the horses' pain and suffering, not re-create an Old West roundup for the excitement and spectacle.

To the north, the herds were as calm as sleeping cattle. They somehow knew we were not after them. To the south, in the capture area, horses scattered like bird-shot pigeons. The path of our choppers had signaled a change in our behavior. The roar of our engines and our low altitude activated their prey response. The same thing happened to prey I had watched in Tanzania during the great wildebeest migrations. When the lion slept, no matter how close, prey foraged nearby. But when the lion stirred and began to stalk in the high grass, turning his face toward them, those same animals would flee. It isn't the presence of the predator, but his behavior and eye contact that cause the prey to react. Whenever we needed to change the horses' direction, we moved in like predators and used the horses' instinct to flee. By dropping our altitude and closing in

on them from the sides, we would funnel them all toward some pre-
determined gathering point.

Today's gathering point for the many individual herds was a spot
three miles directly south of the front gate of the capture pens at the
western tip of the lava flow. All herds being pushed from the north,
west, and south would be driven to that spot. As we planned, each
pilot would descend to the altitude that provoked horse movement
in our intended direction, the early speed determined by the dominant old mares in the group. Once a group was running in the general direction we wanted, the pilot would pull up and move toward
another band. In theory, the plan was solid.

The early morning sun reflected off the fine particles of dust in the
air. If freedom had a color, it was that golden hue. I loved it. It was
like being in the middle of an evolving work of art. Just then, I
knew that I was inside the ring of fire. Our paper plan had come to
life, and now there was no stopping it. From above, the desert
seemed to take on a whole new life. Dust tails emanated from small
pinpoints, bands of horses off in the distance. As the dust clouds
rose and caught the wind, they created various shapes, some
corkscrews, some waving flags. I had to keep track of these various
dust clouds and watch for any change that would require us to react
and adjust our dragnet.

Within three miles of each side of the capture site, several hundred horses in small bands of five to twenty were streaming along,
dust whirling from their hooves. Circling over the herds, I kept a
lookout for young ones. My biggest worry was that those nursing
babies might not be able to keep up with their mothers the whole
distance, and at that age they were incapable of surviving out in the
desert alone. Coyotes would move in on them within minutes if
they were left behind. I was relieved to see that there were only a
few newborn foals.

Below us, we saw a band of more than twenty, huge, dark
horses—and moved in. As we approached them, to start them running south, Tom had to lower our craft until he was only yards from

the horses before they took off at a run. But then they'd stop just far enough away to get a good look back at the chopper. These horses were going to be a challenge. Unafraid of our big bird, they seemed angry at being disturbed. They pinned their ears and some of them kicked a furious hind end at the chopper. The old matriarch in this band was bay and white and was waving her head furiously at us, shaking her mane around like a whip, as if the chopper were just a big horsefly. We approached again from just above the mesquite trees, and when we were almost on the ground the horses took off in earnest— but in the wrong direction. Our herd was headed west instead of south. It was post time, and we needed Les and his team's biker skills to help turn back this herd. I called him on the two-way radio.

Shortly Les and Gary located our galloping herd of wrong-way mares and friends several miles west of the gathering point, insisting on their western route rather than joining the growing southbound river of horses. Les took matters into his experienced hands and broke north close to the herd's right side, and Gary accelerated to get near the lead horse, the mare. Trying to pressure the mare into a slow, gradual turn south, Gary cruised about a hundred yards away from the herd while Les, back a quarter mile, attempted to group the stragglers with the main bunch so that we could turn the horses all at one time. Until a mare leading a group is satisfied that a turn is her idea, she likely won't succumb to any pressure. And this one refused to head south. Sometimes even a solid wall or cliff won't stop a stampede.

Simply to ride on the sand dunes on the missile range took the kind of skill that can't be found even in guys who race dirt bikes for pay. To ride while herding wild horses took experience and sheer guts. Les and Gary, another native cowboy of the area, were the best team of bikers I'd ever seen. Gary had the strength of a gorilla, earned from a life of roping, hard labor, and arm-wrestling. But these guys were pursuing formidable wild horses into mesquite forests whose trees had two-inch thorns that could pierce rhino hide. And among those mesquite forests were prickly-pear cactus patches that sometimes stretched a quarter mile across.

Gary raced his engine, but the best he could do was to turn the herd slightly southwest. Slowing down was not on the mare's mind. The stalemate coursed over five furious miles, the horses shifting right and left. The bikers surged forward, closing the gap, and then lost ground in the loose, shifting sand. From the south side, more horses joined the wrong-direction outlaws until a group of about one hundred horses had coalesced. I couldn't believe it. We were losing the race. And if we arrived at the lava flow short about one hundred equines, the television cameras would duly note it. Failure was not something any of us were accustomed to.

Les flew up and over a ten-foot-tall mound of sand and yucca plants, airborne. It seemed forever before he came down. But he kept going until he'd raced farther to the right of the stampeding herd and was able to speed to the front, ahead of Gary. From our vantage point in the chopper, the bikers were gaining on the matriarch and would catch up with her in a mile or two. Gary tapped on his fuel tank, asking Les if his fuel was all right, and Les signaled a thumbs-up. Now, Tom wanted us to get in on the chase and help, but I signaled for him to wait.

Les and Gary found some hard-packed sand and at full-throttle gained advantage on the herd, darting forward and out front of the lead mare. They veered toward the wide-eyed old girl and with that maneuver finally managed to slow all the horses. The wily mare decelerated to a trot and looked south, where she saw no apparent menace by air or land. That's what we all wanted. Sensing escape, she bolted south and sped to a gallop again. Les looked up at us and jabbed his finger south, and that was our cue to re-engage on the far south side of the herd. From there we could start the horses moving back east, toward the central gathering area south of the lava point. Tom tipped the chopper down and we dived a thousand feet. My heart jumped up into my throat. Then he called for Patrick's chopper to help put pressure on the stragglers, and in ten minutes we had us a nice little bunch of horses headed east.

Once headed in the right direction, the horses needed occasional pressure from the chopper to continue east and slightly north, so we moved up and down, in and out, for almost two hours. The small bands of animals within the large herd shifted and rushed and calmed, the wise old mares trying every imaginable trick to dart back west and out of the larger group. They knew something wasn't right, but while they were adept at guiding their small families, they couldn't turn the tide of the whole galloping herd. We all felt relieved but stayed alert to the possibility of small maverick break-aways.

As all bands being driven by the three choppers began to merge at the gathering point, three miles south of the lava flow, the real fireworks started. Most of the groups were composed of a stallion and his harem, though a few contained only stallions. When our wayward group joined the large herd at the gathering point, the stallions seemed to forget all about the helicopters and turned their attention on each other. It was their nature to fight off any intruding male, and the stress of the chase and the adrenaline generated by the run triggered them into ferocious battles. They reared on their hind legs, struck and pounded each other with their heavy hooves, and gnashed their teeth as they defended their own. With teeth bared, jaws crunched, blood began to flow, and fur flew. We had expected some of this behavior—all White Sands stallions were covered with scars from just such matches—but I was amazed at their disregard for the helicopters. As Tom and the other pilots tried to urge the herd forward, they could nearly touch the stallions with the runners beneath the choppers. The immense horses had no intention of letting another stallion—or a big metal machine—take away their harems.

A big bay stallion raced alongside his harem, head and neck curved toward the ground. Desperately, he tried to lean in and turn his "girls" around. But each time he pressed the herd to turn back, Tom moved the chopper in closer to push them on. After a while, the stallion gave up his attempts to remove all his eight mares and their colts, spun around, and bolted off south on his own. In what seemed like a second he was completely out of sight. Our rear pilot pulled up and began to go back for him, but I told Tom to call him off. That stallion would be back.

Sure enough, in a few minutes, the massive stallion had swung far wide, rethought his position, and come back from the north. He wouldn't abandon his family, no matter where they were going. Their bonds and instincts were too strong.

As I leaned forward to get a better look at the galloping herd, I saw a chestnut mare, pregnant and running hard. For a healthy wild horse, a ten-mile run is barely enough to get winded, but this one was struggling to keep up and was getting tense. I told Tom to pull up and radioed Les below.

"Gililland, do you read me?"

"Loud and clear."

"There's a heavy mare bringing up the rear on the far left of the harem that just came in. She may have had enough. Get her in your sights."

"Ten-four."

Tom drifted up a hundred feet and I looked back at the expec-

Herding along the southeast face of the lava wall during the first roundup.
The Sacramento Mountains are in the distance. The gates are
camouflaged on the right about 1000 yards west.
Courtesy of White Sands Missile Range.

tant mother to see if this was enough distance for her. Her relief was evident as she slowed but forged on in the direction of the herd.

"Les, back off a minute and see how she does." If the herd held together with less pressure from the choppers, she ought to be able to make it to the capture site. If she didn't, we'd be coming back for her and her foal another day. For the moment, she was comfortable enough to keep up the reduced pace.

When we got within two miles of the capture site, the combined herd numbered close to 160 horses. It was an incredible sight to watch them run together, flowing steadily along, a powerful tide surging toward the lava bed.

Back at the capture site, in the brisk winds of the desert morning, the reporters and photographers had arrived on their buses. With the help of the MPs, they took up perches on the lava flow, hiding among the formations there, and waited under the seemingly endless, brilliant blue sky. To the south and east, stark white sand dunes shifted with the wind and the dust cloud over the moving herd drew closer. The mountains to the west were breathtaking, looming against the stark foreground. Blocking their view of the herd, due south, just beyond a bare stretch of desert, was a mesquite forest we were approaching from the far side with the horses.

The horses plunged into the trees, twisting and turning to get through them, and vanishing from our sight from the choppers, since we were now hanging back aways. The only evidence of them was the cloud of dust that continued to rise in their wake. When at last the cloud began to emerge from the far side of the mesquite and roll down the last slow hill before the desert stretch leading to the lava walls, we could also make out the long, broad, black liquid line of horses. Our herd was running full out, wave upon wave coming together in a mass that poured through the low trees, up and down the small rises in the dunes, darting in and out of the shallow arroyos, and then out onto the flat sand just a mile from the southern base of the lava flow.

As the last of the horses emerged from the brushy rise, our three

helicopters lifted up over the outcrop and showed ourselves to them
again. At the same time, the ATV riders came into sight from out
the low mesquite trees, driving the horses up to and along the lava
wall, ever closer to the gates. One mistake now—a biker out of position, an overly wide gap between the ground crew, a chopper suddenly out of fuel, an anxious cameraman shifting on the ridge to get
a better angle, a voice from the lava flow, a glimmer of glass, anything
that spelled danger to an old mare—and the herd would scatter. It
would be chaos, every horse for itself. Babies could be killed, stallions crippled, mares ripped to shreds on the jagged lava. And the
grisly tragedy would be captured on national television news.

As the herd flowed at nearly ten miles an hour directly toward
the lava, the people waiting could begin to make out individual
horses. Even in the melee of this last, full-out run, I had been able
to keep an eye on the pregnant mare that had concerned me. I
couldn't stop her now. The herd was moving too fast and too tightly
for even the most skilled range rider to get inside and cull out a
horse. But I said a silent prayer that I had judged correctly, that she
would be all right, that she would not collapse. I knew of no other
way to capture this many horses in this kind of environment, but
any injuries would be entirely my fault. I strained forward in my
seat, heart pounding, watching for any sign that this drive might fall
apart in the home stretch.

As they neared the lava flow, the horses took the only viable
route, the long slow curve right along the formation's wall that led
directly to the first set of gates. A quarter-mile wing fence draped
in green tank camouflage ran straight out from the gates, and it
blocked a left-flank escape effort as the horses turned into the gated
opening. They were almost there. Could they stay on track, or
would they get bottlenecked at the gate? Everyone in our team held
his breath.

The horses crossed the finish line and raced toward the open cavity
of the natural holding pen in the lava flow. The reporters and photographers gasped as the animals came galloping into the enclo-

sure—several even screamed. For a minute, it looked like the horses wouldn't stop, but within a few feet of the steep, jagged black wall, they finally halted. Horses that had probably never seen one another before found themselves in close quarters, and immediately milled about trying to find their own bands. Heads swung from left to right, stallions tried desperately to regroup their harems, and mares called wildly to their foals.

I radioed "good job" to my tremendous crew and had Tom land our helicopter some distance away from the corral. My legs a little rubbery from the adrenaline rush, I made my way slowly back to the site to sit quietly in my truck. Hugely relieved, but still worried and anxious, I replayed our success in my head. I waited as the media boarded their buses and left the range, as closely supervised as they had been coming in. I closed my eyes and thanked the powers in heaven, over and over.

Inside the lava corral after the first aerial roundup.
The San Andres Mountains in the background, the beginning of
the sorting pens on the right.
Courtesy of White Sands Missile Range.

With the outsiders gone, I scaled the lava flow to find a point where I could crouch behind a grove of boulders and observe the new captives from a safe distance. Walking safely on the top of the flow took "lava-legs," good footing, much like getting sea-legs in a small boat on water, so it took me a cautious while to climb, after the fast action of the drive. The brilliant black shine of the lava emitted a seemingly unnatural heat. The surface of the flow was uneven and had huge pitted sinkholes twenty yards across, like a black, jagged, glassy moonscape. The fractured edges were sharp as fine pieces of shattered glass and a fall meant bloody cuts and scrapes, even broken bones. Finally, on top of the flow, I got my first real close-up look at the mystical White Sands wild horses.

A small sea of horses stretched out below me, but I didn't spend more than a moment in appreciation. Scanning the lava corral one small section at a time, I looked for any animal that seemed injured and for any new foals on the ground. I located the sweaty mare I had been watching from the helicopter, and was relieved to see she was still heavy with her colt, upright, and appeared to be breathing easily.

After I was satisfied that the horses were safe and uninjured, I sat for a long time to admire their diversity, strength of breeding, and awe-inspiring stamina. The predominant characteristics that this group shared were a strong draft-horse build and classic feathering of the hair around the ankle. I wasn't surprised at the predominance of plow-horse features in this herd, as we were only a few miles from Tres Rios, or Three Rivers, where sugar beets had been a major farm crop at the turn of the century. Even in their thin, diminished condition, these were strong, thick-necked, muscular horses built for work.

Draft horses were bred to pull draft, or weight, like heavy wagons or plows. Workhorses, or warmbloods, as the Europeans call them, are a combination of draft horse and throughbred. They can pull weight, but less than draft horses can. Workhorses also are used as human transport and work cattle on long distances like trail drives. Quarter horses were bred as "saddle horses" for close work in confined spaces like corrals. The quarter horse is known for its short-distance speed. The American quarter horse is a mix of old Middle Eastern breeds crossed with horses from Ireland and England and is heavily muscled and athletic. Smart, alert, and with fox ears, he is named for his ability to run a quarter of a mile faster than any other horse in the world. A thoroughbred by contrast is fast and sleek.

In fact, these horses' speed astonishes me. In full flesh, the larger stallions could carry seventeen hundred pounds and stand at sixteen hands, or more. Many of the stallions were proportioned head and neck, body and rump like a draft horse stallion, only slightly smaller. It wasn't hard to see that quarter-horse genes had also been introduced into the workhorse stock, which made these horses shorter, but faster. Trade in ranch horses had been a bustling affair at the turn of the century. Sheriff Pat Garrett was even reported to have brought in some racing thoroughbreds from his earlier work in Uvalde, Texas, to his final home on White Sands. Garrett's horses had been free-roaming after he was murdered. I took pride in helping to keep his horses alive.

The horses' hooves most impressed me, however. No blacksmith was needed out here. The sand had shaped the feet to perfection, thick-walled, perfect slope, balanced as I'd never seen before. The whole mass of horses searching the corners of the lava enclosure had hooves that looked freshly trimmed, polished like steel.

One of the smaller, younger horses looked tentatively into a trough of water Les had put in the enclosure. We didn't know whether these horses would drink from troughs, or if we'd have to re-create a drinking hole by filling in a patch of desert with water. In past roundups, I had sometimes introduced what mustangers refer to as a "Judas horse"—a trained gelding that would drink water or eat food any way we served it and set an example for the rest of the animals. In this space, though, with so many raging stallions and so much tension among the large numbers of different bands, I was afraid they'd kill a tamed horse. Instead, I trusted that the younger horses and any who had already drunk water from troughs on the range to set a good example. The young horse did just that, taking a big drink and looking around at his interested, sweat-stained peers. A few other young ones slowly followed his lead. Tomorrow we would try to introduce some food. I expected that the young horses would be on our side then, too. For the first time since I'd pulled on my boots at four that morning, I started to relax.

The horses' smells drifted up from the corral—a grassy, sweaty smell mixed with ammonias and fertilizer. There were short bursts of squeaking as the mares that weren't in heat fended off the advances of young studs. Foals and mares called back and forth to each other. More worrisome were some brief scuffles between stallions as they sorted out their harems.

The problem I couldn't solve that evening was the sorting of the stallions from the rest of the herd. Their fighting could cause injuries, even deaths, the longer they stayed with the females. But sorting wild horses required moving the herd into the metal corrals and the chutes Les had built. Separating stallions from the others would take an entire day and would be another stressful process. These animals had just run as much as twenty miles, most of it at a fast clip, and darkness was just minutes away. Separating the horses in the morning would allow us to eyeball them up close, to check for signs of disease or injury. And I would also be looking for evidence of any strange toxicity. The mystery of the dead Mound Springs herd still troubled me. I still could not swallow that starvation and dehydration was the cause of death for so many horses at one time, all in the same few acres around a dried-up watering hole, while nursing foals wandered around healthy as the day they were born.

Satisfied that the horses would survive the night, I stood up to leave and began making my way gingerly across the lava flow to a spot where I could get back down to the ground. Ten paces away from my perch I spotted another man sitting in a crevice atop the formation, cigarette smoke drifting up. His back was to me, but I knew from his hat and build that it was Les. Still and silent, he leaned against the lava flow, surveying the horses. He scanned their ranks, shook his head, and then fixed his gaze on them again. He took his hat off and laid it across his knees, then put it back on and adjusted the brim. Then he looked off into the distance, back toward the mesquite forest he had blazed through hours before on the four-wheeler. He was still there as I made my way down the steep wall of the lava flow, to my truck, and out onto the road that would take me off the range until morning. I knew Les wanted to move the stallions, too. He was a damn good cowboy even if his ride that day had been steel and rubber and his foreman in a chopper. As Rhodes would have put it, he would've been glad to see Les "come a saunterin' along when I was in a tight."

Chapter 6

The Great Escape

I was back on the missile range at five in the morning and headed straight for the lava flow as soon as I cleared security. The desert dawn was radiant, its purples and pinks streaking across the sky. But the sight was nothing compared to that other natural glory—the wild river of horses that I had seen yesterday. As a cowboy and an equine veterinarian, I reveled in the company of horses, and now I had more than a hundred of them out in the desert to care for, rough and wild. I was eager to check on them, hoping that they'd all still be healthy. Yesterday they had been stressed, sweat-stained, and tired, but not hurt. Any number of problems could have developed overnight, though, and I ran through them all in my head as I drove, willing each one to be just a possibility and not a reality waiting for me inside the lava flow.

One fear that I kept pushing out of my mind is that some of the stallions could have killed each other. Days were lengthening and breeding season nearing in the southwest, and stallions inevitably fight in such close quarters. I just hoped that they wouldn't fight to mortal injury. The older stallions, those more than three years old, would calm down after I had separated them from the mares. That was my first chore, and as I sped along the old Army road, I scoured my memory of the pens and the alleyways Les had built and mentally put the horses through the maze in a dry run. Running wild horses from pen to pen was not unlike a capture. They'd move more easily if they thought the route was their idea. I envisioned the position of the crew and the opening and closing of the gates, one at a time. One failed step, one gate left unlatched, one wrong gate opened, a man's silhouette inside the pen or in the alley, and it could all go to hell.

But just in case something did go wrong, every stage had a built-in safety factor, for man and horse. You could more easily stop an M-1 tank than a charging stallion. When a horse is trying to flee, yelling at it and waving your arms won't help at all. To save your life, you have to climb completely out of reach of his powerful legs, hard hooves, long neck, and mouth full of sharp teeth. All the crew had been instructed in the crude art of climbing to safety. And we had narrowed the alleys between the pens and covered them with solid, green army tarp to prevent a stallion from turning around or being able to see through the fence to the mares and suddenly deciding he preferred to stay with them.

As I approached the corrals, I also worried about whether the horses had rejected the water in the troughs, since it was so different from the salty water they were used to. I hoped they had followed the lead of the younger animals. In their dehydrated, malnourished state, they couldn't afford to go without water for too long, though food could wait until later today. I'd had specially ordered Oklahoma bluestem hay trucked in from eight hundred miles away. It would begin to rebuild their strength, but its main purpose was to avoid causing the digestion problems that can frequently occur when an animal's diet is suddenly changed. These horses were going from nearly nothing on the desert to good-quality hay.

The horses' gut is an evolutionary contradiction. It is made of seventy-five feet of pipe going in one direction, leading to the chamber where gas usually forms, at about forty-five feet toward the end. If leafy forage, like alfalfa, is suddenly introduced to a previously bland diet, the horse's gut becomes a balloon, and every balloon has its limit. This gaseous condition is called colic, and it can be fatal. For the wild captives, colic would be a human-caused disaster.

Some new foals might have been born in the night. There was a chance that, with the stress of capture and confinement, and so many other horses close by, a mother might reject her baby or get separated from it. She might also have delivery problems. If foals were wandering around aimlessly, I would take them out of the general pen and put them in one of the smaller corrals that the team had prepared ahead of time for orphans.

I slowed my Ford truck, turned off the cracked pavement and onto the hard-packed sand just outside the lava enclosure. Rolling slowly toward the gates, I relived the capture from the day before. I saw the heart-stopping rebelliousness of the old mares determined to escape, the aggressive stallions protecting their harems, the choppers and the dust and clouds rising over it all. Anxious and excited, I parked outside the lava flow, walked around the metal pens, and climbed carefully to the top of the lava formation to take a look at the horses.

The lava corral was empty.

Where yesterday a hundred-plus horses had milled around, there was how only one scrawny, dark-chestnut foal. I scrambled down the lava in record time and got to the enclosure's gate. Crying, the foal hobbled on its unsteady legs up to me and banged right into me. His hooves still had the wispy shards of newborn feet, which generally can take twelve hours to a day and a half to dry out. I put an arm around his neck to steady him and continued to look around for more animals. Not one was visible. All but the foal had vanished.

The baby was tiny, maybe seventy pounds, and about an inch of umbilical cord still dangled, broken off from the placenta at exactly the right spot. This meant that the birthing had gone well. He was covered with dried sweat and dirt, but in the pale early dawn light I could make out a white blaze and white stockings. The lack of blood on his body meant that the mare had cared for him after he was born. He was just hours old, and so tired that he even stopped bleating for his mother as he continued to lean his weight against me. As I looked below the pretty blaze on his face and into his eyes, however, pure white corneas looked blankly back at me. He was blind.

Wherever the rest of his herd had gone, the baby could not follow. I squinted and slowly turned around in the enclosure, balancing the foal as I did so, trying to figure out what had happened. I feared the worst and I didn't even know what that was. If they'd died, there'd be bodies and there was none. Who the hell could steal more than one-hundred wild horses, in six hours? I saw no truck tracks or hoof prints heading out the gate. Had I dreamed yesterday's events? Stranger things had happened to me. The fences were still intact and covered with camouflage, the gates shut tight and locked, and the lava flow still high, steep, sharp, dotted with boulders, and seemingly impassable. But the horses we had so carefully and arduously captured yesterday had disappeared.

My mind jumped back to the horses I'd seen at the end of my first day on White Sands as I was touring the range. They'd been standing just a few yards from me, but when I looked away for a second and then turned to see them again, they'd disappeared. Standing alone in the corral, supporting the listing foal and glancing around at the eerie landscape in the dawn light, I heard Maynard's voice in my mind. Maybe they'd all been ghosts, just shadows of the mustangs and quarter horses and draft horses that had populated this land along with the cowboys and outlaws. I shook my head to clear those thoughts. I coughed and the little foal jumped. I soothed him with a calm, easy hand and mindlessly apologized to him. This foal was real, flesh and blood, and those other horses had been, too. They had to be somewhere. Maybe there was a blind canyon hidden behind a huge boulder or a cave we had overlooked. I strained to see more in the dim light, but found nothing except a soft, furry nose.

I knelt and wrapped one arm around the baby's neck and the other around his rear, lifted him up and carried him to a small, separate enclosure near my truck where he'd be safe from the scuffles and commotion between stallions in the herd, if and when they returned to this enclosure. I sniffed his muzzle to see if he'd nursed, but couldn't smell any milk. That wasn't good. Not only was he hungry, he didn't have the benefit of the antibodies from his mother's milk to keep him healthy and allow him to be with other horses. The little guy nuzzled my ear hopefully.

I went to my truck, grabbed a bottle, some frozen mare's milk, and a blanket, and draped the blanket over his narrow back to give him a little sense of security. Though I've never been much of a babysitter, I knew this little one would be my responsibility if we couldn't find the mother. He'd been left behind because of the capture I designed, and I needed to bottle-feed him until he learned to take milk from a bucket. As soon as possible, I would probably need to pass a stomach tube into his little nostril, through his esophagus, and down to his stomach to see if he had gotten his mother's first milk. If he hadn't, as I suspected, I'd have to give him some of the mare's milk. He needed the antibodies within twenty-four hours of birth, but after six hours, the absorption would slow dramatically.

"I'll be back to feed you in a little while," I told the foal as I closed the pen. "Let me see if I can find your mom, first." I set a container of the frozen milk on the warm truck hood to thaw and turned my full attention to the escapees.

Planning to take a shortcut to a high outcropping on the top of the lava flow for a good look around the area, I headed for the front gate. Rounding the corner of the capture sight, I found Les scurrying down a wall of lava boulders. He stopped to glare at me, a cigarette hanging as usual from the corner of his mouth, stretched his lanky frame to his full height, and held my gaze. Then he strode gracefully along the lava edge, and jumped down to the ground fifteen feet from me.

I glared back, suddenly wondering if maybe Les—or someone else who had a vested interest in keeping horses on White Sands—had just thrown open the gates and set the horses free during the night. I glanced for a split second at the keys clanking in his hand. He didn't hide them. To my knowledge, Les had been the last person to leave the night before, and he'd apparently been the first to arrive this morning. I hadn't seen his truck when I arrived, but there were many places along the lava flow to hide vehicles. Hiding a herd of horses was another matter. Les had been such a determined, effective leader of the ground crew, I could hardly imagine he would have thrown away all of that effort by turning the horses loose. He knew as well as I did that they'd have to be recaptured, and we might not be as lucky again.

"How's the foal?" he asked as he headed back into the holding tank in the rear of the formation and started his ascent on the big rocks. I wasn't surprised that he knew about the blind baby.

"What the hell happened to those horses?" I followed him like a young goat, not knowing if I should grab him and shake him.

"Looks like they went for a walk." He leaned into the rock and strode hard toward the back to the pile of boulders, then climbed from rock to rock up onto the lava flow again. He stopped, picked up a piece of horse hoof and tossed it down the hill in my direction. My stomach turned at the thought of all those horses risking their necks to take this route to freedom, but as I watched him, I knew he had the right idea. Single file, taking their time, those horses had mountain-climbed their way out of our holding tank. I hoped they were still up on that treacherous ground, because once up on top of the bed, there are very few ways off it until the end where the lava tapers toward the sand. That was miles west from where I was standing. It occurred to me that the blind foal's mother had followed the herd up the dangerous path and, once in line, could not turn around and head back down. That piece of hoof might have been hers, torn loose as she fretted nervously at the edge of the rim trying to return to the foal. Unless she was following an experienced, surefooted stallion, she probably couldn't find her way back down. She might be frantically trying to find a route off the lava and back to her baby right then. That meant that the herd was on the move.

The horses would not be able to make fast time up on the lava surface, which gave me hope that we could find them before they found their way down to the desert floor. Slick and sharp, the obsidian was also scarred in many places with deep crevices and pits, some dropping straight down fifteen feet or more. In a best-case scenario, the horses would have nicks and cuts on their lower legs and feet. Some might not make it at all. The top of the lava flow was the worst terrain on the entire missile range. Could more than a hundred horses as conditioned to unfriendly ground and difficult passages as these wild ones really cross it for miles?

If the horses had "gone for a walk" and had not been released, they had to be up there. Which horse, I wondered, had been the first one to dare to scale that ledge? One of the brazen stallions? Or one of the wise old mares? That horse had endangered every one of the others in his prison break. I don't suppose he thought about that.

The worst thing we could do would be to track the horses in the same direction they were traveling. If they sensed men coming up behind them, they'd try to move faster, which would increase their risk of injury and accidental falls. I yelled for Les that I was going to drop to the sand and circle around to the south and west where I could make double-time. I was sure he was a wise enough cowboy to climb down and circle around the lava flow on the other side north and head west to get ahead of the escapees.

I went on foot, worried that the noise of a truck or an ATV would spook the horses into moving faster. Being a runner, I figured that at a fast walk or a slow jog there was a good chance I could overtake them. The newness of the blind foal told me they had about a two-hour head start. Having started in the dark, they could move at only a snail's pace, carefully finding their footing for every step. The passage was only wide enough for one or two abreast, so they were going slow, but now that the sun was almost up they could improve their pace.

In my Western boots, I jogged for fifteen minutes, then walked fast for twenty more. My feet soon ached. In my rush to get ahead of the horses, I'd also left my water in the truck. The crew was due to arrive within the hour and they'd sure as hell be working in the capture site, right in the wrong place when, and if, Les and I could turn the horses and send them back down the narrow footpath into the lava flow corral again. If the horses saw men filling the water tanks or spreading hay, or heard them pounding metal somewhere, they would turn back on Les and me. That could be painful. With that thought, I had the fuel to run again, nearing the spot where the top of the lava flow was closest to the sand.

After a few more minutes, I stopped, looking in amazement at the odd, silent parade of silhouettes above and in front of me. More than one hundred horses in one long, snaking line moved with great care and deliberate steps west, away from the corral. High above me, with no chance of climbing down, they kept pushing forward. Not a sound came from the entire group. No stallions challenged one another or snorted, no mares nickered, no foals whinnied. It was as if they were all holding their breath as they made their dangerous break for freedom.

I debated my next move. In another half mile, the horses would reach a drop-off where they could climb down and head back onto the desert. If I climbed up on the lava flow ahead, the horses would have two choices: go over me, or turn around and go back. My guess was that they would turn, but a lot of that decision would depend on the leader at the front of the line. Many of the stallions would likely plow right over me in a heartbeat. They weren't afraid of confronting one another, and were surely not afraid of me. I hoped a mare was leading the way, as she'd be less inclined to trample me.

I had no other option. I had to take my chances and try to get the herd to turn. Staying close along the lava walls, parallel to them, but out of sight and hearing. I ran again, hard and quick and quiet to get ahead of them. When I had passed the front of the line, I began looking for a place where I could scale the lava flow and get up in front of them about two hundred yards. Finally, I saw my spot—a climbable wall. I scrambled up and waited, silently puffing up and willing myself to look big.

I glanced around behind me and realized I was not the only human on the formation. A short twenty yards away, I could see Les taking careful steps along the flow, puffing a freshly lit cigarette. I wondered how in the world a guy who had smoked all his life had the stamina to beat me to the herd cutoff point. But there he was, making his way in my direction, and he didn't look nearly as tired as I felt. An hour earlier I might have suspected that he had set the horses free himself, but now I was just grateful to not be up there facing that herd alone.

As the horses approached, I was relieved to see two mares leading the way. One had large, full mammary glands and small globules of milk dripped freely from them. That was not good. I needed that milk in the belly of the little blind foal. Time really was of the essence. Les and I stood blocking their path, and the entire equine parade came to a halt as the mares considered the situation. I took two steps toward the horses, and Les did the same. The mares stepped back. I took another step. Les stayed in place and the first of the two mares turned slightly, positioning herself sideways across the lava flow. I advanced again, and she rotated again and found herself facing back the way she came. Les moved forward, and the mare moved back toward the rest of the herd. The second mare turned around. With a deep sigh, I continued to creep slightly forward and watch as the line of horses that extended almost as far as I could see followed the lead of the horses closest to us and began to turn back in the direction of the holding tank. As the mares nearest us moved that way, the whole herd began to retrace its steps. I'll never know what the signal was from horse to horse, but each horse stepped so carefully that they rarely bumped. These animals knew the seriousness of their situation. They were all in the business of saving their own lives.

Les and I carefully maintained a safe distance from the horses all the way back to the holding pen. The last thing I wanted was to spook them and lose any of the animals on the lava flow. The path curved tortuously, cutting back and forth around the sinkholes and across a narrow divide in the surface. It was supremely dangerous. If any of us fell into that crevasse, man or beast, the sharp volcanic rocks certainly would ensure the fall would be fatal. We slowly followed behind, stopping to wait at times for the new lead horses to decide the direction. Whether by sight or smell or memory, they knew where they had just come from. Horses always know their way back.

Back at the pen, I stood by helplessly watching the horses scale back down the walls into the enclosure. It was terrifying, but we had no other way to get them back. By mercy and grace, not one horse appeared wounded from the march or from yesterday's captures.

Two hours had passed and the horses had descended safely back into the enclosure. While the crew of cowboys set about blocking their access to the top of the lava flow with a new fence, I returned my attention to the blind foal alone in the corral. His legs were out of all proportion with the rest of his thin body and his impossibly long eyelashes looked like they belonged on a deer. He was lying down and looked awfully frail. Surely dehydrated, he now desperately needed milk. I shook the now-thawed container of mare's milk that had heated on my Ford Turbo's hood. Ford Tough, as the hood of the truck advised, was something the little horse was going to have to be. I poured the milk into a bottle, checked the temperature, and added a little cold water to cool it to 100 degrees Fahrenheit. I screwed a rubber nipple on the bottle and went back to the exhausted little guy. I urged him to his feet, put the nipple near his muzzle and dribbled a few drops of the sticky stuff on his lips. For a good while he fussed, snorted, and gagged, and in general refused it, but eventually he swallowed the portion I forced in his mouth. Then he sucked a bit, making a mess of himself and me. I was relieved. If he hadn't given in and nursed on his own, I would have been forced to pass the stomach tube. In a few minutes he seemed to regain some life force, and in a few more minutes he lubricated the area around himself and fertilized it as well. I hoped that his intestines would absorb the big protein antibodies that he needed to survive the many viral and bacterial insults his little body would encounter. It would be nearly three months before he developed immunities of his own.

I fed him a bit more a few minutes later until he totally refused, arguing well enough to lead me to believe that he might be full. He looked rejuvenated, so I set him inside the farthest corner of the back holding tank with the newly reclaimed herd, then hid in the rock formation above the corral to see if his mother came to claim him. Despite his blindness, the tiny horse wobbled his way across the pen to the area where most of the horses clustered as far as possible from the men who were working on the fence. He bleated as he neared them, and then wove his way through the crowd, crying for his mother.

All of the horses let the baby pass, but not one nuzzled him or acknowledged him. He nudged at the mare with the full milk glands, but she moved away. He nudged another, but she nipped at his ears and sent him running off. I watched him for almost an hour, trying to find a home in the herd. I could not tell which mare was his mother, but it really didn't matter, because if she didn't want to take care of him there was nothing I could do to make her. With cows, you can herd the balky mother into a stanchion, lock her head in it, and help the calf learn to suckle. No such luck with horses. Grafting an orphan or a rejected baby onto a mare is near impossible. In most cases, the foal will be injured or worse before the mare relents.

After a while the foal seemed to give up, but instead of lingering near his own kind inside the fence, he came back near the place where I had put him and began to cry again. It seemed pretty clear that he was calling for me. I climbed down, hoisted him out of the pen, and carried him back to the small corral. "Guess you'll need a name." I said. "How about Sam from Salt Creek?"

I decided to call him Salt Creek Sam, and then started trying to figure out how long it might take to get him to feed from a bucket instead of a bottle. In the meantime, it would be the two of us in that corral, every few hours for at least the next several days. I'd learn what nightlife was like in the January desert, thirty-five miles from a warm bed. Pat Garrett had nothing on me there.

As darkness began to settle over the beautiful, deserted land, the fence crew packed up and went home. The work was nearly complete, and even though I doubted the herd would figure out how to skirt the new construction to make another great escape, I wasn't about to underestimate them a second time or trust that they would hang around. I decided to pull my truck up closer to the corral and sleep inside where I could see the herd and tend to Salt Creek Sam. Without the protection of his mother or the rest of the horses around him, he would be easy prey for the crafty coyotes that could wander into the capture site to have a look around. Creatures much larger and fiercer than a scrawny foal had been known to fall prey to their attacks. In fact, one of the stories about how Jornada del Muerto got its name tells of a German trader who ran out of water while crossing the desert. Five weeks after his disappearance, a group of travelers came across his dead horse still tied to a tree. All that was left of the man were several ribs scattered across the ground and a mass of hair. The Journey of the Dead Man memorializes him and other ill-fated travelers who didn't survive the crossing from the Pecos to the Rio Grande rivers, over land adjacent to what is now White Sands Missile Range.

I wasn't the only camper on the range that night. Les, who hadn't said a single word to me since we'd walked the herd back into the holding tank, pulled his own truck around and parked it about fifty yards from mine. Apparently he wasn't sure that I could keep track of the horses. Like me, he had a folding chair, and he sat alongside his truck and grumbled a quiet, "Evenin'" in my direction. When I started to make a fire and he looked like he was going to build one of his own, I had to try to break the impasse.

"How about if I make it here?" I asked, glancing his way.

"Too close to that corral."

I stepped back a foot, just to be agreeable, and set to work. Les stood in the shadow of his truck, lit a cigarette, and watched. In a few minutes, he moved nearby. There was a long, awkward silence, and then he casually offered, "You can go on. I'll stay the night here." His voice was dismissive, as if I was trying to take responsibility for something that belonged to him.

"I think I'll stay. The foal will need to be fed."

After another long silence, I eased into a different kind of conversation, thinking that it might make this less miserable for both of us.

"Ever spend the night out here before?"

"Sure," he paused for so long I thought was done speaking, but then he continued, "Lots of times. Hell, I slept on the range every night when I was a kid."

"What year did your family have to move off?"

He glared into the fire. "Well, depends on which part of the family you ask about. We had seven ranches I was kin to. My uncles, my granddad, my dad, my grandmother's family. They moved them all off at different times. It was pretty much the same, though. The government would ask them to leave for a year or so, and then they wouldn't let them come back. Then they wanted a twenty-five-year lease, and there was nothing to do but give it to them."

I considered the uncomfortable idea of a whole extended family being evicted from its homes and livelihood. "They were all ranchers?"

"No, they were bird-watchers."

I cringed at the stupidity of my question. "What'd they do after?"

"Grandaddy hired on as a city policeman in Alamogordo." He smiled to himself.

"Jim Gililland?"

"Yep."

"He was an outlaw for a while, wasn't he?"

"Yes, he was."

Jim Gililland had found his way into the history books of the Old West, first for cattle rustling, which was a crime many men of the day participated in. His claim to fame, the reason I knew the name, was that he and another rancher, Oliver Lee, had been tried for one of the most notorious crimes in the history of the West— the murders of attorney Colonel Albert Fountain and his young son. They'd been killed in 1896 along one of the roads that cuts across the modern-day missile range. In a closed society rife with all kinds of crime, the murder of the boy was an act that broke the moral codes, not just of the cowboys and the lawmen, but of the outlaws as well. But no one ever claimed responsibility for the murders, and the bodies of the victims were never found. It seemed obvious to many at the time that Fall, rancher Lee, and his friend Jim Gililland were somehow involved. The murder almost undoubtedly grew out of a personal and political feud between Fountain, a Southeastern New Mexico Stock Growers' Association Republican supporter, and Albert Fall, a Democrat said to be associated with cattle thieves. Fall was known to have served time both as a cabinet secretary in the Warren G. Harding administration and as an inmate for accepting bribes creating the Teapot Dome Scandal. Fall opposed Fountain's efforts to punish cattle thieves. Investigations into the murders led to nothing but partisan argument, with Sheriff Garrett caught square in the middle.

Eugene Rhodes claimed that he had ridden with the men while they were on the lam and had helped hide them in and around the Jornada, all of them feasting on beef none of them owned. Sheriff Pat Garrett had said that Rhodes hid them, fed them stolen cattle, but that he really didn't mind. Since Lee was a prominent old family rancher in the area, Garrett knew it was just a matter of time, probably about calving time, that Lee and Gililland would find their way back to Lee's own corrals and Garrett would nab them then.

Back then, all of the men in the territory were either friends or had worked together at one time or another, including outlaws like Billy the Kid. Months later, Lee and Gililland turned themselves in, were tried and acquitted, but the crime was never solved. Later in 1908, the same Albert Fall would successfully defend another man against charges for the vicious murder of Sheriff Pat Garrett. Oliver Lee and Jim Gililland were thought to be accomplices to the Garrett murder, too. One motive for the murder may have been that they didn't want Pat to sell his ranch, which had coveted spring water.

All of these mysteries had unfolded a few mere miles south and west from where I now sat at a sparking fire with Jim Gililland's grandson, Les. Everybody loves an outlaw, but it seemed a little ironic that Jim Gililland would have ended up carrying a city policeman's badge. Neither *city* nor *policeman* jibed with the legend created around him.

"What did your dad do?" I asked, very interested now in Les's family tree.

"Went to work for the phone company as a lineman after he couldn't ranch anymore."

It was a huge leap from being a self-sufficient rancher, living off your own land, no matter how hard that life might be, to working for the phone company. I'd never really felt tied to any one place, always going where my work took me, but I respected the kind of life that ranchers make for themselves, scratching out a living no matter what. It seemed like a harsh injustice. I hoped they'd been well paid for their property, but I doubted it.

"What happened at the end of the twenty-five years?" I wondered aloud.

"Well, then the government said the land was too polluted for anybody to live on it. So they condemned it and kept it."

"Damn."

I got up to make one more bottle for Salt Creek Sam, and he stirred and came up to the fence to meet me. He bumped against it, and I put a hand out to pat his head while he drank. I wondered if he would have survived if we hadn't conducted the capture. A blind foal is at a great disadvantage, but many do survive to adulthood. If his mother had abandoned him on the range, he wouldn't have made it through the day, but I knew she hadn't just left him. The stress of our aerial assault had separated them. Like all of the captives, he was my responsibility now.

Done with the bottle, he banged his nose against me, asking for more. "That's it for you," I told him and rubbed his ears. "Get to bed."

Les grunted behind me, I guessed in scorn that I was talking to the foal. Whatever coldness he bore toward me, though, I knew it didn't extend to this foal or any other horse on the range. Patrick had told me that Les had carried the foals away from the site of the die-off after it had been discovered. He'd put them, one at a time, in the cab of his truck, thrown an arm around them, and taken them home. He had been the one on bottle duty then, and he had managed to find homes for them all.

I waited a while, and Les was silent, but there was one more question I wanted to ask. "Were you living out here when they tested the bomb?"

"I'm not that old."

I waited.

"My parents were in bed, and the whole world lit up, just like the sun was shining. They didn't know what was going on. They saw the light—and the mushroom cloud. Daddy's always told me that the cows that were lying down in the field, turned white on the side that was facing the sky, and stayed that way. Three of my uncles that lived out here came up with cancer the same year, after the bomb."

"Did you stay in Tularosa all along?"

"Nah. I joined the Navy. When I got out I stayed east, managing farms and working horses. I had two saddles, and after sixteen years I got tired of them always being wet, and I got tired of the cold, so I came home and signed on to work out here."

"Tomorrow we need to separate the stallions," I mumbled. Les nodded as if we should have done it that day, but the corrals were not completed and we would have had a train wreck on our hands if we'd tried.

Les smoked and watched the little horse.

"A lot of the Mescalaros around here think that a stallion's ghost haunts the mesquite, name of Midnight. They say he travels with seven other stallions. I know his descendants still roam this missile range. Two of them are in that lava pen behind us."

"You been talking to Maynard, Mescalaro Apache." Les crushed out his cigarette and flicked it into our fire. "Ghosts?"

"You know the Mescalero?"

"I'm too lousy a cowboy to know anything." Without another word he got up and eased toward his truck. That was the end of our conversation for the night and for some time afterward. Les had

been more open than he had been with me during the whole operation, though I could tell he really didn't want to answer questions
about his past or about the past in general. And he didn't ask any.
But Les's way with horses did not come from a book or video or
even from some fellow cowboy. His way was inborn and honed by
miles on horseback, the only way to learn this rough trade. Les
knew where a horse would head and about how far. I intended to
learn as much as I could from him, but I also intended to watch out
for him; he was as cagey and tough as any wild horse.

Les opened the truck door as quiet as a desert mouse, spat,
loaded the corner of his mouth with another Camel, and slid in
behind the wheel. I watched him as he lit the cigarette. The glow
highlighted his face and I swore I saw a tear run down his western-
tanned face. I'd never ask him about it, but I'm sure of what I saw.
He turned the truck's ignition and started to back out. I assumed
that he was headed home, but I didn't know just where home was
in Les's mind. I stared up at the billions of stars broadcast across the
clear, southern New Mexico sky, moved closer to the corral and
Salt Creek Sam, and kept watch on the foal and his remarkably quiet
family until dawn.

Chapter 7

Trust All Horses,
But None Too Much

At the prison training program we had worked primarily with individual horses, while at White Sands Missile Range we worked horses mostly in groups. That required additional sets of skills. For all of his deficiencies in human relations, Les was damn good at making horses follow instructions. He avoided charging stallions with a gazellelike quickness and yet could be as tender with a foal as its own mother would be. Les's crew adopted his excellent horseman principles and technique to move the groups of horses from the large lava corral safely toward and through the processing chutes. Each man was equipped with a thin, five-foot-long pole with a plastic grocery sack duct-taped to the end of it. The plastic made a noise that the horses hated and would try to avoid, so the men used the plastic bags to stimulate groups of horses to move in one direction or another, or to separate individual horses from the herd. Where the first horse darted most of the others followed. If propelled properly, the herds moved like flowing water. The key was to get the correct animal to dart the correct way at the correct time coupled with appropriate use of the plastic bag. We counted on help from their herd instinct, behavior based on their inherent need to be in social groups, which was as malleable and usable for large groups of horses as it was for training the individual animal. We tried to create a window for the horses and then get out of the way and let their instinct take over. It was no different from training any horse, or even any school kid. The men watched the horse's eyes, and if the horse thought that it was his idea to move to a certain place, he went there like melted butter.

The working corrals we used at the lava flow site were constructed from stout, portable horse panels. I always used the WW Livestock Manufacturing brand for corralling, because it was the toughest, safest system I knew. The six-foot-tall gates were made of two-inch metal tubing with three vertical bars, one on each side with one in the middle, and six horizontal bars. We covered the panels with solid, Army-green tarp so that the horses would have a limited field of vision. Les designed the corralling in a circular fashion for maximum efficiency and safety. The corral looked like a small pie with gates on its perimeter, inside a larger pie that was divided into pens. The larger circle was about one hundred feet in diameter and the interior circle was about sixty feet in diameter. An alley ran through the center of it all to end at a processing chute in the middle of the inner circle. A gate from the lava corral holding tank opened into the alley, a straight shot to that processing chute. Horses were funneled down the alley, single-file, toward the chute, with one horse processed in the chute at a time.

Processing consisted of a medical examination. I and my veterinary associates would reach through any one of four two-feet square side doors to give common viral vaccinations and de-worming medication, make identifications for paperwork, apply a painless freeze brand, and take blood for lab tests. Once processed, the horse was released into the inner circular corral and directed through various gates into the outer circle of pie-shaped pens.

In the outer circle pens, we held processed horses: mares and foals together, stallions with stallions, and adolescents together. Les's system moved horses with a minimum of harassment and required seven to eleven men at any given time to make it all work efficiently.

Chasing a wild horse across the desert on an all-terrain vehicle meets a modern cowboy's visceral need for speed, but trapping a fourteen-hundred-pound stallion in a livestock stanchion to treat him demands experience as well as quickness and agility. It also requires steeled nerves and the hand–eye coordination of an explosives expert. We were thirty-five miles from the nearest electrical outlet, so we had to power our mechanical squeeze chute manually, which didn't exactly give us the level of control of a hydraulic chute. The length of our chute, actually a modified, mechanical bison alleyway, was about eight feet with a sliding door on each end. That was just enough to hold a full-size stallion and it had the unique feature of closing evenly on the sides, which narrowed the horse's lateral movement. Though that was safer for the horse, it was not as safe for the men who provided the treatments or freeze-branding. The wild horse is a capable adversary and any confinement short of general anesthesia merely meant cornered, to him. Though far better than a lariat dallied. Around a snubbing-pole, our chute left his head and teeth, shoulders, and sand-honed hooves free to use as weapons. He could also slam his full weight forward against the head rails and crush a human arm against the front door or catapult backward with a wallop against the back door and launch forward again. The noise of a kick against the back door was deafening—the mares were twice as fast, three times more frightened, and deadly accurate. Les used to say that the "mares could kick the starch out of a biscuit."

Working around wild horses in confinement was no place for amateurs or the foolhardy. Many a day Les and I left for home splintered, battered, bruised, and stung. Though it is written that the horse evolved a vegetarian, I have seen that whatever a horse bites off, it swallows, plant or animal.

The first order of business the morning after the recapture required that we drive the entire herd through the alleyway to the processing chute in order to separate out the stallions. It also enabled me to examine each animal, up-close and personal. The second order of business was the neutering of any male over three years old. To help with the process, I hired a local equine veterinarian, Dr. Becky Washburn, from Capitan, New Mexico, as an assistant. Becky had grown up a cowgirl and become an enviable racehorse jockey in New Mexico before she had taken the long stride into the profession of veterinary medicine. A week before, Les Gililland had told me about Becky and said that she was as good a roper and horseperson as had ever slung a calf-rope, and that impressed me. The proverbial rope, ride, and wrangle fit her résumé better than most men's. She and I had spoken and then met bright and early one morning at a lonely café in Tularosa, and she was hired. When her big veterinary truck rolled into the parking lot at five o'clock on the morning we planned to separate the horses, the back window boasted a well-coiled, used lariat.

Besides her throwing arm, Dr. Washburn had two more assets that helped me as the White Sands veterinary health adviser. She was a sight for a cowboy's sore eyes, and her equine medical ability was up there with the best. Becky Washburn was memorable eye-candy in her wrangler's jeans—her Western manner had a way of purifying the desert.

Dr. Höglund fills out paperwork in preparation
for transport to Oklahoma Ranches.
Courtesy of Don Höglund.

All of the horses were tucked in the back corral against the far wall, and it would be difficult to drive them to the chutes in groups. Les and Gary went to the back corral to run the entire herd through the gate that separated the holding pen from the alleyways. The men, with plastic grocery sacks tied to a stick, ushered the horses gently from the back lava corral through a set of gates leading to the wide part of the alley where they would be held temporarily with plenty of room for movement. Les entered that dangerous area and began pushing a few horses at a time down the alley. Crewmen hid behind each open gate along the alley and as the first horse entered the alley, the gateman called out "fire-in-the-hole." No one could afford to let their guard down at any time.

The horses entered the tarp-covered alleys at a fast trot, single-file, and coursed in a straight line toward the processing chute. One horse was captured in the chute, and four individual horses were isolated, one behind the other, in the alleyway. They snorted and squealed, and the foals tried to stick to their mares' flanks. Les paid special attention to the safety of the foals.

The sound of the hooves produced a staccato echo that bounced off the walls of the lava flow. The horses' large size still amazed me. They were nothing short of magnificent. Fierce and powerful, they didn't move like their hearts were full of terror—until they got into the individual chutes.

We got the animals into the chute with the least amount of stimulus possible. I had banned Western hats, because the sight of a cowboy hat raises the level of horse anxiety tremendously. We also avoided staring directly at the horses because that created a predator-and-prey environment, though doing that was sometimes unavoidable. The horse cannot focus well on anything close to his eye, so it is advisable not to get in his face. Otherwise, we risked suffering a nasty bite, perhaps even losing body parts. Finally, it was best not to climb above the horses along the alley. They are particularly afraid of predators above them and are likely to try to turn around in the alley and hurt themselves. Herding them in the alleyway was done with a plastic sack at their feet. That worked well to move the horses along the alleys and it was safe for everyone, except the plastic sack.

The sorting took nearly the entire morning, but once completed, Becky and I promptly began our veterinary examinations of the stallions. We evaluated each animal's health generally, assessed his adoptability and suitability, vaccinated him for various viral diseases, and drew blood to check for an infectious red-blood-cell disease. Inserting a thick-bore needle through the rhinolike hide of the stallion's neck and into his tightly stretched jugular vein is dangerous. The horses are generally frightened to the point of holding their breath, which can lead to near fainting, for both them and us humans. They also tended to throw their weight around the close confines of the chute, making every task more difficult.

I had had at least ten thousand cases of evaluating wild horses under my belt before I had taken on the White Sands capture. So, I gave Dr. Washburn a short history on my approach. Confinement breeds panic in a wild horse, which can mean death for one that's mishandled. The White Sands horses struggled to escape the chutes with a ferocity that could only signify genuine terror. One big sorrel-red stallion kicked with his hind legs, struck with his front hooves, and tried to rear up in the small space, screeching the whole time. I felt so sorry for him, truly, that for a split second I questioned our right to be doing this stuff. He was such a completely wild thing.

Wild horses know that people have two hands, so it's always best to touch them with both hands, one at a time, while attempting to insert a needle into the skin. *Quick and smooth* was the key to safety. The main sensory branches of the nerves are in the skin. I told my new crew to get through the skin quickly and not stand there gingerly poking the needle in and out of the nerves. Becky nodded politely, even though she already knew that bad veterinary technique meant a human could get stomped, kicked, struck, or body-slammed. I hoped she believed me.

When the first huge, beautiful horse stomped into the chute—a commanding brown stallion with neck skin thickened from years of fighting—I got ready to stick him. A needle remained sharp for only one use so any failed attempt to penetrate the skin demanded a new needle. Holding the large syringe firmly in my grip, I slid the wide-bore needle down the horse's neck toward the narrow part just below the jaw and quietly admonished anyone who'd listen that "any hand that got near the head, usually got eaten." The giant snapped at my arm and I instantly retracted. His hot breath and the sweat on his chin hairs poured over my fingers. A near-miss. As I put both hands back in and began the slow, firm glide toward his throat-latch and the bulging jugular vein there, I continued, "Any hand that gets more than a few inches below the neck hair usually gets struck with a front foot and any hand left inside the chute, near the horse when he startles, usually gets broke." I pressed the needle's tip under the first layers of tough skin and dull-red liquid spurted back into the syringe. I pulled the plunger steadily back as the horse trembled with pent-up energy. He shook and the stanchion rumbled with him, the metal joints clanking loudly, but he stood nicely for the long minute that it took to gather adequate blood for the test. I quietly retracted both the needle and my hands. He and I both sighed deeply and I stepped back. But I failed to close the two-foot by two-foot side door in time, and to everyone's astonishment, the fourteen-hundred-pound bay stallion poked his huge head out of the opening and tried to crawl out of a hole I just knew he could not. We all stepped back and watched. I was wrong. The horse acted like a mouse, squeezing one shoulder followed by a leg at a time through the examination door. After a short struggle, he pulled his hindquarters free and pranced off toward the closed front gate. I would not have believed what I had just seen if anyone had tried to tell me it was possible. I looked at Les. He was just as amazed as the rest of us.

When it was Becky's turn with the syringe, she performed well. Her technique of two hands on the neck of the new stallion, the fingers of the lower hand clamping both jugular veins and the other hand slowly advancing the needle, quickly through the skin and with the bevel of the needle always up, on into the vein in one sure stroke went perfectly. But she left her right hand on the horse when she looked back at the crewman processing the blood specimens, and her short ponytail brushed the face of the tense horse. The stallion ducked and dropped to his knees, his brute shoulder slamming against the inside wall of the iron chute, trapping her hand between. She dropped to a knee, gasping as she retrieved her crumpled wing. She grabbed and covered the injured hand with the other hand, back-pedaled to the veterinary truck, bent over in agony, but didn't scream. I did it for her.

When I pleaded for her to let me see the damage, she finally uncovered it and I saw that the entire layer of skin on the top of her hand from her wrist to the knuckles of all four bones was folded over and dangling in one large piece of bloody epidermis. It made me sick to look at it. But she wrapped the skin back in place with a medical bandage, never complained, and continued the day's long exercise of collecting blood from one hundred similar wild stallions. The procedure went slowly and the price of love, that day, proved high. My weak stomach made me feel pretty small for the next long while, though it didn't stop me from spending considerable time with the brave, appealing young veterinarian over the next several weeks.

Becky's injury put off until the next day the "attitude adjustment," or gelding of the males. Because it was no easy task, it was usually done as the first procedure, the first time the animal was touched by human hands. Gelding a wild horse is many times more difficult than the same procedure for a domesticated equine. I preferred to geld recreational or competition horses at less than one year of age, and I usually did it while the horse was sedated with what we called a "cocktail," which left him standing so that he could be pressed against a solid fence or stall wall. Good technique and a long reach helped complete the procedure in twenty minutes.

The same surgery for an untouched wild stallion was not as simple. It required a general anesthetic, since I rarely used ropes or halters on the head of a wild horse—too much restraint is worse than too little. Wild stallions who have never felt the touch of a human are saturated with adrenaline. In fact it required two needles: a sedative injection into muscle and then a large-bore needle injection in the terrified horse's neck. And we had to keep the second needle in long enough to infuse forty milliliters of expensive sedative anesthetic. A horse can feel something as light as a housefly perch on his hair, which causes him to twitch the skin muscles. So it's no wonder that he jumps the moment heavy human hands touch him. If my hand-needle coordination and angle of descent through the skin and into the vessel are poor, the horse will either snap at my hands, lunge forward, slam backward, jerk up, or drop like a lead weight to his knees. Often it was a combination of all of this at once and if I were foolish enough to hold on, I'd injure arms and hands. Technique meant everything. A slow, firm touch is far better when dealing with a wild horse than soft, wispy fingers and repeated stabbing on the skin of a wild animal poised for flight.

As soon as the horse was properly injected, the needles, withdrawn, and the side door closed, the horse was released into the corral and ushered to an unoccupied pen. There, in silence with only eyes peering through the slim cracks in the tarps draped over the fences, the stallion slowly succumbed to the effects of ketamine hydrochloride and the profound sedative and pain-dulling properties of xylazine. The stallion would sit back on his haunches like a dog, and then ease over onto his side.

Quickly my team of experienced cowboys opened the gate and rushed in. One covered the horse's eyes with a thick towel and cradled the brute's head in his lap to keep dirt out of his eyes, and another placed a lariat around the upper hind leg. I washed the sur-

Midnight colt in the alleyway leading to the processing chute. *Courtesy of White Sands Missile Range.*

gical site with surgical scrub, rinsed it with clean water, and in three minutes cut in and neutered the stallion. A third assistant handed me another small dose of sedative to slow the recovery and four fresh syringes containing vaccinations. Branding, for him, would come later. In one fell-swoop, the animal was identified, castrated, vaccinated, and examined closely. In twenty minutes, without fail, in the quiet confinement of that clean, safe pen, the horse would stand on wobbly legs and view his White Sands world from a different perspective.

We freeze-branded the entire herd on their left hips for permanent identification and also attached a numbered tag on a thin nylon collar around their necks. This cowboy version of epidermal cryosurgery required clipping the hair over the skin where the brand was to be applied. That was one of Les's jobs. After spraying rubbing alcohol on the spot and completely immersing the branding irons in liquid nitrogen, Les would hold the metal letters *US* and a number corresponding to the neck tag against the skin of the horse for forty seconds. The branding left a small white indentation which inflamed to a half inch afterward. Within thirty days the covering skin would fall off painlessly, leaving a permanent white brand. It was a simple process, unless of course the horse threw a fit, and then it could take more than a half hour.

After all of this touchy stuff was completed, the horses were vaccinated against several viral diseases they might encounter in domestic life. I also fed them Strongid C, a good parasiticide, in their hay.

These were long arduous days of treatment, but the satisfaction of providing for the health needs of the horses and preparing them for adoptions left us with a sense of accomplishment. Just touching each of the horses, the most beautiful, magnificent animals I'd known, brought a feeling to me that I was sure my heroes Eugene Rhodes and Pat Garrett would recognize.

Maynard and I met regularly in the comfortable bar at the Alamogordo Holiday Inn. Though I invited him out to see the wild

Midnight stallions fighting after the capture.
Courtesy of Tony O'Brien.

horses, he shrugged off my offers. We always sat with a bar stool separating our high-backed chairs, in the eerily dark side of the bar along the far wall. I decided that the separation was Maynard's way of creating a safe distance. I never really got to know him well, despite all of the time we spent together, but his extensive knowledge of the land of the Tularosa Basin interested me.

I told Maynard about the horses' great escape over the dangerous lava. I believed that something had told those horses where to climb the steep-walled lava corral. I was sure that the horses had been called to from above the corral floor, but I didn't know by what. Then I told him about the blind foal and the troubles of handling an orphaned baby horse in the midst of capturing and processing captive wild horses who had not forgotten that they preferred freedom over what we offered.

Maynard squinted, sucked air, and looked around the bar. Suddenly he folded his tobacco pouch fast and rose from his seat, Tabasco drink and popcorn in hand, and waved with his elbow and chin for me to follow him over to a set of soft easy chairs in the corner farthest from the bar and the door. It seemed that Maynard wanted a quiet, undisturbed place to hear more about what I just told him. He seemed almost uneasy as he sat in the chair darkened by shadows, and I sat in the light facing the far-off door.

"You've come into contact with the spirit world," he said. Maynard smoothed the long, black braids that fell around his rotund midsection. "Did you capture any gray horses?"

"Just two," I said.

"Mares?" he asked.

"No. Stallions."

"Big horses?" Maynard's eyes widened.

"Too young to tell," I responded. "Probably going to be big."

"Why is that little horse blind?" He was avoiding answering my question, I could tell. He had something brewing.

"I don't know yet." I rubbed my chin and pictured Salt Creek Sam clearly in my mind, how he had an appealing face despite the clouded eyes. "That surely is a problem."

The old Indian eased around to face a little more in my direction. "If a problem has a solution, why worry about it?" he asked. I didn't quite know what he was getting at. He talked in riddles. I nodded in friendly agreement and grabbed a handful of popcorn.

"If a problem has no solution, why worry about it?" he repeated.

I took my silver-bellied Western hat from my head and placed it on my crossed knee. I crunched on a popcorn kernel. "So, what's the problem we're talking about?" I asked.

"When are you going to work the horses?" Maynard asked, without answering a single question of mine.

"In the morning," I said.

"Les gonna help you?"

"I suppose," I said. I wondered why Maynard was seemingly evasive.

"Tell me more about Midnight."

I frowned at the lack of answers, but I liked to talk about Midnight, so I found myself drifting into a lengthy monologue about the origins and proliferation of this distinguished contributor of our modern quarter-horse bloodlines. Midnight was born jet black in

1916 in Texas, the only son of a horse named Badger, sometimes known as Gray Badger. Badger sired only two known foals, and the female foal dropped into obscurity.

My own story of Midnight was best told starting with my horse barn at home. My cutting horse, Belle, a horse trained to sort cattle in pens, was a daughter, an own-daughter, as horse people refer to direct offspring, of a super cow-horse known as Peppy San Badger, three time world champion cutting horse. The American Quarter Horse Association, which formed in the 1940s, had its antecedents in people who had drifted around on horseback in the nineteenth century, irritating cattle in the lush green pastures of Oklahoma and Texas. The ones who were inclined to have good horses came from the vast expanses of dry rangeland, like west Texas, the panhandle of Oklahoma, and southern New Mexico, where I now sat sipping a bitter, diluted Tabasco drink, talking to Maynard.

Any critter sporting the name *Badger* or having any Badger in his lineage came by it because he was related to the original Badger, and if he was related to Badger, he had to come from Midnight. The same went for nearly any modern horse registered by the AQHA with *Midnight* or *Belle of Midnight* somewhere in their name. Those horses are spread across North America and also live and work in Europe, especially in Italy, where Western horses are popular.

No quarter horse did more for the development of the breed than Midnight. After he had matured, it was tough to match him in races. In 1921, he destroyed the up-and-coming reputation of horses thought to be winners, including a horse from the massive Texas cattle company, the Three D Waggoner Ranch. After Midnight romped across the finish line, far ahead of their horse, the Waggoner people purchased him on the spot. Midnight was five years old then, and had turned storm gray, with a yellowish mane and tail. He stood fourteen and a half hands high and weighed 1,150 pounds, a stout, powerful running horse with a dominant gene for black foals that, like him, turned gray, nearly white, at maturity.

Midnight ran for the Waggoner outfit for several years and then was turned out with the mares. Sometime later he was purchased by the JA Ranch, established by Charles Goodnight, the celebrated cattle drover. From 1922 to 1933, a lot of cowboys trucked their mares to breed with the master of speed, Midnight. After serving the JA Ranch for several years in Texas and Colorado Midnight was purchased by Aubra Bowers and taken to his final home in Allison, Texas. Bowers took good care of the old horse and got several colt crops from Midnight before he died in 1933 or 1936 (depending on the source). Walter Merrick bought Midnight's last known colt and named him Midnight Jr. He won sixteen straight match races and then found a happy life at stud.

All in all, Midnight had his heyday before the formation of the AQHA, but when it first came together the association registered twenty-three of his offspring. His grandsons and great grandsons included Easy Jet, winner of the All-American Futurity, the richest horse race in the world, and Peppy San Badger, the third-leading quarter horse sire for money winners in Western horse competitions.

Maynard listened carefully and pointed out that Midnight had surely bred with some of the great-granddaughters and great-great-granddaughters of the Palo Duro mares that the Calvary hadn't slaughtered back in 1874. He surmised that old man Charles Good-night had gotten possession of some of the original Comanche mares and bred them to good stallions. With their large collection of good horses, Goodnight and Loving drove hundreds of thou-sands of cattle on the trail later named after them, and the New Mexico part of that trail glided just over the hill from where we sat in Alamogordo. I allowed that it was possible that Comanche horse blood flowed through the veins of some of the horses we'd just caught and penned, and I knew for sure that Midnight blood was all over that missile range. Gray horses born black with a light, flame-yellow mane and tail are rare, and I'd just seen dozens of them from the air in the left seat of an Army chopper and two of them inches from my face in the processing stanchion at the lava corral.

Maynard stood and stretched his legs, covered a yawn, and offered me one more piece of advice. "The solution to all of your

Four-year-old Midnight, just beginning to turn gray-white. *Photo by Don Höglund.*

Midnight stallion at about seven years of age. Note the small fox-like ears and the 903 paint brand on his back. *Photo by Don Höglund.*

problems is to let Les Gililland think everything is his own idea." Like we did with our wild horses.

All the way out to the guard shack at the Tularosa entrance of the missile range, I thought about the old quarter horses of the West and their blood-link to the horses we'd rescued. I passed an old carcass of a whitetail deer just off the side of the road, which jogged my memory of the die-off.

One hundred and twenty-two horses all died in the same manner at about the same time, in the same place. With the drought, the temperature was always above 60 degrees Fahrenheit. The carcasses were desiccated, eviscerated by scavengers, no rigor mortis. But the baby horses hadn't died. At least I didn't see photos or remnants of any dead foals and hadn't read that any perished during the die-off. There was a long list of possible causes, including immune disorders caused by radiation or chemicals, like steroids and toxins. The list also included bacteria like anthrax and viruses. That bugged me.

I had recently acquired an audio CD from the Center for Disease Control on anthrax, and I popped it into my tape deck to listen to recent revelations about research into the disease. I needed a refresher on that nasty bug. *Bacillus anthracis* had been reported in the United States back in the nineteenth century, but Robert Koch, a Nobel winner in 1905 for medicine and physiology, first showed it to be the cause of disease in 1877. Primarily affecting domesticated and wild animals—particularly herbivores such as cattle and horses—anthrax was used as a biological weapon a couple thousand years ago by Greek and Roman armies, and that usage had been revived as such in the twentieth century. Vaccine research and production for anthrax started in the 1920s in Michigan.

In humans, natural infection by the anthrax bug was reasonably rare. Normally infection causes a skin lesion near the surface that is easily treated with antibiotics. The inhaled form, known as wool sorter's disease, mostly a sheep shearer's concern, is more abrupt and often fatal. In the late 1950s, it was thought that the numbers of bacilli found in blood vessels of anthrax victims caused a logjam of sorts, and the patient died from a coronary clog. It was later discovered, however, that the toxin that anthrax produces causes many problems in the hearts, lungs, and blood vessels of mammals, which together lead to shock and death.

As I listened to the tape I remembered that the hardy little bug produced spores, like fungi, that can be dried and used as the "killer" agent in a biological weapon. After suffering a fluctuating fever and difficult asthmaticlike breathing and shock, a victim dies painfully in twenty to thirty-six hours. I sat back in the comfortable seat of my new truck and listened soberly as I cruised toward Salt Creek Sam.

Anthrax spores remain viable in soil for decades and are easily dispersed by wind or water, the tape revealed. The bacteria becomes a problem when a large dose of spores or toxins hits an animal's or a human's lungs or intestines. A vaccine of six not-too-painful shots and a yearly vaccination booster are typically administered to Army troops and food animals, but not to civilians or horses. I wondered if I needed a vaccination. I wondered if every man, woman, and child in America should be required to get a vaccination. I let myself ponder some conspiracy theories, but as I listened I couldn't make the leap to anthrax as a possible explanation or how horses might have contracted anthrax, if that was indeed what had killed 122 horses at one place, in one night. I needed a clue about how to prove that anthrax was the culprit.

I drove along, thinking about the horses and all their suffering, wondering why a wildlife biologist, Patrick Morrow, was heading up a wild horse capture when the Army had hundreds of in-house veterinarians. Sure, he was a supervisor in the Environmental Protection Division, but I wondered if maybe the federal and state government veterinarians were . . . lying low?

I turned off the paved Army road onto the hard-packed sand just in front of the lava capture corrals. Coyotes scurried back and forth across the road in the dark, desolate expanse. They had excellent night vision, but the moonshine lit the tranquil mesquite and cactus forest and made it bright in places and dark in others. Travel for experienced night-stalkers, like coyotes, was enhanced by smell. Their shadows grew and collapsed, casting for unusually long distances as they skulked back and forth with ghostlike searching and hunting movements, trying to avoid my headlights. I was alone— not really scared—but alone, and I didn't like the possibility of being attacked when I left the truck for Salt Creek Sam's corral. I'd never known coyotes to attack people, but there was the story of the German traveler on the Jornada. He'd probably died of dehydration, and then the prairie wolves made short work of him and his horse.

All of a sudden, eight forms appeared outside the corrals, sixteen prominent eyes reflected in my headlamps. Tall horses like none I'd ever seen—massive, muscular stallions. The coyotes also saw the stallions and disappeared. Then the horses vanished into the darkness. I stopped, rolled down my window, and killed the loud diesel engine. Where'd those stallions go? But I couldn't see through the moonlight's reflection on my windshield, so I opened the door, stepped out into the chilly air, and immediately smelled them. Definitely, there were stallions nearby.

The star-filled sky was brilliantly lit and full of flocks of nocturnal scavengers on the wing, vultures perhaps, unusually active at night, circling, but nowhere near the gate leading to the corral. The stallions were probably attracted by the mares we had in the corrals. But near mares, what were they doing in their own band? Stallions on the prowl didn't want other stallions around, and their first order of business would be to chase or fight other males out of their territory.

I walked a few paces and listened, but I heard nothing unusual in the sounds of the desert. I needed to get to Salt Creek Sam as soon as I could, but I also wanted to see what the heck was going on. Where were those horses? Then I saw a dead coyote, then several of them, torn to shreds.

I walked cautiously toward the entrance of the corral. The giant horses did not reappear. The birds also veered off. I recalled the phantom horses that Maynard had told me about, the legendary band of stallions that roamed White Sands. But ghosts can't stomp coyotes to shreds. The hair on my neck stood straight out and I got gooseflesh.

Then that stallion smell drifted on the air toward me once again, a pungent, musky odor. I stopped cold and backtracked toward the truck. I felt a tingling in my hands that made my arms weak. I wasn't normally afraid of horses, but White Sands stallions were extraordinarily aggressive, and I didn't want to be vulnerable to them.

The moon's glow exposed the desert basin. It was remarkably beautiful, but tonight it felt menacing, too. I was again aware that I was really alone out there, no partner, no dog, no gun. I was more afraid of the truth of the desert lore just then than of the horses and the coyotes. Though I wasn't a true believer in the legends, a part of me fought my rational side. I felt like I was being watched.

Back at the truck, I smelled the maleness again and something told me to get back inside. It was like the smell of a bull elk, though much stronger, more urine and musk. I stood firm. I couldn't help it. I needed to know. Then I saw a big gray horse. The moonlight set off the pale, flame-yellow mane and tail drifting in the slight breeze. His sudden appearance nearly catapulted me backward, but I balanced against the front of the truck, scared to death and awed. His large, black magnetic eyes skewered me. He was hypnotic, magnificent, and fearless, his presence overpowering. This massive stallion had to be the patriarch. I sensed that the beast had no encoding for *retreat*.

Why I didn't just turn and hightail my inferior human butt out of danger, I don't know. But I was elated. I felt a sort of pride in knowing the truth behind what others thought was nonsense. The stallions in a stud band were real. They did look like specters, nearly shamanic.

The stallion stepped closer as I stood motionless. My idle truck pinged as its steel cylinders cooled. He did not show the fear I thought he should at the sound. He didn't appear vicious, though I knew he could attack at any moment. He lifted his muzzle slightly, sensing the space between us. He didn't snort a warning as stallions usually do, probably because I posed no threat to him. His ears were back, but he did not appear incensed. Rather, he seemed lost in thought or listening to something behind him.

Why wasn't I as dead as the coyotes? It was a sign, it had to be. I didn't put any stock in omens, but in that instant, I became a believer. I was meant to be there, to see him.

Within moments, seven more huge grayish bodies appeared out of the darkness from all sides. Their black eyes surrounded a retinal green reflection from the truck headlamps and their nostrils flared. They circled me but came no closer than twenty paces. There was no sound except their soft breathing. Like monolithic granite statues, they stood, powerful and unafraid.

I could see subtle differences in each face, though all were long-muzzled and refined, with short, fox-like ears. I wanted to run then but was frozen to the spot. My heart thumped and my pulse jumped under my skin. I felt weak, like a condemned man. White-knuckled, my clenched fists began to grow numb and my arms drew up toward my shoulders in the body's natural reaction to fear. A large branch snapped behind me and I jolted and turned around to look—nothing. When I turned back toward the horses, they were gone.

I swayed and then caught myself and strode forward to look for hoof prints. There were so many from the recent capture that I couldn't tell fresh from day old. I sat on a large lava boulder stuck in the white gypsum sand and ran the experience over in my mind. I shivered. I felt chosen to have seen that band of stallions and got teary-eyed at the privilege. I don't know why they didn't kill me.

For the first time, I really knew why I was brought to White Sands. It didn't have anything to do with who I knew or my experience—not really, not on a cosmic level. I was here because I was meant to help these horses. I'd find out what happened to them and I'd save them. I didn't care how long it took.

Chapter 8

Liver-colored Survivor

One of the big liver-colored stallions had one hell of a tumor. About thirteen hundred pounds, he was a little bony, probably twenty years old. The grotesque, bloody tumor hung like a large melon on the left side of his long neck, about a third of the way from his otherwise beautifully refined head. Probably a fat cell tumor, it dripped a serumlike liquid as the horse moved, but other than being ugly, it didn't seem to be a problem for the horse. He didn't seem to notice it hanging there. However, it did limit the big stud's adoptability. I waited at the processing chutes where we had him corralled as Les eased around to get a closer look at the bloody lump. I decided that Les and I would trailer the massive horse thirty miles west and turn him free where Les said he came from. In wild-horse years, the old guy had probably outlived his herd-mates and didn't have all that much time left anyway, maybe a few years at best, though I'd been fooled before. We gelded him, so he wouldn't contribute to the growing population on the range, even if we managed to miss a mare or two in our roundups.

The trip west with the tumor horse in tow was long and forsaken. The desert looked like the same painting over and over, miles of low scrub and sand whipping by at fifty miles an hour. As usual, Les didn't utter a word, he just drove and smoked. Actually Les would have preferred to go alone, but I wanted to see the place where the horse would be released and scout west for future captures.

After forty minutes, we'd arrived. Les chose an old abandoned
ranch site to turn the trailer around. The few sun-bleached buildings were backed by low-cropped salt grass punctuated by tall
mesquite trees. The low-slung, deserted ranch house gave me an
empty feeling as I stared into the blackness behind the cracked and
broken windows. No doubt this ranch had been snatched from its
long-gone owners by the government. It couldn't have happened
any other way. Les came to a careful stop and I stepped out of the
pickup into the sand.

When we opened the tailgate, the tumor horse hesitated for ten
seconds, getting his bearings, and then flew out of the back of the
trailer, kicking up dust. The tumor certainly didn't slow him down,
but his old bones made him run like a pickup with square tires.
Even so, he disappeared in seconds in the dense dust he'd raised by
galloping away, slipping into the safety of the mesquite trees he had
probably foraged his entire life. I imagined that he was thrilled to
be back out there in the wilds of home again. Les had already
slipped off to rummage around the old homestead, but I stared into
the settling dust, then closed my eyes and tried mentally to photo-
graph the stallion galloping back into the desert.

The faded pinkish adobe walls of the main ranch house were
cracked and weathered, and small splinters of straw poked out from
the clay surface, giving the walls the texture of burlap. The old front
door hung wide open behind a four-foot wooden porch that was
still in good shape, though the paint was all but gone from a century of weathering wind and sand. A small lean-to barn tipped
slightly to the east, its adobe walls and roof weathered severely. It
was firewood at best in that condition and, like the ranch house,
probably more than a hundred years old.

An aged pine-and-metal windmill listed slightly to the east in
front of the large corral gates, which were still in good shape after
all those years. It figures that the ranchers would build a sturdy place
to keep their cattle and horses: The most important part of their
lives was the livestock and the land. The gate to the corral swung
back and forth lazily in the breeze, making a rusted noise like fin-

gernails on a chalkboard. Other than that and the lightly rustling mesquite, the scene was soundless. The open gate made me uneasy. It was force of habit for every cowboy to close a gate behind him, so a gate swinging in the wind felt very unnatural. I had an urge to shut it, but I hesitated and walked the other way instead.

Coyote fences made of six-foot cedar stakes rose side by side lining another small corral, though some of the stakes were missing. I wandered over and found fox and coyote tracks in the gypsum sand. It didn't matter now that these nocturnal creatures had the run of the place, since there was no livestock to worry about, no kids in the yard, no house pets or barn cats to be attacked and killed.

I looked toward the barn, searching for Les, but he had wandered out of sight. Feeling like an intruder, I went up the porch steps and through the open doorway and into the house. There's something about an open door that begs walking through it.

The inside of the house was nearly as shabby as the outside, peeling paint and wallpaper; boards in the floors had risen up here and there, leaving gaps like missing teeth. The breeze whistled through the open windows and gaping kitchen door and gave me a chill. Fine powdery dust covered the floors and spun in opposing circles, and cobwebs hung like crepe in each ceiling corner. Flooded with the southern sun, the well-lit rooms showed that the originally white walls had turned yellow with age. The furniture was gone, but the remains of magazines, old papers, and old books had been swept into one corner of the small living room.

I felt a sense of loss, though I'd never been there before. I had no connection, no kin with ties to the place, no direct reason to feel that way. But I had goose bumps in spite of the desert heat, eighty degrees outside, at least. Maybe I felt an old grief, perhaps for the West itself, for what it once was and what it had become. I was a cowboy, after all, and that connected me to a tradition as old as range cows themselves. I felt the same sorrow whenever I saw an arrowhead on my property near Santa Fe or a four-hundred-year-old sword behind glass at the Louvre. The old ranch yard evoked visions of good men and true intentions. I hoped that I had the moral fiber and strength of character to have been one of them, to have ridden with them.

This ranch might have once been a home for a family who loved this land, even with its challenges and deficiencies. It wasn't easy land to ranch, but as I looked deep into the old walls and splintered floorboards, I felt reverence for the family that had lived here. They were a tough breed in a tough place. They had created a life out of whole cloth, doing everything for themselves. The split walls and the rusted windmill fan had had a lot of use left in them back when the family was asked to leave in 1942. Even now, it could be fixed up into a workable, comfortable, and safe place.

A little elbow grease, new stucco, a wire strung here and there, and this ranch could be usable. The old homestead had seen herds of cattle driven to market, outlaws like Billy the Kid who had stayed here, and even the mushroom cloud from the bomb. About mid-way from Carrizozo to Las Cruces, the ranch had had fresh water, and wild game and beef aplenty. I felt almost as if I had returned home after twenty years to find the old house ramshackle and empty, the grandparents' gravestones toppled in the backyard, the tree in front cut down to a stump. I gave my own meaning to the scribbled messages on the walls. Out in the desert sand, I could envision the cattle in the once-sturdy barn, swatting at flies and lazing about, chewing their cud. The calves and a goat would have been held in by the coyote fences, which had been set by hand. They would have been festooned with squash vines and morning glories. I wanted to see the families and to know them personally. We were all a part of a whole, a continuum of life, they before me, and others after me. I felt the old energy of this place and wished the walls could talk to me and tell me the truth of the land and the people. Then I envisioned the MPs stepping down from their dusty military jeep in 1942, the eviction papers they held rattling in the breeze. I had not been as sad as in that moment in a very long time.

I bent over and picked up a small handful of folded papers on top of a pile of old things in the corner of the living room and sifted through old advertisements in the newspapers and magazines, *Life* and *The Saturday Evening Post*. Dated from around the mid-thirties, the periodicals and catalogs were selling cold cures, elixirs, and remedies of one kind or another. Gardening and farm implement sales and ads for gimmicks littered the pages. I found an old checkbook that listed salaries paid to the migrant laborers—five dollars for this work, two dollars for that fence line, twenty-seven dollars for a month for everyone at calving season. There was an old stub for a Model-T Ford purchase from down in El Paso in 1925 for $1,000. The trip to drive the pickup to the ranch took seven hours, according to the neatly handwritten notes, all delicately aligned in the space provided. It gave me the impression that a woman's hand, soft and sure, had described the trip for other than financial reasons when she wrote in the margin, "Dad so proud."

I found a letter, smartly written and addressed to a family in Ketchum, Idaho. The author, a woman again, dated it at the top, October 28, 1929. She mentioned that the sugar-beet crop had been good a few years prior. A ten-year drought had passed and the "rain had been plentiful for some time."

The letter went on to describe how the young Anglo lad of the ranch had received a new high-powered Remington rifle and how there were now a few bear and fewer wildcats around the Tularosa valley. The mother had given special care to a Mexican laborer who had been injured in some infighting among the laborers. The letter also spoke of the family's quandary of "what to do with the profits" from the crops as the stock market had been "acting funny" and "Dad" was not about to buy into the "risky market." The next day was Black Tuesday in financial mythology. The stock market crashed that day beginning the Great Depression. It was signed *McDonald, Tularosa, New Mexico*. No clue about how it had returned to the Southwest. I tucked the letter in my shirt, then went outside. I would give it to Les, when I found him.

I poked my head into the old root cellar or "fraidy-shack," as we from the tornado lands would call it. As I stepped down the stairs into the half-darkness I felt a surprising dampness in the air. A couple of old wooden barrels stood in one corner, probably once used to store potatoes or turnips. Empty shelves lined the walls for the preserves and pickled vegetables that the woman of the house would have stored here in mason jars.

Something glimmered in the far corner, and I went to investigate. Bottles of old vaccines were lined evenly along the hand-honed beam that supported the sod roof, just as they looked in the medicine ads from the sun-dried newspapers in the house. Curious about their age and contents, I squinted at the bottles in the low light and saw that they were labeled BA-13S, a vaccine of sorts for *Bacillus anthracis*—anthrax. They were empty—not opened, but empty. The contents must have dehydrated through the seals.

Something in the medical part of my mind stirred, and I wiped my hand on a rag I carried in my pocket, just in case the vial had once contained dangerous organisms. I'd never used anthrax vaccines, didn't know if the anthrax organism could regenerate once outside the bottle, even though it would've been heat treated and killed before being sealed, but I didn't want to learn about the disease the hard way. I didn't like the feeling I had in that dark shack, and I turned and climbed back out and into the desert. I knelt down and drilled my hand into the powdery sands a dozen times to scrape off anything I'd picked up off the bottle. I blew my nose noisily and drilled my hands again. Could those old anthrax vaccines have any link to the deaths of the horses at Mound Springs? It seemed unlikely, but fatigue and the isolation of the range were getting to me.

I wiped off my hands again and glanced up at the Sacramento Mountains. Dog Canyon was on the east slopes, and the Mescalero reservation near the top. Maynard's village was spread out like an Andrew Wyeth painting on the mountain, smoke drifting from a few chimneys, windows sparkling in the afternoon sun. I wondered if Gene Rhodes had ever stood where I stood right then. He would have been furious that the ranchers had been forced to give up their good land. I was.

I meandered over to the edge of the homestead property, looking for Les. I spotted an old forged branding iron hanging on the fence, and was approaching it as Les came out of nowhere and grasped the rod from under my nose. He picked it up and turned toward me, pounding the end of the iron in his huge hand. I was as vulnerable as a cornered mouse, thirty miles out in uninhabited desert, defenseless, with a man who didn't like me. I looked around and saw nothing that I could use for protection, so I stepped back, out of swinging reach of that branding iron. Les examined the iron and pounded it in his palm again. The usual smoldering cigarette was anchored in the corner of his creviced, weathered lips. He approached me almost casually, and I could imagine my head split open in the dirt. I breathed heavily.

"Hey, Les," I said, backing up toward the truck, "got something there?" He swung the brand abruptly at me and I tried not to flinch—he was holding up the end so I could see it.

"This was my grandfather's," Les said as he spun the old metal hot-rod in his hands. "I've been out here a million times and never saw it. See it, the end there? Dad'll love to see this. Bet he used it when he was a kid."

He continued to tap the iron threateningly in his cupped hand as he approached me. I backed up and studied his crooked smile. After months, I still didn't know the guy, and right then I wished I'd never met him. He stepped faster and then just blew by me and headed directly for the truck, opened the driver's door, and slid clean as a whistle in behind the steering wheel. Shaken, I slipped into the passenger seat and tossed the McDonald letter onto his lap.

I must have dozed off on the ride back, because I woke with a start as the truck rattled on the washboards near the front gates of the capture site. I didn't recognize the place for a moment, but as I cleared out the cobwebs, I saw that people were feeding horses and filling the big aluminum water troughs. A huge tanker truck—commandeered for hauling water from the springs to the capture pens—rumbled past. Les had ordered water from the water holes where the horses drank to hasten their acclimation to captivity. A loud Army-diesel forklift lumbered by with a stack of five thousand-pound bales of hay teetering aloft. I blinked to get better focus. I suddenly realized how tired I was—this job demanded nearly twenty-four-hour attention. I went to bed at ten at night, after finishing a mountain of paperwork, and rose at 3:30 A.M. or before. When forced off-site because of some military exercises, I ordered chemicals and vaccines, sent blood to the lab for tests, met with Patrick, arranged adoptions, talked to Maynard, or fed the orphan foal.

After the horses first escaped over the lava flow, we assigned a range rider to check the fences daily. Range riders also looked for wandering foals searching for their mothers, and they took special notice whenever a foal wandered up to the front gates to spy on the human activity. Those horses would be particularly trainable and adoptable.

As I got out of the truck I could tell that Salt Creek Sam knew that his two-hour food bell was about to ring. He trotted back and forth in front of the gate, never missing a beat. He was an archetypal bottle-feeder, always standing in the same spot in his corral waiting for someone to arrive with his food, sometimes bucking impatiently and neighing as loudly as a little horse could. He would throw back his regal head and crane his little neck just as he would as a stallion. But he was an easy foal to handle, and because he was the first orphan at the capture site, he was everybody's friend. Most of the men liked to feed Sam, which solved my problem in the daytime, but not the nighttime. That was my time. Sammy must have sensed the rings under my eyes, because after a week he took to drinking formula from a bucket like a herd of kittens. In no time, the skinny baby horse became fat and sassy.

The next day we had to process a whole new group of horses that we had just rounded up and brought in. They were wild-eyed and terrified, and I felt like we were starting all over again, which of course, we were. Each new group went through the same process, and each horse supplied his or her own challenges. When they could hear or smell the mares, most of the stallions threatened to dismantle every enclosure we kept them in. They kicked and

bucked and screeched and rattled the walls of the pens, nearly bust-
ing the joints holding them together. Mares were slightly better, but
not by much. Youngsters calmed down more quickly, but if we got
a high-strung colt in the pen, he might kick and fuss for almost an
hour before we had him calm enough to make our exam. We separated horses all that afternoon and well into the night. Sleep came
none too soon.

At dawn the next morning, I drove slowly around the curve in the
outer fence and up to the unopened front gates at the capture pens.
I rattled the big Army-issue lock, inserted the key, and pushed the
heavy gates open. There he stood, inside the inescapable walls of
the natural lava corral—Tumor Horse had returned. I looked at
the lock and heavy logging chain in my hands for any sign of tam-
pering. There was none. I wrinkled my forehead and hummed to
myself. In less than twenty-four hours, Tumor Horse had traveled
the thirty-odd miles from where Les and I had deposited him to
return to the capture pens, none the worse for his trip and hungry as hell. He was munching hay from the huge stack of one of
the thousand-pound bales of grass hay. Tumor Horse was a break-
ing-and-entering artist. He was not the least concerned with the
female horses, nor me. There was no worn channel of hoof prints
around the female corrals—he had not spent time even looking at
the girls.

Tumor Horse would have to be taken somewhere else, far, far
away from his known territory, and that meant that he would have
to fight his way along new bands of horses and new resident stallions and maybe he'd just find new stomping grounds. I would send
him with Les, northeast this time. There was a lot of forage farther
north, just not much water. But he apparently didn't require much
water. He looked as fit as when we dropped him off at the ranch.
The tumor was still hanging and dripping, but he didn't care a whit
about it. I felt a little sad about exiling the old stud. He was friendly
enough and evidently smart as hell. I didn't like sending him back
into the wild when we had a veritable grocery store for him right

here. Then, it occurred to me, he came back for his family. I wondered how all of it would end for him.

I often marveled at a horse's ability to navigate across vast tracts of land. Even in new territory, horses can make their way back to temporary campsites or a barn that they have left by another route. Smell, sight, horizon, familiarity, and instinct cannot fully explain their extraordinary sense of place and direction. Maybe they have a prehistoric homing device located somewhere in their brain that science still hasn't located. Geese have one; whales have an auditory bone that helps them—so why not the horse?

Smell, noise, and the horizon were probably factors that brought back old Tumor Horse. Actually, he probably knew the whole missile range. This time Les would take him forty-five miles away. I leaned on the corral panel, amazed, and watched Les trailer the beast as if leading him with a rope and halter, and drive out through the front gate of the lava corral. I hoped that this wasn't the last time I ever saw the old codger. I was getting pretty fond of him.

Chapter 9

Nowhere to Run

We were engaged in another aerial chase to capture horses from the east range that had been too wise to be swept up in the first capture. The chopper cruised back and forth in front of a stubborn sorrel mare, but she refused to respect it. This educated old lady merely ducked and ran in the opposite direction beneath the hovering craft, between the runners. She was ruining everything for us. Once the elderly lady cut back, the other one hundred head turned and split, too. It was like trying to herd cats.

The horses thundered beneath us and we dropped so low in our failed attempt to block their retreat that they scattered sand over the front window-screen of the chopper. If they hadn't abruptly slanted off in front of the aircraft they would have trampled me where I sat in the left seat of the OH-58.

More than thirty of them, a good-sized group including the old matriarch, were circling back away from the lava corral. I didn't want to lose them. We were being outsmarted by one dang mare. No matter what we did, we couldn't keep that old girl and her band headed toward the lava corral. The guys on the ground on their ATVs could do nothing but scatter after the various bands and follow the horses' dust in a senseless journey.

Two hours at eight-hundred dollars an hour for the aircraft and the pilot, three choppers total, three fuel stops, two complete days of planning, not to mention the crewmen's salaries, and we had not captured one single animal by the time we got back to the lava flow hours after an early morning start. All five ATV riders sensed the futility of the chase and puttered in through the front gate, the guys with their helmets off, their heads hanging, sweat soaked, dirty, and frustrated. Everyone was exhausted, demoralized by not having finished our mission for the day. We needed a better strategy.

"Follow them south," I said into my microphone from where I sat in the chopper and thumbed backward. "I need to know where they're headed." I asked the other pilots to refuel and wait at the lava corrals. My pilot and I would follow the escaped bunch for a few minutes, come back, and try again on other horses. The other choppers retired as we lifted up and out. At two thousand feet, we flew toward Holloman Air Force Base, hoping to catch the herd led by that crafty little mare. In two minutes—one-half mile south of the lava corrals—we found the main herd, but they had already started to break into harems as the alpha stallions fought off repeated attempts by other suitors to thieve their mates. The distance between the lead horse and the tail horse strung out to well over two miles. After a short reconnaissance, I signaled the pilot to quit.

Suddenly, to the right of the chopper, I saw a coal-black newborn foal wobbling badly. The baby's mare and the only other horse, a huge gray stallion, kept on running full steam south. The pilot saw them, too, and aimed the craft to hover at two hundred feet above the foal. Skillfully, the pilot tipped the chopper nearly on its side and circled tightly around the baby. Dangling in my seat, I got a better view of the damage. It looked like the little guy had run plumb out of fuel—glucose. His muscles had bound up, maybe from lactic acidosis, or from overexertion, which could result in a condition called rhabdomyolysis, a severe muscle problem. He wasn't going to go anywhere, fast or slow.

The small black baby with four white stockings stood trembling and confused. He had decided to stop at the start of a stretch of rolling desert. A defenseless newborn stood a poor chance of survival for even a few hours. The omnipresent coyotes recognized frailty, and the mare and stallion were long gone, leaving the foal an easy mark.

"It's your call, Doc," the pilot said, his attention on stabilizing the craft.

"Can't leave him," I said.

"Prairie wolves?" he asked.

"Ten four," I said. Then, almost as if we had manifested them, three figures started skulking across the desert toward the baby. It was then or never. We had to do something.

"Please set me down, Captain," I requested. The coyotes hunted in packs here in the basin and were expert at their work. They could devour an entire adult horse in one night. I couldn't allow that to happen to this little foal if I could help it, especially since my failed attempt to capture the group resulted in this disaster.

The pilot guided the craft away from the baby a few hundred feet and then down, but not so close that we'd spook the foal into the thorny brush.

"I'll hop out and grab the foal, he's small," I said as the pilot set the chopper down softly on the desert surface.

The pilot gave me a thumbs-up, as I released my shoulder harness and belly strap. I twisted and dropped out of the seat, landing deep in the sand. Ducking under the rotors, I pressed my cap down and secured my sunglasses, then hustled toward the exhausted little horse. The coyotes halted their advance and hid behind the nearby mesquite trees. I wasn't worried about them—my pilot had a weapon and I was sure he wasn't afraid to use it.

The pilot lifted the big chopper one hundred feet into the air and waited patiently as I calmly approached the trembling foal. The colt was exhausted and favoring every muscle. Trailing his new mother for several miles had worn down the little creature. Somehow, my appearance wasn't frightening him. Slowly I reached out and firmly placed my arms around his neck and rump, lifted him into my arms, and gradually pulled him toward my chest.

Crusted white stripes of sweat streaked along the sides of his face and flanks. He smelled of milk, his breath rancid and hot. He trembled, his black pupils narrowed, and then his eyelids closed as he collapsed into my grasp, as if he had an idea that he was being rescued. I cradled him in my arms and hefted his body off the sand, a little worried that he might startle and fight for his life and I'd pay for it.

I stopped and thought for a few seconds. I needed a plan, and quick. I couldn't hold this baby here out in the desert all day, and I didn't want the chopper to leave me here with him. I could carry the foal toward the road and await a truck or even call Les Gililland on my radio and request his ATV. The abandoned baby would fuel Les's arguments that we should just leave the rest of the horses alone, but it wasn't in me to leave him stranded.

Now I would have to explain to Patrick why I had chased a mare with a day-old baby. I looked the foal in the face, at his half-closed eyelids and long eyelashes. He was beautiful, whole and perfect—not coyote fodder. How could I not try to save him? The chopper hovered and blew sand down on me and my new recruit. I bent over to shield the foal's eyes when I saw the coyotes again, skulking behind the bushes and cacti nearby. My fortitude began to weaken as the horse started to struggle in my arms. It was hard to keep my grasp on him. He weighed just a little less than I did and he had started fighting a hell of a lot more than a sack of potatoes.

I had an idea that I could put the baby in the chopper compartment with me. It was crazy, and very risky. I looked up and gauged the distance to the front gate of the capture corrals—a couple miles. I considered the road again, probably one-half mile from where I stood. I turned toward the road and started to carry the little guy in my arms, but he felt as heavy as an elephant and he was kicking his hard hooves against my legs. I decided he wasn't afraid, but was having muscle spasms. I felt his stiff muscles and rubbed the cramping knots, trying to get them to release, all the while talking in a low voice to soothe him.

Struggling to take every step, I was soon soaked with sweat. I wondered why I hadn't just gone to medical school and specialized in dermatology, so I could sleep at night, without dreams of coyotes and corpses of horses in the desert. I labored to set one foot in front of the other without tripping and falling on the foal. I stumbled over the sand hills and rounded the cactus patches and then walked through the thick, dangerous mesquite thorns. The chopper hovered patiently above me, the pilot watching each step. I could see him talking calmly on his radio and figured he realized that the road was my target and had called someone, perhaps Les.

Suddenly the pilot swerved hard to the right, and I looked up. Without warning, as if appearing out of the thin air, the giant gray stallion who had been with the baby's mare appeared from behind a small mesquite tree, twenty yards in front of me. I had just cleared a treacherous yucca field with the foal slipping in my arms.

The stallion was damn angry, and his nostrils flared. His ears were pinned forward assessing me, and he snorted fiercely and stomped the powdered desert floor. Plumes of dust rose as each powerful hoof smashed the ground, each a threat-gesture for me to take seriously. He wanted me gone. His brawny neck stretched taut, his muscles quivered. He snorted again and looked away to glance quickly at something. Abruptly the mare appeared on the opposite side of the tree.

I froze in place, the foal still in my arms. Holy crap. It was my only thought.

Unafraid of the loud helicopter engine, the enormous gray stallion stood his ground, prepared for battle. He stomped again and appeared to boil with rage. He gritted his teeth, licked his lips, and chewed rapidly. I lost my grip on the little horse as my knees weakened. The stallion was about to charge. I had seen it a thousand times at the prison. I was completely vulnerable, without so much as a stick for protection. All I had was this beast's baby, and he wanted him back.

I let go of the baby and then looked for a place to run, but the stallion would either outrun me, or I'd run right into a thatch of mesquite thorns. Climbing a tree was not an option. I stepped a half-foot backward and judged the end of my very life. I searched for footing with my boot. Everything except for the ringing in my ears seemed to stop. An awful pins-and-needles feeling crept into my fingers and my eyes blurred. The foal put all four hooves on the ground and managed shakily to hold himself up.

I could smell this horse's maleness on the breeze—he was that close as he lunged and retreated. This was no ghost horse, and I was as good as dead if I even so much as flinched again. I needed to face him and stare him down. If I turned my eyes away, he would take me. I needed to keep his fear of man-on-foot, a predator, alive in his brain. It was my only hope.

I could feel his hatred for me. I couldn't move. The stallion snorted loudly again and lunged, but stopped and stomped. That was the last time; the bluffing and posturing were over. He stood frozen, but he would charge at any second and it would no longer be intimidation. It would be the real thing. The show of force was over. Now he was going to take me. Abruptly, he stormed at me, his teeth bared. His sharp hooves reached for me.

The chopper slammed against the desert floor squarely between me and the charging stud, bounced awkwardly, and the pilot deftly righted it on the runners. I raced to the hovering aircraft for all I was worth and hurled myself into the open door. The pilot jerked the yoke back and quickly lifted above the crazed stallion, just as he swung around the runner and grasped the very bottom of the cuff of my Wrangler jeans with his teeth and tore them, leaving a scrap of fabric dangling by my boot. The chopper whirled, its nose facing upward. I righted myself, breathing heavily, and strapped my shaking body into the seat. The pilot began to speak, but I couldn't hear anything and I waved him off. I had seen stallions bite and tear flesh from their handlers, but I'd never had a horse actually try to eat me.

Below, the baby horse lumbered clumsily after the mare. The giant stallion herded them, his nose close to the sand, into the quiet, calm desert afternoon. From nowhere, other horses melted into the tranquil scene and the baby eased in next to his mare's side and nudged her to stop and nurse. She refused and he tottered on with her. I hoped he would fare well in his journey. Just as subtly as they came, the horses blended into a peaceful, desert mirage. I sat back, closed my eyes, and breathed deeply.

The chopper flew back toward the capture site. Deep in thought the whole ride, I kept playing the scene over in my mind. I admitted to myself that I had been humiliated and humbled. After training hundreds of untamed wild or feral horses, I had never had a horse actually attack me in a place where I didn't have the upper hand. As confident as I was about horses, I recognized that the equine had managed its fifty-million-year evolution without my help. It was the world's oldest surviving a land mammal and I figured, right then, that I was the dumbest.

The old adage kept banging around in my head, "Whatever you do, do no harm." I nearly had made the critical and unforgivable mistake, but I had been given the chance to redeem my shortsightedness, my thoughtlessness, my ignorance. I needed to learn a sense of restraint. I had tried to play God and damn near paid for it. And yet, why hadn't the stallion killed me? If he had charged when he had the chance, I'd be gone. This place was becoming hazardous to my health.

Chapter 10

Nowhere to Hide

Back at the lava corral, we had put the geldings in large groups again, preparing to ship them out for adoption in Tularosa in a few days. They'd fight little, if at all, not because there was less hormone floating around in the blood of the altered males— that would take a few months to work out of their systems—but because they were sore from their recent surgery. All of the captives were eating well, and that pleased me. It was always a good indica- tion of improvement when an animal was willing to eat. The day was bright and clear and warm. I requested the assistance of the ATVs to push the horses from the large lava corral into the metal pens where they could be processed one final time before adoption. The engines revved as the riders prepared for herding. I was certain that the motors escalated the horses' nervousness, but the bikes were essential in the three-acre holding tank because each successive trip to the chutes had become more difficult. After the first experience in the chute, the animals knew that another round of slamming of the gates and confinement, poking, prodding, needles, and branding was on their horizon, and they became very agitated. Men on foot near the gates would be in danger from horses that turned back, so the noise and the speed of the ATV was essential for herding horses through the last fifty yards and past the gate.

The horses' apprehension heightened, and the men knew it. Picking my way down the uneven, jagged lava cascade toward the very back of the natural corral, I carried one of Les's five-foot fiber-glass sticks with a plastic grocery sack duct-taped to the end. I slowly eased down onto the desert floor of the holding tank, staying close to the wall for safety. The horses kept their safe distance and moved away from me and into the center of the pen. I herded the nearly two hundred horses around a left-hand curve, and started them down the easy slope to the metal pens two hundred yards away.

The roaring of the ATVs heightened and out from behind the lava rubble cruised the four super-charged, all-terrain bikes, with Les in the lead. They circled around and continued the herding toward the chutes. I stayed back but moved to the center of the corral, absorbing the sun and the event, watching the herd race around the edge of the lava outcropping and disappear in dust and fury. They seemed to blend into one giant, annoyed mass of horseflesh as they moved together and out of my sight. I relaxed a little and felt grateful that my crew had pulled together and turned into such a unified, efficient, humane force. I gazed up at the twenty-foot-high black rock sides and marveled at the natural force, seven hundred and fifty thousand years earlier, that had sent such a lava stream from the distant peak of the Sacramento Mountains. The volcanic explosion must have resembled the detonation of an atom bomb, or a hundred of them. The engines of the ATVs revved, and I heard voices shouting above the roar from near the chutes.

No sooner had I wrested my attention back to the ground than the horses came rampaging back at me, almost two hundred strong. They burst through the dense dust cloud that they had left behind only moments before, and in seconds they were upon me. The wall of charging equines gave me nowhere to hide.

The sharp lava stockade, intended to confine the horses, now trapped me. The horses came as their own cavalry, a screeching, lurching, lathered bombardment. A firing squad of ragged hooves shot at me and I had no rock piles to hide behind, no trees, no ditches, no crevasse in the lava wall, no chopper to aid in escape, and no time to think. I faced them, one-hundred and ninety-nine beasts, and the fury in their eyes. Lord, I thought, things have turned sour. Life looked short.

The first gelding flew by and I judged his speed in nanoseconds. One monstrous hoof after another struck the ground with a force that scattered the gypsum like a shotgun blast. A group of even larger geldings ripped past and I felt the wind they created. I stepped instinctively and quickly side to side, and avoided them by the slimmest of margins. It seemed they were avoiding me as much as I was avoiding them. Then the next group was upon me, hundreds of eyes and legs, and we did an odd dance, the horses and I, weaving and shimmying around one another. Grit hit my face and stung my skin and eyes and I yelled out in fright and to try to scare them away. But there was no off ramp for this stampede.

One after the other they flew by, sometimes slamming me on the shoulders, sometimes knocking me to one side or back to the other. Their buffeting seemed to hold me upright. I could barely see them coming anymore because of the blinding sandstorm they raised around me. Horse after horse winged past, their hooves crashing down on the hard desert sand—but not on me. My stick and plastic sack tore from my hands and danced off like a spear, out of control. I spun, twirled, whirled wildly around, and spun back. I did not have time now to balance, or even yell for help from God, or from anyone. Their sweat and lather flew all over my face and instinctively I put my arms up to try to deflect a blow to the head. A split second later the field appeared cleared, then a blow crashed against my shoulder and spun me around and immediately after another hit the back of my head. I said to myself as I bounced on the sand from the impact, "That was too hard." And then everything went black.

The room was cold, lights were bright, and the noises unfamiliar. People were talking, but I couldn't understand them. Patrick and Gary Hooper, one of my ATV crew, were talking. My head throbbed and my left leg ached deeply. I smelled medicine and antiseptic and lemony floor cleaner. I felt my head with a hand and noticed that I lay on a bag of ice. My arm flopped back down on the bed.

Then I remembered parts of the fast and dangerous ride to the hospital. I had held my left leg the whole trip. I don't remember what I said, but I know I was shouting orders and laughing in that stupid way that pain causes. Gary had a look of fear and remorse on his face while he drove the truck like a crazy man. It jolted over every patch on the old road and each bump sent a shock of pain through my whole body. My leg was broken, I knew it.

My face stung. Salt-and-pepper grains of sand and dust were everywhere, in my eyes and in my nose, in my teeth, in the bed. Patrick stood at the side of my bed in the emergency room and held his worn, white ball cap. He looked tormented with worry. The physician stood next to him and tried to examine my eyes, but the little light was annoying, I thought. Where were my pants?

"Doc, are you in pain?" Patrick asked. I opened my eyes and stared at him and pondered the question. "Doc, can you hear me?" he asked again.

"He's still groggy," the MD said as he turned to look at the x-rays of my head.

"No visible fractures."

"Concussion?" Patrick asked.

"None apparent, but we want to watch him," the doctor responded.

"My left leg is broken," I said as I looked over at the MD. "I heard the crack."

"Ah, good, you're responding," the MD said, checking my eyes with his little light again.

"You look like a pigpen," Patrick said.

"Where's Les?" I asked. Not knowing why it was important to me at the moment, but like always, I wanted answers.

"At the capture pens," Patrick responded. "He's fine."

"Shoot a picture of my leg, please," I told the doctor. He frowned at the order, but turned and left and started the process of getting a bedside radiograph.

"Who turned the horses back on me?" I asked Patrick when we were alone.

"Doc, we'll worry about that later."

"How did the horses turn back?" I wanted to know. I had to know. My gate configuration and my plan was such that an accident like this was impossible.

"Nobody opened the gate to let them into the working pens," Patrick said. I knew what that meant. The horses were coming, someone saw me there, and didn't open the gates so that the horses would turn back on me. Who was supposed to be at those gates, I wondered? Les Gililland was in charge.

Patrick was clearly frightened. He cared about people and he cared about safety. But now, I knew he cared that I now had a vendetta.

I awoke with a start at midnight. The door to my hotel room was open and I could see out into the lit corridor. My leg throbbed and my butt and head hurt just about the same. I refused the painkillers. My mind swirled as I felt the pain of injury and frustration of inca-pacitation. I hated being hurt because it stopped the world—or at least, it stopped my world. I had thrown in my lot to save the horses, and now I was out of it, dizzy, broken and slowed way down. I real-ized, in my fogged mind, that I should have been dead. I ought to be damn glad I wasn't, because most of those wild horses had some-how missed me—only one horse had hit me, the last damn horse in the herd. I could just as easily have been hamburger. I felt sure that the lone mare at the rear of the herd meant to get me. She had swerved from far right to my left, shifted back and forth like a run-ning ostrich. She aimed straight at my head as she stomped down with all four hooves. I could be wrong, but it sure felt that way at the time.

I didn't blame the horse. She was probably trying to get to her foal, who had already passed me by. Oddly, I remembered that her brand number was 478. I had branded her the week before and had seen it just before I blacked out.

I was mad at myself. I had given the horses no choice. I was their captor, after all. What in the hell was I thinking? How in the world is a man with my experience going to explain this kind of stupidity? I rolled over, groaning. I ached everywhere. The trucks were waiting to load the horses for the adoption in Tularosa, I thought. I had to get out of there. Before I could move, I drifted off again.

It's time to cowboy up, Doc. I thought I heard a voice, but realized it was my own. I had been talking to myself. My head spun. *I don't give a damn if you got clobbered. It was your own fault. Those people and those horses are counting on you.* I turned to rise from the bed and stepped down on my fractured leg. I wailed. Moving slowly to the closet, I shivered and reached out for the two doorknobs on the closet—everything was in twos and threes. Painfully I retrieved my clothes, slid my legs into my pants, and slung a shirt over my shoulders. I had refused a cast and even a temporary splint. Leaning against the wall, breathing rapidly through the stifling pain, I rested my head against the wall and let out a real scream. I lifted my leg, shook it slightly, and held the back of my head as tears rolled down my face. *Now I know what those horses feel like.* I pressed my cheek against the cold door to the hospital room as sweat dripped from my face.

It was after midnight, and the swelling was getting worse and the trek down the back elevator of the hotel did not help. In my mind, I had no choice. The livestock inspector was due to arrive at the capture site in six hours. Weeks of planning and sixteen-hour days and fifty thousand dollars of John Q's money would be all for naught if the paperwork for the movement of horses from the missile range was not signed. Leg be damned, I could deal with it later. I had to sign the paperwork myself because I had drawn the blood for the tests. Dozens of people—federal, state, and local—would be present at this first transport, and I had to be there. The advertisement for the planned adoption was done, radio airwaves were filled with the adjectives describing the splendor of owning part of the nation's great history, and I could not allow one broken bone to stop the months of work everyone had put into this. I stumbled out to the truck that had been left for me and drove painfully from the hospital to my hotel, gathered in three hours of tossing and gripping in pain and then retraced my steps back to the truck and headed for the capture site.

The first thing I sought when I crossed through the gates on the bumpy road and into the lava corrals, was a gleaming trough of desert-cold water. I stuffed my broken leg into it and bit my lip. The water was numbing and that helped lessen the pain. I didn't want to take painkillers. I needed my senses, and narcotics would screw me up. If a horse got hurt I needed to handle the situation. I was an orthopedic surgeon the same as the guy who had x-rayed my broken leg, and I knew that the inevitable swelling that occurs under a cast would cause huge pain. Besides, I was resourceful.

Heaving my leg out of the trough, I gimped my way to the truck and its medical supplies. I rolled my coveralls up and cut a hole in the side of my faded Wranglers just next to the middle of my left calf. I took a needle, aspirated a moderate quantity of lidocaine from a clear glass vial, and injected the spot near the fractured bone. The nerve block could deaden the pain around the break in the fibula, which was not a major load-bearing structure. I would pay for it later with additional swelling, but right then I needed the lidocaine to stay in my right mind, and the pain was making it difficult to think. In a short while, I placed the bottle back in my black medical bag and hobbled in pain around the pens and down to the loading chute. I needed to stalk a tall cowboy.

Chapter 11

Rhodes Canyon Rescue

I pointed the nose of my truck at the fast-food restaurant in the heart of Holloman Air Force Base just as a Stealth F–117A fighter aircraft lifted its sleekness from the tarmac. The huge bat look-alike roared and rattled my eyeteeth. I had a hastily arranged private gathering with Patrick Morrow in the parking lot of the local restaurant, and he knew I would pull in with blood in my eyes for Les Gililland. I hadn't found him the night before, but I felt I could kill him for turning the horses back on me. They could have killed me, and now it was Les's turn to feel the effects of that stampede.

Les had known better than anyone that a man would have no refuge if the horses returned. The last moment that I saw Les, he was eyeballing me from just around the edge of the lava flow where the horses would hang a left and leave me dead-center in that holding tank. If the horses were to turn back, they'd be camouflaged by the dust cloud. The ATVs would then be behind them, inadvertently chasing them back to the far end of the lava corral, where I stood daydreaming about all the success and the greatness of the effort, seconds before that crazy black mare clobbered me.

Patrick rose up from the hood of his pickup and stood directly in the path of my onslaught. I'd give him an earful and Les a busted nose. A bone for a bone, sort of a macho thing among cowboys, I figured.

"Where's Les?" I called out as I swung my crutches out the truck door and faltered on my exit, missing my armpit with a crutch and nearly toppling over on my head. My silver-bellied Western hat danced on its brim and headed directly under my truck, resting squarely in a slick oil patch. I felt sorry for myself.

Patrick put his hands up in a "hold'er steady" manner and said, "You're way off, Doc."

"I'll be way off in about thirty seconds." I pointed at the Stealth fighter and then rubbed my leg. "Where is that Wild West refugee?"

Patrick was diplomatic, but direct, "Doc, you are stepping past your authority."

"What authority?" I belched back.

"If there's discipline needed, I'll do it." Patrick squared off at me and his broad shoulders gave me full view of his athletic ability. He was no slouch. "This is my project."

I reared up and got a big hump in my back. My fingers waved around like flags. "I have technical control of the captures, complete health-care responsibilities, food, transport, adoption control." I puffed up. "What the hell is left for *you* to do?"

"You look like you haven't slept in a year." Patrick brushed past the insult and tried to reason with me.

"I own those horses the minute they enter that freaking corral out there." I pointed east. "Your idea, not mine."

Buying time, Patrick corrected me, pointing north. It took the edge off my argument. Knowing direction was everything in the desert, and I'd just shown Patrick I was out of control. I said, "You haven't seen a horse in six weeks."

"Look, you're right on that." Patrick put his hands up to surrender that point, a tactical diplomacy. He gave in a bit, but not too much. "I was handed a wetlands emergency, and I've been fighting those problems twenty-four-seven for over a month."

"I would not be here if you hadn't told me you were in dire need." I blurted at him. "Then you abandoned me."

"The general's command was at stake. He's a good man and he solved the problem," Patrick continued. "We're right on schedule, doing great."

"I'm not military," I said.

"What does that mean?" Patrick wrinkled his nose.

"You GIs got to have a thousand veterinarians in the Army." I entered that old argument into our airspace, intentionally. "Where the hell are they, anyway?"

"I'm not military either." Patrick tried to find common ground. "Military veterinarians are involved, but wild horses aren't in the training manual."

"Why didn't the foals die?"

"Foals?" Patrick frowned.

"Mound Springs?" I shouted. I wanted a fight even though Patrick really wasn't on my radar. That frustrated me.

"That's old business, Doc." Patrick leaned back on the truck. He wouldn't play the game.

"Why didn't Les Gililland come here with you?" I jabbed at the ground. "That's new business."

"I ordered him to go to the pens instead," Patrick said as a matter of fact.

"Afraid of me?"

Patrick looked down at my leg and then at the crutches. "Not hardly."

I breathed heavily but I had to admit it: I was the technical consultant, had all of the responsibility—and none of the authority. I was fighting for the control I felt I needed and to some degree the situation demanded. But if I had to revert to demanding anything, I'd already lost command. Cowboys sometimes revert to getting physical when hurt and frustrated.

Patrick knew what I was about, and he did what he could to defuse the situation. I was, frankly, a bit relieved. Fighting with Les when I was healthy was going to be a whole-day project. Hell, I hadn't even brought a lunch.

Just as I started to retort, Patrick squelched it. "Les wasn't responsible for the accident."

My lungful of air leaked out as I squinted at Patrick, my mouth framing a *"What?"*

Another sleek F-117A blasted down the runway, and the ear-splitting rumble bombed our confrontation, giving me just enough time to cool my jets. Patrick slid under the truck and retrieved my stained hat.

Dusting it off as best he could, he placed my 20X Resistol gingerly on my bruised head and said, "One of Les's crewmen didn't follow his order to open the gate and latch it." Patrick shrugged. "It wasn't an easy mistake for Les to take, but it was a mistake." Patrick looked off toward the desert and spoke softly, "He's very sad about all of it, Doc. He takes full responsibility." Patrick stepped back and intoned, "Les would never shoot anyone in the back."

I had learned that Les might be confrontational, a bit tangential with lip, but he wasn't counterfeit. My assault instantly changed direction. I pointed at my leg. "Who did it?"

"He's been disciplined," Patrick said. "Reassigned."

Patrick had taken all the wind out of my quarrel. I leaned back on the truck and thought of a family affected or a man's reputation destroyed over that closed gate. Though I could fire from the hip at times, I also shut off the moment I got satisfaction. I stared at the sign for a cup of coffee and a scrambled eggs and green chili-burrito and suddenly, I got my appetite back. I needed a fix, to *"eat the heat,"* and distract me from the damn pounding in my leg.

"Anyway, I should have known better than to stand in the center of that lava corral," I said as my way of giving quarter. I turned and tossed the crutches in the cab of my truck. "I'm hungry."

Patrick smiled and put his hand on my bobbling shoulder as I hopped toward the front door of the fast-food emporium. I had a cold feeling and was looking for something hot. We had a long day ahead of us.

About three weeks after the accident, I decided that I'd be better off without those damn crutches. I got around painfully by hopping and putting little weight on the leg. I refused the cast, even ten days later when I went back to the hospital for a follow-up. I spent as much time as I could with my leg in the cold water troughs, one by the front sorting pen, another by Sammy. The water helped reduce the swelling. My leg turned all shades of blue and black and then a sick bile color, yellow-green. It looked awful, but I could get around on it, and that's all I cared about. I wasn't going to let a broken bone—or anything else—stop me from getting my job done.

One morning before our next planned capture at Rhodes Canyon, I pulled my dripping wet leg out of the water trough and piled into Les's truck. Without a word about the stampede or the broken bone, we slipped out the front gates of Fort Gililland, as I'd named the capture site, and headed for headquarters and a brief recap meeting with Patrick. Among other things that he told me was that less than 1 percent of White Sands Missile Range, which was more than thirty-two hundred square miles of open desert, had been used for target practice. After that session with Patrick, we headed for Rhodes Canyon. I needed a firsthand look at our next capture area in order to understand the many constraints that would be placed on our movements for this operation. The path to the capture pens that I'd proposed would drive horses across some environmentally sensitive range, and I needed to scope out the horses' condition there. Rhodes Canyon rips down the eastern side of the San Andres Mountains and cuts into the expanse of white sands, opening into an alkali flat. About twenty-five miles north of the missile range headquarters, it faces due east. The climb into the canyon was difficult with my healing leg, and each step gave me a painful jolt, but it was worth it for the clear, wide view of the mesquite-laden foothills. The Rhodes herd there numbered around four hundred head and was scattered over the flat eastern side of the hilly slope near the four-mile-wide opening.

The horses stayed around the mouth of the canyon for the water and forage, and wandered not much more than five miles north or south of it. They often stayed against the hills, west of Range Road 9, the basin's western road, as it coursed north and south along that slope of the San Andres Mountain chain. The road acted as a psychological barrier, which the horses were unlikely to cross, just as cattle can be fooled into avoiding painted lines on a macadam road—a poor-man's cattle guard.

The horses had about one hundred square miles of range before they encountered the rapid rise in the foothills that coursed northward to meet Mockingbird Gap, as the old ranchers referred to it, about twenty miles south of Trinity Site, where the atomic bomb was first detonated. From there, it was five more miles to North Gate, the end of the Army-owned property on the Albuquerque side.

"It takes a tough critter to grow up to be a wild horse," I mumbled to myself as we got back in the truck to drive the long miles west, up the canyon.

Les smirked as he chewed on the stump of his long-spent cigarette butt. His grandfather, Jim Gililland, had roamed and pulled a living with Eugene Rhodes near this canyon and on the Jornada at the turn of the century. Back then, representatives of the British army traveled around the Western world to buy horses for the Boer Wars of 1899–1902 in South Africa. Les told me that Rhodes had refused to sell any of his red horses for that "indecent war," so the ancestors of many of the White Sands herds were, in great part, chestnut or sorrel in color. Eugene Rhodes had bred, raised, and broken light-red ranch stock with brownish tails, and nearly one hundred years later the Rhodes Canyon herd was predominately light red with white on the head and legs, "chrome" as Les referred to it, and a light-brown or flaxen tail.

Because Les's grandfather was a close friend of Rhodes's, Les felt a kinship to these horses that was more than just how a cowboy feels about his ride. These were *his* horses, *his* birthright. He felt they had been stolen by the Army, and now they were being snatched off his family's former land. The horses were a living symbol that gave the land a richness in meaning to him. On one hand, he didn't want the horses dying out there in the desert. On the other, he didn't want us to tamper with his life working on the range, which he had been doing well for many years. He still thought that one day the government would give back the land and he'd have a cattle ranch again. He'd need horses, and where better to get them from than his huge backyard, as he called the Tularosa.

The way Les figured it, the horse die-off was not the first time the animals on White Sands had seen hard times. In 1890, cattle had died inexplicably by the hundreds in the Tularosa Basin. Water holes were full of dead animals and the mud was full of maggots. Range wars and shooting were common back then, and water was the prize everyone sought. Rustling and brand blotting were at an all-time high. The agony of that drought, which held on until 1893, haunted old Gene Rhodes for the rest his life, even after he left the desert for the East Coast. But Les thought we ought to just let the horses be; he'd take care of them the old way.

When we got back to base camp, Les and I discussed the planning and logistics of a grueling wild horse chase from Rhodes Canyon across thirty-five miles of desert, a considerable distance compared to the simpler first capture. The terrain was different, much rockier, with longer distances upslope, and deeper sand that made each step more difficult and more costly in energy, especially for the fat mares. The potential for injuries was much higher, and with many of the mares having dropped foals in the past few weeks, we'd have a lot of tired babies to contend with. Some of the mares were still heavy with foals and might not be able to traverse the terrain in that condition. There was also the nuisance of passing through other herds and their hostile, irritated sires. Some of the groups would join in to our capture herd, others would create confusion. I was sure that the large herd would fall apart many times and that and the number of chopper refueling stops would increase proportionally. Rhodes Canyon was also prime oryx habitat, and we'd have to deal with herds of these dangerous beasts converging with the horses. On top of all of this, we had to find a gathering spot to group the initial herd away from the splinted bands, and it needed to be a safe distance from the sand-blasted brush, mesquite thorns, prickly pear, and tall ocotillo cacti.

Once we had found a suitable spot east of Range Road 9 for the herd rendezvous, the roundup of the Rhodes Canyon horses started the same as the other aerial captures. At first, choppers worked independently of one another—one five miles north of the Rhodes Canyon opening, one far south, and the other at the mouth of the canyon, a barrier that opened east. The mostly chestnut and bay horses with full blazes and chromed legs often tried to circle back west and disperse into their original bands, so the choppers worked continuously to keep them on an easterly course.

After a twenty-five-mile jaunt across dribbling creeks and around dry lakes, interrupted by several orchestrated chopper fuelings, the four hundred horses were reported by the pilots to have entered the five-mile radius from the front gates of the lava capture corrals. Patrick Morrow, Les Gililland, Gary Hooper, two MPs, and I started our ATVs' engines and began a slow arc west toward the herd. His usual high-spirited self, Gary took the lead south and around to the west, and I followed. I would not want to prove it, but I think that sly guy tampered with his engine's carburetor and might have used a more potent fuel for more power. Gary knew all kinds of mysteries and had a visceral need for speed. He always stood on the floorboard of the bike with bent knees, never sitting. When he thumbed the throttle lever, it was futile trying to keep up with him. He was the Dale Earnhardt of the southwestern desert.

Les arced north and west at a stable pace, his path pockmarked with low bushes and small mesquite. Ocotillo cacti stood like wood stakes with fine, menacing spines. Yucca seemed to lean away as he sped past, but shot back to grab the next unsuspecting rider. Patrick swung wide and sped to the outside of Les on flat ground, moving well ahead, while the MPs went to the middle north. The whole of it looked like a free-for-all motocross, no restrictions—just get there and get it done. I overheard the MPs chuckling as they mounted their bikes, *"No one would be left behind."* One MP pointed at the other. "I've got your backside." They gave each other the thumbs-up.

The middle ground north and to the west of Salt Creek was dangerous. Several of the gradual arroyos leading to it had walls ten feet high and it was too wide to jump, even with the supercharged all-terrain Army vehicles. Their engines warmed, the GIs began their first sand-dunes chase.

My leg ached, and I knew I was no match for Gary. My plan was to follow for as far as I could to meet the charging herd, listening on my two-way radio to the pilots as they chattered back and forth about the horses' positions and the target poles to watch for at two o'clock, or seven o'clock. The pilots were amazed at how well the tiny foals handled the chase, their little legs keeping pace with the adults.

I found a mound from which I could watch the horse drive at times with the naked eye and at times with my Army binoculars. Occasionally I barked orders on my handheld radio. But I mostly enjoyed the fact that the pilots and Les had learned from the several earlier chases. I had to watch the course of the bikers by their dust contrails; usually the mounds and the bushes hid them from view. With binoculars, I could see the dust of the horses as they approached the five-mile point. The choppers were just visible on the horizon, like tiny dragonflies in the distance.

The stallions from different bands fought ferociously to keep their harems together, rearing at each other, threatening and pummeling for an advantage. When the dominant stallions with mares encountered an all-stallion band, the result was incendiary: bodies slammed together, weaker horses smashed to the ground. The males frothed at the mouth, heads low to the ground trying to bite rivals' front legs and throw each other side to side. The kicking was brutal and fast and repeated until blood flowed and hide flew. The screaming carried for miles and confused the mares and the young. We tried to use the choppers to deter the stallions' fighting, which mostly kept them moving at a dead run. Even then, some stallions would continue to fight at a full gallop.

Unlike the scattered herds of the first capture, the Rhodes Canyon horses had a kinship. Together, they formed a magnificent ruddy-colored blanket, covering the land. Bright-eyed, in good flesh and health, the herd might have survived a millennium without a drought. The capture of the Rhodes Canyon herds went perfectly, an Old West movie played out before my eyes, in real time.

Then, just as the herd arrived at the west side of a dry salt-lake bed, a playa, they stopped dead in their tracks. The drought had left the salt lake, normally fed by the Malpais Spring, a dry, shallow dish of about one mile across. There, the four hundred head of horses swarmed around like a school of fish. Perhaps it was their last attempt to reject the push and head back home to Rhodes Canyon. More likely, the horses thought the lake bed had water and did not want to enter it. Gary, to get them moving again, approached first on the south side and Patrick on the far north. Les pulled up in the middle, and each biker found a slot among the three choppers. The choppers roared their engines and the ATVs gunned their throttles, but the horses continued to mill around in place. The GIs arrived to join the line and block the horses' retreat. The three choppers hovered two feet off the ground, swinging sideways to broaden their reach, the ATVs gunned forward to try to startle the horses into taking the first step. But the frantic herd continued to circle in one large group. Minutes seemed like eternity. None of the horses would move out onto the dried lake bed. When it looked as though one old sorrel mare was about to break through the metal and human road block, Les suddenly pulled out a plastic bag from his shirt pocket. One simple food-store sack and the mare melted back into the herd. Once again Les's horse instincts were right on target.

The horses flirted with the dry salt bed, a few at a time, and then started moving again as a herd, but always following along the salt bed, not in it, with the bikes and choppers herding and pressuring the horses around to the south. As they approached the opposite side, the mass of equine protoplasm turned east toward the lava wall. They must have thought that the lake was a trap and must have had a history of problems with it. Perhaps when it was full of water, it had proved treacherous and they remembered it was dangerous.

From that point on into the lava corral, the capture was smooth. We all patted each other on the backs and congratulated ourselves on the good job. Patrick sat on his ATV, his helmet in his lap, and grinned at the success. He had put together a group made up of twenty individuals, but the Rhodes Canyon rescue had brought us all together as a team.

Chapter 12

Little Midnight

"Royal gold" would have been a great name for the color of the sun that lazed behind the small San Andres Mountain chain separating me from Las Cruces, New Mexico. I had thirty or more miles of peaceful cruising along Range Road 9 on the western side of White Sands Missile Range for time to reflect. I was headed for Army headquarters and a meeting with Patrick Morrow, wild horse magistrate, about the upcoming adoptions—our first—at the fairground in Alamogordo only two weeks away. Every step in between had to go right. Even though the mares and foals would stay together, separation of herd-mates created anxiety in the horses, which made them suspicious of every man on foot, every truck, and every bird in the air. That made life at the capture corrals stimulating, where I, too, now jumped at the first sound of a pounding hoof.

Capturing horses that hated confinement bothered me. All horses are programmed to graze and forage twelve to eighteen hours a day. That penchant, fixed deep in their DNA, had ruled their behavior, and that of their extinct ancestor, little eohippus, since the Lower Eocene era. We kept an average-quality forage in front of them all the time. But they needed to be adopted or gotten back to pasture as soon as possible. Even though the recent drought was over, dry spells in the Tularosa Basin ran in cycles of decades. Next year could be worse. An additional four hundred babies might be added to the herds in that time.

The International Society for the Protection of Equines threat-ened all kinds of bad things including litigation if three hundred head of unique horse genetics were not left on the range. This misguided argument for posterity created more frustration and headache for the commanding general of White Sands Missile Range, whose annoyance steamrolled downhill to us. One fertile mare can set off a line of births through her offspring that could lead to twelve additional horses in ten years, even with normal mortal-ity. Three hundred horses today, half of them female, meant more than one thousand horses in ten short years. No higher-math skill was required to figure that, and those thousand horses would be back in a predictable, repetitious drought, again needing rescue.

Other animal rights groups wanted hundreds of these horses moved to their own sanctuaries, which I couldn't support because I doubted that they had the wherewithal to care for and feed the horses long-term. The horses' numbers at these proposed sanctu-aries could also grow out of control. Ranch horses, or any other horse returned to free roaming, will readopt the same wild traits as their ancestors. It is programmed in their genetic code. Though wild horses are best left in the wild, the White Sands horses had to be rescued. Turning them loose on public lands was not a legal option at the time. I felt responsible for them as a cowboy, a horse doctor, and an American who loved the lore of the Old West. I chuckled when I thought about coming face-to-face with rabble-rousing Eugene Rhodes, in the next life, and having to answer to him about the poor job I'd done stewarding his property and pro-tecting his horses.

Off in the distance. I could see the lonely remains of the old homestead. My mind drifted back to a conversation a few years before with an actor friend of mine, a good rider and owner of horses who had mused that he acted roles in movies that I worked in and lived in real life. Back then, I was actually not working as a cowboy but helping to produce a Wild West show, which was the kind of work that men and women of the West had turned to after their frontier way of life had vanished. When there were no more open ranges and no large herds of bison or wild cattle to irritate, Buffalo Bill and Sitting Bull, the 101 Ranch, Pawnee Bill and his Wild West Extravaganza, and dozens of other re-creations hired former cowboys and displaced Indians. The parallel to my own situation hit me hard. My skills as a wild-horse trainer were being relegated to entertainment. After that realization I became determined to prove that I could still pursue an authentic Western life. The day I concluded my tour with that Wild West show, I returned to live my life again doing real work with the horses I loved.

A little melancholy, I decided to pull into the ranch again. I slipped out of my bright red pickup and headed for that dingy root cellar. I wanted one of those vaccine bottles of BA-13S that had sat undisturbed for so many years and I wanted to get it off to the lab upstate. I was determined to ferret out the cause of death for so many horses, members of our national historic treasure.

The horses around the Mound Springs die-off site were going to have to be captured, even though their watering hole was now replenished. But, to chase that stressed group would be unconscionable. None of us wanted to give those horses any more discomfort.

About fifteen miles north of the lava capture site, Mound Springs is a series of three calcium carbonate natural springs within five miles of each other. After we had made several low-flight reconnaissance passes near the salty puddles, we knew that the horses were not going to leave the site easily. As far as they knew, no other water existed anywhere. To them, a trip away from the salty pools would be their own little Jornada del Muerto, a journey of the dead horse. Their instinct to stay home in their territory might have killed 122 of them, but if I had anything to say about their future, they would soon be headed for greener pastures east of New Mexico. And I was going to find out what happened to their friends and family. Since I was about to spend a month hanging around the water hole where 122 horses died, on the most notorious munitions proving ground in the world, I wanted some answers.

Trapping the horses around the water, we all agreed, was the best strategy for these herds. Les proposed that he build a corral around the entire natural spring using freshly acquired portable WW Livestock panels. That would eliminate the need to chase the stressed horses around the desert. Les had foreseen that because some of the Mound Springs herd didn't fear the choppers, we would need to capture them the old-fashioned way: entice them into a trap. Les planned to install a one-way gate of his creation in the corral to enclose the horses around their natural water source. Besides, the horses were much too clever to be tricked into moving away from the spring toward the lava flow. And even if all of them survived a slow push, one shot is all that could be expected to work, and the first failure might not present a second attempt. Impressed by the guy's logic and understanding of the horses and their predicament, I agreed to the plan. I wouldn't have thought of that solution if I had had another ten years to ponder on the problem.

We figured that the plan would take three to four days to accomplish, but surrounding the horses with WW horse panels for three days in a row would make the remaining five hundred horses outside the panels damn thirsty and damn cantankerous, no doubt. Four days was too long, so we determined that we would do it in three.

"No problem," Les responded. "We'll see how many horses are standing around looking for water when thirty hours is over."

"If it's fewer than twenty, we can go to four days," I said, bridling a little at Les taking command of the project. The water trap was his idea, sure, but if something happened to those horses it was going to come out of my hide. I couldn't afford to have too many cooks in this kitchen and I could tell from his stance and tone that he wanted to have the ladle in his hand. "If it's more than twenty, we'll open the trap and capture them."

"Got to have it your way." Les smirked. "Ain't that right, Doc?"

"It's my ass if it fails."

"My horses die"—Les glared at my head—"if you fail."

"If we fail," I said. We stood nose-to-nose as Les thought it over.

For a few long seconds, Les held a deadly grin and then as if a bell went off in his thick skull, he backed up, walked off, and checked the rubber tire on the wing gate. From that point on, Les was a different man toward me. I'm not sure, but maybe he changed because it was the first time I ever told Les he was part of the success. Maybe I needed to learn that instead of assuming a man understands that he is respected, I need to show him he is, and even tell him.

The corral took two weeks to build around all of the springs in the area. Thirty-six hours after the gate in the corral had been locked, Les tied a rubber tire to the top of the gate so that it wouldn't close completely. The gate would open four feet but then it would spring. Horses could push in but they couldn't push out.

"The fighting's going to be bad between stallions of different bands, both inside and outside of the water trap," I told the crew. "And that means we need to empty the pen every day."

The crew and I drove back to a rise about a half mile away and watched for any signs of life returning to the springs. Within minutes an old bay mare with several younger animals and a dark bay stallion strung out behind her walked straight to the fence. She studied it for several minutes, walked the perimeter around toward the gate, found the gate, saw the gap, and then pushed through like she had designed it herself. The others followed the mare like baby pigs, or like piglets. It was obvious that her need for water, especially with a foal glued to her teats, was greater than any fear she had for the strange new panels. We celebrated quietly from our position on the rocks and watched herd instinct fill the corrals with beautiful wild horses.

"What happens if we catch an oryx?" I asked Les, concerned.

"Let him out as soon as possible or he'll tear the capture site apart," Les said.

No sooner had I said that than Les broke out his binoculars and focused in on the gate. "We just caught ten oryx, and they've destroyed three of our bull panels," he said. These specially thick steel panels were normally used in rodeos for bull containment. The power and strength of the exotic antelope amazed all of us. By the time we had run to the truck and made our way back to the water trap, all of them had either jumped over, slunk under, and in two cases, crawled straight through livestock corrals that I would have wagered were impenetrable. I was glad that the brutes got out on their own; I was sure they wouldn't have respected a plastic grocery sack duct-taped to a cattle prod.

Within twelve hours, two hundred horses had meandered inside the water capture site. Two hundred would have been sufficient for the third adoption, but way too many for the water trap. On our way back around to the water trap, Les opened the panels at a nearby spring to water the wild horses who had remained outside and closed and locked the wing gate at the trap. When we pulled alongside the trap, stallions were fighting furiously to maintain their harems inside the trap. We could barely hear each other over the deafening squall, so Les and Gary quickly loaded the trapped horses into a stock trailer and transported twelve to fifteen horses at a time to the lava capture holding tank.

The next morning I hobbled to a favorite flat spot on the lava flow overlooking the newly trapped Mound Springs herd. The thin, sharp rays of the early dawn light streamed down from atop the Sacramento peaks and struck the pointed magma rocks, which scattered the sunbeams in a dazzling spectrum of crosses. I had gone out alone to the pens on that Sunday morning to feed my feisty little Sam, and I was enjoying the solitude of the day.

The lava stockade had become a second home to me with its familiar sounds of horses and desert. The flitting wings of small desert finches punctuated the contented sounds of the horses, who were segregated in different groups, fed and watered. It all mixed together peacefully, a natural symphony of sorts. Being among all creatures great and small made me happy that I was a veterinarian doing veterinary things.

Then my daydream shifted into gloomy thoughts about the die-off, which no one but me seemed to think needed further investigation. I suspected that Les had seen and heard a lot more than he let on in his job out on the range, perhaps including rumors about the Mound Springs herd.

I pulled my mind back to my charges who were very much alive and scanned the capture corral from one side to another, looking into the nooks and crannies to make sure the horses seemed as contented as they sounded. A smart-looking little colt with a jet-black coat pushed his way through the horses and trotted around the perimeter of the holding tank, looking distressed. Late the evening before, Les had unloaded the last of the Mound Springs captures, a group of about twelve, and put them in with other, recently trapped mamas and babies. This new colt was as black as the obsidian I sat on, with long legs ending in dark hooves, and even though he couldn't have been more than two months old, he was already acting studlike. He pranced and pushed the other little guys around— he pushed even the older horses out of the way—and forced himself through the herd like he owned it. None of the adults or larger juveniles argued with him, and that caught my attention.

Suddenly I recognized that he was the foal I had tried to rescue from the chopper and whose daddy had nearly cleaned my clock. He had grown to about one hundred and fifty pounds. I leaned forward to study him and look for his mare. He was still of nursing size, maybe just toward the end of it, but he was already feeding on the scattered hay set out for the horses and even drank from the water trough. Regal-looking, he was full of himself, parading around. He was looking for something.

A subtle grinding sound jolted me out of my admiration of the foal. I looked around. Where was that coming from? It was the sound of unshod hooves on a hard surface, of pieces of obsidian glass crumbling into granules. I could hear it faintly, but perfectly. The phantom stallions, as I called them, must be stirring around on the lava above me. I couldn't see them, but I could feel them, and now I could smell them, the distinctive male drift of musk and urine. I pulled my leg around so that I could sit more comfortably and I listened carefully in the other direction.

Quietly, I got up and hobbled toward the noise. I had to find them and see them in the daylight to prove that they were real. I started out over the top of the volcanic rim, stepping gingerly on the razor-sharp, slick surface. Something glinted off to my right, and I spotted the ass-end of an unexploded six-inch-diameter rocket, its nose buried in the lava, tail fins out. I gave it a clear berth.

When I got to the top of the lava flow, I could see most of the Tularosa Basin. Mockingbird Gap, and the cut in the mountains that led to Trinity Site twenty miles to the north. West was Rhodes Canyon. I limped up to a huge open pit in the rock. About two hundred yards in diameter, it dipped way down in front of me. I peered cautiously into it. Eight adult gray males and two younger, solid black horses calmly fed on green grass at the bottom of the pit. My ghost horses, the night guardians, the coyote killers. The were flesh and blood, real. And they were home.

In the pit was a refuge and pasture. The surface of the rock had channeled any water into the same places that the wind had blown sand and grass seeds. Lush, healthy grass grew in the walls, best in the shade. So, this was where the stallions had tried to call the captured herd that first night. I was elated to have found them but deeply sad that we were disrupting their lives.

With a start, I recognized the stallion who had tried to jerk me from the chopper. He was three hundred pounds heavier than the others in his group and quite distinguishable from them, with a distinctively powerful build, coloring, and feathering on his fetlocks. He hadn't seen me and I didn't want him to. When we captured his harem at Mound Springs, he had probably returned to the stallion band. I didn't ever want to trap these horses.

Huge and confident, the stallions fed without concern, in no great hurry. They acted as if they were alone, though I'm sure they knew I was there, so I stepped back, hunkered down, and watched, fascinated. Two miles away was what we had thought was the perfect natural capture site. Yet the entire lava flow was just as much their home as the desert.

From out of nowhere a thunderous clap knocked me backward

and levitated me what felt like two feet. I smacked the back of my head on the rough lava rocks and damn near fell off the ledge. The sharp rocks opened up my head and small drops of blood splattered on my sleeveless arms. The military had just dropped a huge bomb in the desert, five miles away, though it seemed as if it had been right on top of me. An enormous dust cloud erupted at the point of impact and boiled up. It grew and began to blow in my direction. I rolled over, grabbed my head, and stood as best I could. My whole body vibrated and every hair stood on end.

The land continued to rumble back and forth, from one vast escarpment on the west over to the east at the face of the Sacramento Mountains, and then back again. Each echo went right through me. I shook my head, dizzy and confused. So that was why the guards had told me earlier in the morning to stay east of Range Road 7. Damn glad I followed instructions for once in my argumentative life.

Down in the huge pit in the lava flow, to my great surprise, the stallions continued grazing, unmoved and unrattled by the bomb. Worried about more explosions, I lumbered back toward the capture pens, marveling at the growing dust cloud as it drifted off to the south. I kept low like a GI in a firefight, and double-timed it back to check on the captured horses.

I ran from pen to pen looking at each group. Everything was as calm as when I'd left and in spite of the irritating aches in my head and leg, I had to smile at the horses' nonchalance.

When I saw the little black colt again, I right then named him Little Midnight. Rubbing my sore skull, I stopped for a moment and admired him. I wanted that colt for my own.

After surveying my wards, I stuffed my ugly, sore leg into a cold water trough and dunked my bruised head in there, too. An hour later, with Little Midnight standing quietly staring at me from the holding tank side of the tall horse panels, I opened the panels and led the friendly, almost doglike colt into Sammy's quarters. He quickly scampered through the gate, investigating and smelling everything, including Sammy.

Within hours, Little Midnight and Salt Creek Sam had become fast buddies. It encouraged me immensely that they cooperated this way, considering that I wanted to keep both of them for my own. Fighting and dominance between the two would have made my life and theirs miserable. But they had a good amount of space to play and stay civil. Twenty feet in diameter, the corral that made Sammy's living quarters was mostly round, so the foals had a condo fit for kings.

Sammy in fact had emerged as the king of the lava corrals. He was the first to be greeted each morning by everyone, and he was well spoiled, as orphan foals often are. He treated every milk-provider, groomer, and corral-cleaner as his dedicated playmate. Being virtually blind, Sam wouldn't tolerate a change in furniture or fixtures or schedules, and he hopped around like a kitten, striking the air and chasing his own tail within minutes of an empty milk pail or if his hay bucket wasn't loaded to the brim. Sammy liked powdered milk-replacer with a sweet feed mixed in. He liked to crunch on the little pieces of corn and checked that bucket as often as a nursing foal checked his mama for a new load of warm milk. He had turned into a spirited little hellion.

Since Sammy knew the ropes, he taught Little Midnight to take to the milk bucket properly, instead of slopping in it, and to eat the grain straightaway even though grain is foreign to a wild horse. Sammy thought that every approaching crewman was headed in his direction and he whinnied and faced the familiar footsteps or the clanking of the powdered-milk barrel, and he got excited upon hearing a voice he preferred. My voice, unfortunately, wasn't one of the chosen. He remembered me as the one who had administered "the ouch" in the rump that came with his first vitamin injections, tetanus antitoxin, and protective vaccinations. Because I poked here and prodded there, to his considerable distaste, he generally turned up his nose at my approach or snorted and scampered to the far wall. My odor was heavy with vitamins and medicine, and Sammy smelled me coming before I even rounded the corner of the covered wall. He stood at the back of the condo when I entered the front gates each morning, and he taught Little Midnight to do so, too. It was no fun being persona non grata to the little kings of the lava corral.

Little Midnight seemed to know that Sammy was visually challenged, as one worker put it, and the two of them mixed well. Sammy tended to recline often, which worked well for Sammy, but Little Midnight learned that lying around could be hazardous to his health: Sammy walked wherever his nose pointed him and often collided with anything that wasn't in its place. Little Midnight learned to sleep standing until he was so tired that he just fell over. His afternoon nap was always going to be precisely the same length as Sammy's.

Since it was a Sunday morning and my chores at the corral were done for the day, I limped over to my truck and slid in behind the wheel. I left the radio off, and just sat there and marveled at the colts, and at everything that had happened in the past few weeks. What a wonderful life it is when we can spend it with horses. After a good, long reflection, I hit the ignition and directed the truck toward my make-do bedroom, office, and entertainment center at the Holiday Inn, Alamogordo. I was headed for a much needed siesta.

PART III

The Light of Midnight

"The wildest colts make the best horses."

—PLUTARCH

Chapter 13

The Royal Road

As I bounced in a chopper at fifteen hundred feet above the eastern boundary of the missile range, the stark gray of the Jornada, mean stepchild of White Sands desert, loomed on the horizon. I strained my eyes to search beneath our aircraft for tracks said to have been left by covered wagons in the surface, but all I could see were craggy rocks and low scrubland whizzing past below. Patrick Morrow and I were scouring the vast, empty flat surfaces as well as jagged elevations of the escarpment for horses that might have been scattered by our frightening aerial roundups of the past few weeks. We were in the final phase of the rescue, and the capture of the Mound Springs and Oscura Range herds had begun.

The original horses brought by the Spanish, the little *mesteño,* the ownerless mustang, were freed somehow more than three hundred years ago, and had contributed to the genetic pool of all North American horses. Les had told me that mustangs roamed the area around Mound Springs, but I had not noticed any "tiger striping" of the legs seen in the original Spanish Barb lines or the smallness associated with the reintroduced first horses. Instead, the gray and bay-colored animals on the hilly east and west ranges twenty miles north of the capture site were predominantly huge and feathered at the ankles, from their draft horse ancestors. According to the evolutionary record, the horse's long, strong legs had helped it survive by enabling it to escape danger quickly and roam far to find food.

As we looked and spotted small groups of equine survivors, I realized that whoever had said it first, got it right: The only real control any horse has is in the way he reacts to his environment. The wild horses of the White Sands reacted well.

The big view reminded me of the poignant images of the past in the letter I had found and given to Les at the old homestead. I wondered if I had been born a century late, but then realized that, had I ridden the river with Pat Garrett or Charles Goodnight, I would have missed this adventure of a lifetime. At fifteen hundred feet above sand, I glowed with pride in the strength of my fellow human beings as journeymen adventurers. Life had been so hard back then for the natives, settlers, and ranchers. Yet they had survived. Belted to the chair in that chopper and studying the face of the Jornada, I could not divide the natural from the not-natural in the vast desert below. Its emptiness affirmed that we are born with nothing, we leave with nothing, and the time in between is all we have. My rescue mission was my anchor and I saluted every horse and human being who had ever challenged that formidable desert path.

We flew above hills that were once peppered with copper mines; all were now caved in and closed, but their depressions were still visible. Bands of stallions dominated the remaining groups on the missile range, though a few mares, weanlings, yearlings, and foals dotted the northern yucca flats. I guessed that those couple hundred horses had ventured that far north because they were strong and could make the long treks for water. Most had no new foals to provide for or slow them down. Our pilot dipped here and there at Patrick's instruction, and we recorded the numbers in each band, the sex if we could, the apparent ages by new, juvenile, or adult, and plotted their whereabouts on maps. Patrick seemed to record other creatures, as well.

Below us, large whitetail deer grazed on the slopes of the lower foothills. The early morning sunshine threw golden light onto a yellow sky and carpeted the lowlands. Dense foxtail, Indian rice, and Mormon tea grasses alternated on the flats with mesquite and yucca

McDonald Ranch House, 1945. Here was assembled the first A-bomb.
Courtesy of White Sands Missile Range.

McDonald Ranch House, restored in 1982.
Courtesy of White Sands Missile Range.

that looked oddly human. Only the twenty-five-mile-long black volcanic flow interrupted the sameness of the horizon.

The site of the Manhattan Project headquarters was twelve hundred feet below us. Given its historic significance, it didn't look like much—just a restored ranch house formerly owned by the McDonalds, one of the families forced to leave the land so that White Sands could use the area for weapons testing. The "gadget," as they called that first A-bomb, had been assembled in the master bedroom of that unassuming ranch house, which had been commandeered for that secret purpose. The angles of the modest house cast long shadows in the morning sun, like dark fingers reaching out farther and farther over the sand.

Trinity Site, the original ground zero, had been one of eight prospective sites for the detonation of the first atomic bomb, and actually the second choice for Gen. Leslie Groves, director of the Manhattan Project. The first choice had been a California military site, commanded by Gen. George Patton. Since he did not have a

good relationship with Patton, Groves chose New Mexico's rangeland and the isolated tip of the Jornada instead, preferring the site
closest to the Los Alamos laboratories.

Maynard had told me his memories of the world's first atomic
test, which seemed almost surreal. Maynard's parents' home, where
he lived, was on a ridge on a hill near Mescalero, about sixty miles
from Trinity Site. According to Maynard, on that dark, early morning of July 16, 1945, his dog raised her head, clanking the heavy
length of chain with which he kept her tethered and away from the
chickens she liked to hunt and kill. The dog growled and stared
down the hill toward the proving ground where the military practiced aerial bombing. The growling and clanking woke Maynard
from a good dream. As he started out the door, the chicken-killer
glared at him and jerked her head back toward the ridge. Then she
rumbled a drawn-out, guttural growl that sent a chill up his spine.
The dog was more upset than if she were warning of a bear or coyote. Maynard went over to the corral, where one of his dad's young
colts pressed so hard against the ramshackle enclosure that the
twisted wire cut into him. The horse stomped the ground and
reared so high that it fell over backward and carried on like it had
lost its mind, bleeding all over the damn place.

Suddenly, a bright white light flashed and blinded Maynard for
a minute. Then a current of air lifted and carried the wicked smell
of burnt thorn-bush and brushwood to his nostrils. After a while
he felt a wave that was hotter than hell, and Maynard felt darkness
that had found a voice through that wind. At first, he thought the
"destroyer of enemies," the name for the Apache protector, had
come, but then he realized it was something else, something
unknown. Shaking with fear, he crouched to save himself from the
heat that blasted up the stone face of the hill. Then he heard a sound
that he thought was thunder, but it was so hot and loud that it
knocked him to his knees and he banged his head on an ancient
horse trough, a porcelain bathtub.

Holding his head, Maynard grabbed the tub to pull himself back
into a crouch and peered out over the ridge. About thirty miles

away, he saw a big glowing mushroom cloud grow into the sky. Breathless with fear, he flipped over the tub—the water wasn't much—crawled under it, and stared out through a rusted bullet-hole. He thought maybe the Japanese had attacked. Hitler had killed himself just a few weeks before, and an Imperial submarine had recently blasted a rocket at San Francisco, but missed. The twisted juniper trees shuddered, their gin berries scattering and pelting the tub, startling him in the blast's aftermath. The mud-caked walls of the adobe house cracked and the weathered stucco flaked off the walls and banged on the porch. The last thing he remembered was hearing the screen door quiver on its leather latch. It was all too much for him and he fainted.

As Maynard had told me about his firsthand view of that detonation, I wasn't completely sure that he had actually seen it or if he had formed a mental composite of it from all that he had read and heard over the years. I thought he had told me that he was in the war and gone from New Mexico by that date, but his vivid description of the explosion jibed with journal entries of the scientists who were onsite at that fateful moment.

Looking out over the same landscape now, I saw no evidence of the event that had unleashed a new power into the world and marked a new age. From aloft, all could have been well in the world. But returning to earth a couple of hours later, I would have a closer view.

Bright and early on a Thursday morning, two days before the Alamogordo adoption, the lava corrals were buzzing with activity. In preparation for transport, Les, Patrick, and our crew and I had sorted out the healthiest of the horses and penned them in small groups, mothers with their foals, young juveniles together, and geldings with geldings of their own size. Representatives of the state livestock board and the New Mexico Department of Game and Fish joined us in our examinations. Each animal's freeze brand was cross-checked and rechecked to make sure that it matched the transport permit and the health certificates. We had certificates asserting the absence of equine infectious anemia for all animals on

board, and myriad other federal documents and requirements that
we double-checked for accuracy. All i's were dotted, all t's crossed.
Without that precision and thoroughness in the documentation,
officials at the Oklahoma border could reject the load and forbid
us entry to Oklahoma and the Tadpole ranches, one of the Department of the Interior's wild horse sanctuaries that sat knee-deep in
the lush bluestem grass an hour north of Tulsa.

We loaded 450 healthy White Sands horses for Oklahoma—
forty horses to a transport—slowly and carefully on lowboy, semi-
tractor trailers, eight animals to a compartment, five compartments
per truck, three on the lower level. Baby horses loaded with babies,
mares with mares, and juveniles with those of near equal weight so
that no one would be hurt. That kept the nursing foals away from
their mares, but foals often lay down in transport, so the jarring and
jostling and the heavy hooves of the mares were a much greater concern than temporary hunger. Their trip would be a slow thirteen-
hour transport with a two-hour break for dinner at a highway rest
stop in the middle. An additional 130 horses, mostly mares, foals, and
the younger animals, were destined for Alamogordo to be adopted.
Thirty other stout, older juveniles were held in reserve in the event
that more Alamogordo adopters showed than we expected.

As we watched the loading preparations, I talked briefly to the
foreman of the well-known horse transport company we had hired.
He had logged years behind the wheel trucking other government
horses and barked orders to his other drivers, getting them to line
the trucks in an order based on the sizes of the horses, biggest and
strongest first. Thumbs hooked behind his considerable suspenders,
he paid as close attention as if he were organizing a group of school
toddlers for a long field trip. These horses were important to him:
They were his livelihood and he admired wild horses as much as the
rest of us.

Standing on a large pile of lava boulders encrusted with black dust
and white sand next to the working pens, Les had a clear view of
the sorting corral. He had stationed a man with a plastic bag stuffed
in his pocket strategically behind each gate, and as he worked the

gates with one-word commands to the gatekeepers, the horses moved effortlessly from their small pens into the alley and into the central gathering pen. The calm of it all and efficiency were a tribute to Les's skill and knowledge of the horses' intentions and behavior.

Aside from Les's short commands, the only other sounds we heard were the gates opening and closing, heavy breathing, and thudding hooves. From the central pen, the horses took an alley to the loading incline. The animals hit the truck ramp with the full force of their weight, went through the opened trailer door, and bounded into the stippled light inside. A wrangler followed them as they darted up another ramp and crossed a short upper deck. As they went through another narrow door and into the front compartment, a second wrangler hidden in the shadows quickly closed a final door behind them.

Les worked with the alertness of a tiger handler, and the smoothness of the operation eased my fears about the difficult sorting that would follow at the Alamogordo adoption. Soon, he had all 450 horses safely loaded for Oklahoma. An average of thirty-five horses in each of the twelve idling transports shifted and snorted. For the first time in a decade, White Sands wild horses would leave the missile range forever.

The diesels roared, tires ground in the fine sand, and the huge trailers creaked and groaned under the weight of the beautiful animals destined for greener pastures and more dependable weather, and, eventually good homes with horse-loving people. The animals called out to one another, a frightful chorus. They called in dread at their separation from their herd and fear of this unknown. Mothers poured out their hearts for babies and babies called back from the dark compartments just below their mothers. The horses must have felt they were in a dungeon on wheels, all horribly new, all terribly frightening.

All the hardened men and kind women who had worked so diligently to ensure the safe capture of our friends watched tearfully as the trucks moved away and faded into the blue desert morning. Grown men waved good-bye; some shuffled and kicked the ground with pointed boots; each tried to compose himself and blink back tears. I was sad, too, but had been somewhat prepared for the emotions from working on other rescues over the years, and I also felt glad that a better future awaited these fine animals.

After the trucks were gone, I looked around for Les, as we still had to sort and load the Alamogordo groups. He had walked off alone toward the lava flow when the trucks started leaving and had climbed to the top. I spotted his slumped shoulders, head and sweat-stained cap hanging as he watched the progress of the wagon train. One crewman called out for him in a low voice, but I raised my arm to stop a second call. We all knew this was hard on that cowboy in particular.

The other men turned away, each with his own sadness and fond memories. One man went over to the orphans in their corral to offer them a kind hand. Sammy bucked for a jump or two but even he appeared to have lost his spunk. His nose and eyes seemed runny—it looked like milky water, maybe from the chilly morning. Little Midnight nickered and nuzzled the man's empty pocket. We hung a tarpaulin over the corral panel to shield the boys from the nightly breeze.

Atop the lava bed, Les looked out at the open range. He fastened his light jacket, one slow button at a time, then turned the collar up. He pulled a spent cigarette from the crack of his lips, tossed it into a deep black crevice, and put a trembling hand to his face.

The Alamogordo livestock grounds and rodeo arena provided the perfect backdrop for the first of ten White Sands Missile Range wild horse adoptions. It was the only adoption in which I had participated that took on the joyful atmosphere of a carnival. The twenty-acre exhibition center and tall rodeo grandstands stood out on the north end of town. Hundreds of reflections from the windows in homes on the hillside cast a sparkle on the day's event, whose roots lay in the tragic die-off of more than nine months earlier. Press releases, local and regional newspapers, and television newscasts had buzzed for weeks with the news of the first-ever adoption of historic White Sands horses. All previous horse gatherings on the missile range had ended in auctions to the highest bidder, an unsure future for the horses. This controlled adoption would include a defined contract for how the horses could be used and treated.

The phone rang all morning at the White Sands headquarters, and the groups in favor of the adoption talked about positive aspects of the event, while others rallied for the freedom of the "kidnapped." Some groups and private citizens had completely forgotten that more horses would surely perish from lack of food and water if left on the missile range. Some humans had a much shorter, more convenient memory than horses.

All of us at White Sands, civilian and Army alike, had looked forward to the day's excitement, knowing this southwestern community to be full of horse lovers. We had also tried to anticipate anything that might go wrong. I had worried day and night about how this historic adoption would go. It was scary as hell. What if a horse got hurt during the adoption? I still felt like each and every one of the 130 horses was mine—my responsibility—and I loved them all. What if a horse hurt a civilian? A lot could go wrong.

But Les Gililland and his abilities had been my own secret White Sands weapon. I had turned Les loose on anything that needed doing, from the construction of the individual pens along the fence separating people from horses to preparations around the loading chute, where horses would first enter their new life. And he'd done it all to perfection. Les had settled the horses in neat, twelve-foot-by-twelve-foot pens. Each of the sixty little corrals lined the interior of the handsome rodeo grounds, and another fence circled just inside the rim of corrals. That space created an alleyway where Les could coax an adopted horse from a pen of two or three and easily usher it toward the loading chute and open door of its people's waiting trailer. Les was prepared.

I could not say the same for me, especially when Larry Furrow, the chief of the public affairs division of the missile range, approached me. If Larry was within twenty feet of me, he had a concern, usually a serious one.

Dressed in Western jeans and a fine cowboy shirt, Larry eased over to me and asked, "Do you really think you can load those horses into those people's two-horse trailers?" He pointed to the animals milling nervously inside the WW Livestock panels, then swung his formidable arm around the parking lot, opening my eyes to a shocking collection of every conceivable kind of truck, car (even a VW bug with a U-haul hitch rigged to the flimsy bumper), and two-horse trailers. Some trailers were of the cattle stock type and had no roof. Others were so old and dilapidated that they probably would not make it intact out of the rodeo-ground front gate empty, let alone loaded with a wild horse. If these horses got loose in the parking lot or local highways one-half mile from the missile range of their origin, they would scatter like cats at a dog show, and then head home to Mound Springs any way they could. They knew where they were. A picture of that potential disaster erupted in my head like the business end of a missile launch.

I suddenly realized that in my zeal to forget nothing, I had forgotten to include an all-important requirement in the newspaper press release: "All trailers have to be four-horse with no center-divider, a sound floor, a complete roof, and a lockable door." Les was going to tan the hide of Dr. Don Höglund, veterinarian and supposed leader of the band. I grabbed my ten-ton cell phone and started making frantic calls. I needed a flyer laying out these rules made up in the fastest manner possible and a copy of it gotten into the hands of every potential adopter. I was two weeks late, but I had to try. Then I grabbed the auctioneers and let them know we had to make an announcement of these conditions at the start of the adoption proceedings.

The desert morning grew warmer and the crowd grew to fifteen hundred people. The grandstand looked as if it would burst at the seams. Hundreds of smiling horse lovers eagerly lined up at the gates to the rodeo arena infield, all wanting an up-close-and-personal view of these living relics. Under the bright sun, a sea of Western hats—from new straws to old felts, some broken in, others acquired just to take in the Western moment—moved like a steady tide toward the arena. People had come from as far south as El Paso, and as far north as Albuquerque, two hundred miles upstate. Some wanted a pregnant mare, others only a foal. One man wanted to ride his horse out of the arena because as he put it, "No critter could dump me." Anyone who says he has never been bucked off a horse, hasn't ridden many horses. I pointed him toward the outbound gate and advised him to find a suitable truck and trailer.

Little blue-haired ladies gathered at the top of the grandstand and peered through binoculars at the horses; others just sat, smiled, shaded their eyes from the glaring sun, and happily took it all in, eating popcorn and sipping on cold drinks. Still others amused themselves with the wares of street vendors outside the grandstand, where Native Americans sold their artwork, jewelry, turquoise, and silver buckles. Everyone was excited, the people and the horses.

Questions about the history of White Sands and whether the horses were radioactive peppered the staff, and I found myself headed for the silence of my truck many times, to keep myself from saying something harsh. People were surprised at the size and good quality of the horses. In other Western adoptions in Utah and Wyoming, they said, the horses had been "small and thin." Our White Sands horses were "fat and sassy," one lady boasted. She wanted a gelding for her husband, and the big bay from Malpais Springs had also caught her eye. I was proud that we had taken such good care of our friends in the several months since their capture. *Fat* would not have described them a year ago on the drought-stricken range. Selfish use of the public lands in other states placed the wild horse in a predicament that did not show the respect that American wild horses have earned. I told anyone who would listen that our laws governing wild horses had to change. And most true ranchers at the adoption agreed. The wild horse is a friend we must preserve, and help to survive in the wild.

Even the few protesters still arguing for the horses' release soon admitted to the truth of the horse's health and the need for our rescue. Some were seen filling out the paperwork needed for adoption. I smiled at the addictive pull of a good horse. We heard only appreciative, kind comments for the hard work of the White Sands staff and Les's team of handlers, cowboys all. Adopters and husbands, hopeful cowboys and their wives, young children and teens all marveled at the horses, and Les's crew entertained them with little side trips into their lives. Each had a story about outlaws and ranchers and how the horses of the Jornada had survived the atomic bomb by wit and strength. And one of the crew always had a yarn about a certain horse, who had owned the sires of this colt or that mare and the special bloodline it had come from.

In the grandstand, one of my assistants grabbed the microphone and explained the need for the rules in my new handout, apologizing for the late changes, and stating the order of the day. A maximum of four horses could be adopted per location; a driver's license was required. The address and driving directions to the intended new home for the horses had to be hand-drawn on the application beneath the signature and driver's license number of the applicant. The adopter would initial the statements for ability to house and care for a wild horse, that he knew the horse was untamed, and that in no way would he ever allow the horse to be used as bucking stock at a rodeo or to go to slaughter. Each potential adopter then put his name on a small card that went into a tumbler for the drawing to be held at noon, straight up. The price per horse was fixed at $125, a precedent set by the Department of the Interior horse adoptions. A drawing, like a lottery, gave each person a chance at the horse of his dreams. And everyone there was dreaming. Little girls had visible hope in their faces and little boys were loudly declaring this one or that to be their horse. People discussed the merits of one horse over another, some intensely, some cheerfully.

Though we discouraged it, hands stretched into the corrals in hopes of patting a truly wild horse, and I was amazed at the calm nature of the horses we'd chosen for the first adoption. Just as I was about to admonish one rancher's young daughter for petting near the jaw of a young colt who seemed as curious as she, the girl stood back and looked me square in the eyes. To my surprise, she softly said, "I just love horses." I stepped back and in that moment, saw in her face the finest kind of truth. "I love horses, too." I said, smiled at her, and moved on.

When the noon bell struck, all but a few of the stragglers were firmly glued to their seats in the grandstand. By my estimate, more than a thousand people remained to watch and adopt. All had made numbered lists of second and third choices. My team of ladies and cowboys handled all of the paperwork and chose a pretty little African-American child, a GI's daughter, to pick the cards from the tumbler. Eyes wide as could be, the little lady stood in the center of the arena at the foot of the grandstand, inserted her slender arm, and grabbed a single card. All of the people hushed. When she called out the first name, the crowd roared, and my assistant adoptioneer shouted into the stands, "Come on down!" The first adopter yelled out to a friend, "I got the black colt." She nearly fell as she scampered down the grandstands, taking a cross-country route and parting people here and there. A lady at the end of the stands at the very top whimpered and scratched a number from the top of her tally. Sad faces instantly changed to hopeful ones when the little tumbler princess slid her hand into the drum again. The crowd fell quiet once more.

After the numbers were announced, it was Les's turn at the helm. Les repeated the number, a wrangler called out, "Here," or "There," sometimes, "Down yonder way," and pointed appropriately. A gate opened and a sure-footed teammate slipped in and herded the horse with the right number from the pen. When the first number, the little black colt, was isolated in the alley, the team herded him gently toward the loading chute. My heart raced as I watched him. He looked so similar to Little Midnight. I waved at Les, and without moving a step, his eyes wrinkled at me with a friendly smile, and his head wagged a vigorous no.

At the close of the day, the last group of four horses was assembled at the far end of the long alleyway, waiting to be loaded and trucked to their new home. A young Rhodes Canyon sorrel with a full blaze, a tall Malpais Springs bay without a single mark, an old, calm gray mare with a pendulous belly that looked full of baby

hooves and long eyelashes, and a five-year-old Mound Springs gelding all stood with perked ears and questioning looks on their faces.
Les noticed their apprehension and waved the crew off to the side.
Each man respected the request and stepped back twenty paces as
the trailer backed to the ramp and quieted. I opened the trailer gate
and secured it tightly to a corral panel while Les gave the pensive
horses a broad berth and slipped slowly around behind them. I
imagined their wonder and fear, their mates gone, the pens empty
except for the lonely water buckets and uneaten hay. The horses
seemed to look longingly out at the desert, their nostrils flaring
with the lingering scent of vanished companions. Les casually
moved toward them, and they matched his pace, one step at a time.
When they reached the small rise of the incline into the trailer, they
hesitated and snorted. Just when it looked like they would explode
back at Les, he crinkled a plastic sack in his pocket and they turned
away and flew into the trailer, one behind the other. I closed the
trailer gate, locked the door and checked it twice, stepped back, and
offered my hand to Les, which he shook. Quickly he turned away
and headed for his friends, who all mimed an ovation.

A few tear-streaked faces remained in the grandstands. A caring
father cuddled the nice little girl who loved horses and tried as best
he could to soften the pain of not having a horse to take home. I
slipped up to the dejected family and handed them a piece of paper
for a special adoption that Les would hold, one day soon, and they'd
get their horse, sure enough. I told her that she'd get her wish, and
Les would pick a sorrel baby horse with a white blaze, just old
enough to leave his mother, and bring it to their home, special
delivery. When the daughter had stopped crying, the father thanked
me and shook my arm until it went numb.

I strolled off toward my truck and looked over at Les and Patrick
as they gathered for a beer with the guys, and I saw relief through
the sadness in all their eyes. The adoption had been a complete success. I waved and hit the ignition on my truck and slid out of the
parking lot. I needed time to remember.

★   ★   ★

The sun drifted toward the western horizon and outlined the jagged peaks of the Organ Mountains. The white cumulus and other puffs of cottony clouds blew together, and in the north, where I headed, the sky darkened to steel gray. It looked like rain thirty to forty miles toward Carrizozo, and I reached behind my seat and rummaged for my ever-ready raincoat and duster. I switched my Western hat to my older straw one and thought that rain in the desert would be good for all of us, plants and animals.

I enjoyed the day's success and relived the bright moments as I drove. The sight of the desert and its early spring blooms lifted my spirits. Small drops of rain fused into larger globs and plopped on my windshield with a friendly tune. I rolled down my pickup window and breathed in the scent of sage and essence of desert brush. It was a great feeling to be born in the West and to live there. I thought I could live nowhere else, for long, anyway. A full rainbow appeared and stretched its broad bands from the Sacramento Mountains across to the Oscura chain in the north. Then rain came down in sheets, and bursts of wind blew the truck from side to side.

I pulled up to the Tularosa gate, and the old, welcoming guard recognized me and waved me on without opening his window. I waved back a friendly thank-you and headed the fifteen miles to the lava flow. As I crossed the broad expanse of the range, the greens looked greener from the nitrogen produced by the lightning, the reds redder, and the ocotillo seemed to stand tall and defend their turf.

A few oryx lumbered across the faded macadam road and I slowed and enjoyed their carefree manner. They turned and looked at the truck as if it were an insignificant intruder, and the patriarch glowered and shook his horns before clearing off the highway.

Just as the rain ended, I got to the front gates of the capture pens. The gypsum had quickly sucked the wetness from the earth's surface, and in moments all that remained were the darker sand and greener plants. I stopped for few moments and surveyed the area just outside the pen, wishing the band of stallions would return for another look-see. I missed the sight of our wild horses.

I needed to feed Salt Creek Sam and Little Midnight, and the day was heading for sunset. The duo would be hungry. Already at the gate to the big pen, no great surprise, stood the big happy Tumor Horse. I opened the gate to let him get to the monster-size hay bales. Strong and muscular, he looked damn pleased with himself. His tumor even looked smaller.

As usual, Les had beaten me to the lava corrals, but I didn't see him until I looked into the orphan pen for Sam and Little Midnight. Sammy didn't frolic to the front of his compartment as usual, and I assumed he'd given up on me and bedded down for the evening. But when I looked over the top of the tarp on their corral panel, I saw Little Midnight and Les, his back soaked, bent over Sammy, who was lying there in obvious pain.

I hopped the fence and ran over. Sammy looked nearly dead, barely responsive to a gentle embrace by Les, who sought to raise him to his legs. We could see his little heart through his frail chest beating like a rabbit's, another sign of pain. He ground his teeth noisily and though his eyes were open they were sunk in their sockets; his gums were purple. I froze in thought for a moment, ran my hand over my face in dismay, and realized that he must be toxic, septicemic—the plumlike hue rimming his incisors an ominous sign.

Les released Sammy back to the straw bed, where he paddled slightly. His head and neck stretched back over his withers. He was headed for a coma; the aimless leg movement, the rigidity of his body, and the neck maneuver were all signs. I checked for diarrhea but found none. That was good. Then I checked for heat in his ankles and found none. That was very bad. He was way too cold. I took a quick look at his nose, trying to spot the milky stuff I thought I'd seen earlier in the morning, but none was apparent now. I pulled down on his eyelids and saw the pale membranes that meant anemia. That can be symptomatic of a massive worm load in a horse's gut, but in this case that couldn't be the problem because I'd de-wormed him just like the rest of the horses. His stools had always been normal. But worms couldn't cause this acute problem. Maybe he had gastric ulcers—that was a viable potential cause and would be a real problem, because I had no way of performing lab tests out here in the desert, and even if I could, they wouldn't help me help him now. This little guy needed fluids, plasma really, though I had none, and he needed them fast.

I rushed back to the truck to grab my black bag and stethoscope and a stomach tube. I'd seen ulcers dozens of times in private practice when overzealous owners fed foals supplements or heavy grain mixtures hoping to get a growth spurt on their show colts or help puny babies catch up. Pressure-feeding could rip a young horse's gut to shreds. I shot a quick glance over at the grain sack near Sammy's pen but it looked barely touched. My cowboys were careful and I'd schooled them on grain use. I had very little time to save Sammy. If his pain was not caused by a stomach ulcer, then he had a gut bacterial infection from any number of origins. And for that I had no cure.

When Les heard the bang of my truck's tailgate, he scooped up the frail colt in his long arms and ran toward me. Sammy didn't even try to move.

"Hell, he'd been fine as frog-hair in the morning when we loaded the last group of horses," Les blurted. "I didn't suspect nothing wrong."

Everyone kept an eye on Sammy. He had looked low when we sorted the horses for Oklahoma, but though he had watery eyes, he'd eaten like a starved pig at sunrise this morning when we were loading the horses for transport. He'd even pushed around tough Little Midnight, who had grown to twice Sammy's size, and dominated the morning feeding, as usual. What was wrong? What was wrong? My mind was racing. I bent down and opened his mouth carefully to smell his breath. It didn't have a dead tissue odor that is sometimes discernable in stomach infections. Since he needed fluids first, I opted not to stress him with the stomach tube. First things first.

"You gotta help him, Doc. It's Sammy."

I waved for Les to be quiet. I was stumped and disgusted at the limitations of my medical intervention. How could this be happening to the little foal I'd saved just a few months ago? He had been doing so well. But wild horses are what we vets call stoic—they hide problems better than domestic animals, a behavior that evolved to keep them from being noticed by predators. One minute they're fine, the next, they're down and out. What sign had I missed?

I slid my arms under his neck and pushed him back on the tailgate to a more comfortable place. Les folded his jacket. I lifted Sammy's head and Les placed the jacket carefully under the foal's beautiful head. Sam wasn't moving.

"Is he dead?" Les asked. "Doc, is he dead?" he asked again, two seconds later. "Doc, is he dead? I promised my son this colt. We were gonna make a special endurance horse out of him. My boy, Cory, would be his eyes. Cory wants to have horses, like you, Doc."

As surprised as I was at how much Les cared for Sammy and his plans for his son, I just couldn't answer him then. I rummaged through my medical box and found some syringes, needles, a few catheters, and some white medical tape. Then I searched for a blood vessel in Sammy's neck. None was apparent in his weak state. Finally I found one that coursed on the outside of his hind leg across his hock. I grabbed Les's hand and had him clamp the upper part of the foal's leg. The small vessel filled with venous blood. At least his heart was still working. Carefully, methodically, I worked a small-bore catheter into the baby-sized vein, capped it, and taped it to his leg to secure it.

"My boy wants to have horses. Like you, Doc."

I listened with the stethoscope, shook my head at the weak sounds of the heart. I grabbed another syringe and a needle, took a bottle of anticoagulant from a long row of pharmaceuticals in the bag, and injected the clear liquid into Sammy's catheter. I worked to attach a fluids tube to the catheter while injecting it with more anticoagulant. Again I ran through all the different possibilities of what could be wrong. I wanted to save Sammy. How could I stop this dear little foal's quick slide toward death? I grasped Sammy around the chest and gently felt his small ribcage for a heartbeat; listened again with the stethoscope. Nothing. But I could hear Les's anxiety mounting again in his rapid breathing.

"Dead?" he asked.

I injected Sammy with another drug to start or speed his heart and grabbed my stethoscope again. I listened closely. I grabbed his chest again and felt . . . nothing.

"Alive?" Les pleaded. I waved him off again. I was trying to save this little horse and hold on to my composure at the same time.

"Not by much," I finally responded. "I'm working on it. I really am."

"How much?" he asked. I glanced up at him and could see his eyes welling.

"He's bleeding, see?" I said. I pointed at the small, slow drip from the needle in the foal's neck. I was surprised at the blood because I couldn't hear or feel his heart.

"Bleeding . . . is that bad? That's bad, right?" Les cringed.

"It means his pump is working, Les," I said. "His heart's still going. Wait for a minute. Let the medicine kick in."

"Thank you, God." Les clasped his huge hands. I couldn't believe the change in him.

"Stop talking for a minute," I said, as I moved my stethoscope to another part of the little foal's chest.

"Sorry."

"Get a blanket," I said, nearly yelling. I inserted a thermometer into Sammy's rectum and lay his tail over it.

Les rushed off to his truck and brought back a blanket he'd used a million times when he'd slept out on the range. He placed it gingerly over the foal.

"Put your hand underneath the blanket," I said to Les, "and count the number of times he breathes in ten seconds."

Les placed a big hand on the foal's chest and seemed to stop thinking for a moment.

"Two," Les said, keeping his hand where it was.

"Not good," I yelled. "Stay here and watch him." I turned and rummaged in the truck and grabbed a small empty bottle from another bag. With one hand I pulled a small aliquot of liquid into two huge sixty-milliliter syringes. I rushed past Les and the foal, hopped the fence into the orphan pen, and grabbed Little Midnight. Pushing him gently to the corner of the corral, I caught hold of the young colt's neck, inserted the needle into his jugular, pulled on the plunger, and extracted two syringes of whole blood.

I scrambled back over the fence to the tailgate, removed Les's grip on Sammy's leg, and injected the blood into the clear plastic tube leading into the vein. The tube turned crimson as the lifesaving blood rocketed into the baby's veins. Soon it would get to his heart, which would send some to his brain and hopefully keep his gray matter alive. We waited a painful couple of minutes for a sign of improvement, and then I injected the second syringe of blood, all the while watching Sammy take shallow breaths.

"Is he gonna make it, Doc?" Les asked when he could wait not a second longer.

I slowly raised my shoulders to indicate my frustration, fear, and powerlessness. "He never got his mother's first milk." I put my hand on the little foal's head. "He had none of her antibodies for protection from infection." I pulled the thermometer out and read it and frowned. It didn't even read cold.

Les's smile slowly dissolved to agony. He placed his large hand on Sammy's face and softly stroked the fine hair. He looked from Sammy to me and back.

With my hand on Sammy's sternum, I felt deep into his frail chest searching for a sign of life, looking for a breath . . .

I released the little horse and stepped back. "He's gone, Les." I put my hand on Les's shoulder. "Maybe a stomach ulcer or an intestinal infection from no mother's milk."

With a gentleness I didn't know he had, Les ran his long, calloused fingers over the small creature's delicate eyelashes, closing the baby's eyes to protect him, one final time. He blinked away the mist in his eyes, stepped back wordlessly from the tailgate of the truck, and moved quietly to the orphan pen. He looked over the covered panel at Little Midnight, who stood wide-eyed, nickering softly.

I sat on the tailgate and slumped. This traumatic, sometimes violent rollercoaster ride in the desert had jolted to a horrible stop. I kept thinking, "Wild animals should stay in the wild." I wondered how we would comfort Little Midnight.

Chapter 14

Oklahoma to the Rescue

On April 18, 1995, for the first time in three months, I wasn't in a hurry. Sammy had died a few days before. Little Midnight was old enough to be with other colts, so I put him in a new pen to make some friends. He was in good hands at White Sands and I would pick him up soon and take him to Oklahoma, where he would live his first year and a half on the perfected grasslands in the northeast of that state. I drove from White Sands, New Mexico, to Bartlesville, Oklahoma. I needed to meet another load of 450 horses that Les was organizing for transport bound again for the Tadpole ranches. They were scheduled to reach Tadpole at about noon on April 19. John Hughes, owner of the large ranch, had agreed to house up to 1,125 of the White Sands wild horses as long as I organized adoptions throughout the Midwest that would relieve him of the horses by year's end.

I needed the drive and the rest so I took the back roads east past Alamogordo up the mountain to Ruidoso and over to Roswell; where I kept my eyes peeled for an unlikely "incident," an alien spacecraft or a cattle drive. I liked to imagine that either was possible. I daydreamed on the lonely Highway 70 up to Clovis.

Still broken up about poor Sammy's death, I had had to know what killed him, so I had done an animal autopsy before I'd left. I found that Sammy had an infected bowel, probably from an organisms that had taken hold because he hadn't had his mother's milk and her antibodies constantly bathing his insides. Mares' milk is nearly sterile, but Sammy had had to get his through nipples on bottles that we couldn't keep sterile and from milk pails that were exposed to air and bugs. His survival had been uncertain from the day we found him, but we'd all been hopeful that his tough little spirit would pull him through. Even though his death made sense medically, it was hard for all of us at White Sands to accept. He'd been a sort of mascot for our rescue operation, succeeding against the odds.

At Clovis I hung a leisurely right on Highway 60 headed toward Amarillo, Texas. All of the drive went through the famed Llano Estacado, John Chisum and Charles Goodnight country. There, I could see why the writer Hamlin Garland once said, "The trail is poetry; a wagon road is prose; the railroad, arithmetic."

The Llano Estacado comprised the southern part of the High Plains, stepping across the New Mexico–Texas border, sprawling between Interstate 20 on the south line and Interstate 40—my northeastern route into Oklahoma. The lonely country between Amarillo and Odessa contained its immense reach, bounded on the west by the Pecos River and the valley it created, and the east by the rust-colored Permian plains of west Texas. One hundred fifty miles of emptiness east to west, 250 miles north to south, an area of 37,500 square miles, the Llano is nearly horizontal, a semiarid bench, elevating from three thousand feet on the southeast to five thousand feet on the northwest, at ten feet a mile—an imperceptible slope to the eye and to water, if rain ever came. To say that the Llano is treeless understates how uniquely dry it is. Mirages were frequent, and though uninhabitable, the plains were anything but uninteresting.

In 1872, John Chisum, also known to cattlemen as Big John, maintained the title of southwest cattle king for nearly thirty years. After producing beef for eighteen years in Texas, he decided to leave his home base there and head for Bosque Grande, New Mexico, where he claimed a range for more than a hundred miles down the Pecos

River toward Roswell for fattening cattle destined for markets in Kansas, New Mexico, and Arizona. Just after the Civil War, in 1874, he contracted for "beeves" to feed the newly created reservations on the Bosque del Apache, which were near his new claimed territory on the Pecos.

I was particularly interested in Chisum because he had a profitable three-year association with Charles Goodnight, during which Chisum provided ten thousand head annually to Goodnight crews to develop markets and brood stock. Goodnight also had created the John Adair or JA Ranch at Palo Duro Canyon, Texas. On the Palo Duro ranch, Midnight had lived and bred mares in the mid-1920s. Now, I was headed to the famed University of Oklahoma Western History Library in Norman to study the origins of Midnight and other horses that might have populated the vast missile range. The next morning I'd do my research and head for Tadpole to greet the White Sands horses in person.

At the beautiful old library the next day, I made my way up elegant rosewood stairs and along carved bookshelves in the Western History Collections. Frank Phillips, founder of Phillips Petroleum, helped fund the collections starting in 1927. In a wooden cubicle in a corner of the library, I hunched over a stack of four books brought by a regal Native-American librarian who was wearing impeccable white gloves to protect the old books. After making sure that I had no pens or tracing materials, he watched me closely as I turned the pages. I could take notes on the pad of legal paper that I had brought along, but I could not photocopy any of the books' pages, because the light could damage the pictures and text.

I was engrossed in the history of the Tularosa, the migrations of the west Texas ranching families, and accounts of Eugene Manlove Rhodes, when suddenly a loud rumble shook the library. Framed photos of old frontier characters hanging on the mahogany walls rattled. Alarmed, I stood and exchanged questioning looks with the other few people in the library. This had been no ordinary rumble.

A few minutes after the shock, a librarian came by and announced in a wavering voice that the Murrah Building in Oklahoma City had just been bombed. I thought that they were going to close the library, so I left my stack of books and headed out with the others, all of us pale and shaken. I would soon learn that several of my friends on the veterinary staff of the United States Department of Agriculture based in Oklahoma City had been seriously injured.

I headed for my Ford pickup and drove east toward Tulsa to avoid traffic in Oklahoma City. I was so shaken that I couldn't drive for long, though, so I pulled off to the side of the interstate and sat and listened for two hours as the radio voices discussed and speculated about the terror. As the death and injury counts rose, I felt lightheaded, sick.

I started back along the highway and drove until I found a Flying JJ Truck Stop near Tulsa and pulled in. Just then my cell phone rang and I picked up to hear my soon-to-be great friend, Ira "Rose Man" Haughn, splitting my eardrum about the bombing, and telling me to quit dawdling along the road.

Ira had worked for Big John Hughes for twenty-some years as a lowly cowhand; then he became a foreman of Hughes's Tadpole Cattle Company, a series of leased corporate pastures on the east and north sides of Bartlesville. Ira was a "piece of work," as the Oklahoma natives referred to him, a real character. He was a farmer turned cowboy, and also a notable "who's who" in North American rose gardening. His near-inch-thick spectacles hid deep cobalt blue eyes, and his occasional smile fronted the sharpest tongue I've ever known. The man could fillet a whisper. Nobody could find a comeback for the Rose Man.

Ira cared for five thousand head of Tadpole stocker cattle and twenty-five hundred head of wild horses from the Bureau of Land Management's unadoptable horse group. He also believed that since he got paid on the first of every month, he was doing what God had intended him to do.

I had chosen the Tadpole Cattle Company for the White Sands horses because Big John had a good reputation as well as the right place, the cowboys, and the will to handle former wild horses. The

Department of the Army had sent Patrick Morrow and a team of contract officers to see the Tadpole and pore over the deal, rewrite the particulars, and sign the contract, so they must have agreed. Although I hadn't escorted the first 450 head there, I did want to see the arrival of the second load and to prepare for the first Oklahoma adoption.

Arriving in northeastern Oklahoma, the 12,500 acres of knee-deep green grass was a bit of culture shock after White Sands. Ira was right, cattle and horses look much better on a green background. Every head of beef, the horses, and even ostrich I saw on the drive from Norman seemed contented, their faces planted neck-deep into the fertile forage.

At the Tadpole offices in the bank building in Bartlesville, Ira and Big John Hughes greeted me with broad smiles and firm handshakes—strong from twisting well-drilling pipe and feeding large numbers of stocker steers. One of the last cattle kings of Oklahoma, Big John Hughes must have tipped the scales at two hundred and ninety pounds. He had lost an arm as a youngster in an accident at the ranch, but that hadn't held him back. Decades earlier, Big John had taken over his dad's vast ranch, a patchwork of smaller ranches north of Tulsa, and south and west of Bartlesville. Ira said that Big John likened that territory to God's country, since he had cattle companies in all directions and "around those parts, Big John was God." John Hughes may have ruled those rolling, scrub-oak prairies with an iron fist, but he was a glad-hander with gifted political ability and a shrewd business mind.

Farther east of the Hughes place sits Woolaroc, oilman Frank Phillips's retreat, established in 1925 as a thirty-seven-hundred-acre ranch and wildlife preserve and hideaway for family and friends. Phillip's words about preservation had often inspired and encouraged me through the wild horse rescue, "This isn't all a dream about something, but a place where I can get back to nature. The great difficulty with the American people today is that they are getting too far away from the fundamental things in life. Too much time and money are spent on things which leave no record and which add nothing, basically, to the present nor to the future. To build permanently and wisely is to benefit all mankind. The conservation of wildlife now will mean much to future generations."

The next morning, I examined our first group of 450 head of White Sands horses where they lounged peacefully on two thousand acres of rolling pasture. It was a place definitely fit for horses. On schedule, the lowboy transports arrived at the front gates to Tadpole's Adams Road corrals, and Ira and I were there to meet them. Ira liked to talk, sort of like a pinball machine, chattering about everything that entered his sight range. His wide-brimmed black cowboy hat covered most of his head down to his substantial ears and he stood wide-legged with thumbs in his belt, mumbling to himself just loudly enough for me to hear him. Ira narrated the action before it happened.

"Back up to the chute ramp. Come on back, what are you, blind? That's good enough for a wild horse," he muttered out loud.

Ira waved the driver off after the truck had been expertly backed into the unloading ramp. "Now, get out of the truck and look in the trailer for down horses you dummy. You'll kill them if one is down. Check the upper deck too. Watch out, they'll bite you," Ira rumbled along in this vein, though the driver couldn't hear a word of it. This was Ira's way of controlling his environment, and I got a big kick out of his micromanagement rhetoric.

The driver, a portly man in his sixties wearing well-worn old coveralls, must have known Ira, because he stayed out of earshot. He released the latched chain on the side of the trailer and the loading (or in this case unloading) ramp clamored down into perfect connection to the alleyway leading into the corral. He pulled another chain and the back gate opened, and there stood the first of forty-eight wide-eyed wild horses.

Hooves shuffled on the trailer floor, which excited the whole truckload and they all scrambled for better footing. Some called out for each other—mamas calling out to babies, others looking for their herd-mates and friends. Then the first horse poked her head out and blinked her long eyelashes. She pushed back shakily against the others and disappeared into the trailer. We waited for them to decide that it was safe to step down onto the aluminum ramp and out into the daylight and green of Oklahoma.

A juvenile sorrel colt tested the aluminum ramp first. His leg vibrated as he stepped down onto the wavering metal, and he immediately pulled that leg back, unsure. Then he touched the ramp again and planted both feet firmly on it. He looked around but didn't move. Horse chatter started again in the trailer just as the sorrel colt spotted the Judas horse, a gelding that Ira had smartly planted just outside the corral, on the far side. To the colt, that horse equaled security—if that horse could be out there, it must be safe for him, too. One jittery step after another, the White Sands colt made his way down the wobbly thirty-foot ramp into the alleyway leading to solid ground. Once all four feet were planted in the Oklahoma soil he tucked-tail and headed straight for the Judas gelding like it was his long lost buddy. I felt elated.

The driver stepped forward, wanting to move the remaining horses faster out of the trailer, and I quickly tried to wave him off. Ira mumbled in my ear, "Hold up there, you dummy, let him decide, damn it!" I looked at Ira, not knowing who he was talking to, and he saw my frown and jabbed a finger at the driver. He rumbled an Okie colloquialism, "Gonna make my life hell around here for me." He called out, "Let 'em look for themselves," and I relaxed as the driver got the hint and stepped away from the truck.

After some more hesitation, one after the other more horses decided to step out of the trailer. I was proud to see them shining in the Oklahoma sun, and hoped that they could already smell the fragrance of that tall, tasty grass.

Horse by horse, mamas first, foals last, the truck emptied. Separated from their mares for the thirteen-hour ride from White Sands to Bartlesville, the foals were starved and it didn't take thirty seconds of calling before they were paired up with their mares and calmed down. The suckling was the noisiest I'd ever heard.

The former stallions (now geldings) would come later, by them-selves, to another lush pasture five miles away. But from this point, that horse behavior and herd instinct, they way they created bands, would never be the same as at White Sands. Necessary as it was, the capture had disrupted a unique niche and gene pool of wild horses.

Ira had left open a tall, heavy gate at the far end of the two-hundred-foot-square corral. It led to a thousand-acre rolling pasture where the horses would live. There, new shoots of succulent green prairie grass poked up from the dark rich earth and looked inviting, even to me. An old cattle watering tank was kept full at the near end of the corral, and the same dried bluestem grass that we had trucked in for the White Sands horses overflowed a feed bunk along the corral wall.

These Oklahoma corrals invited envy. Used well-drilling pipe was in cheap supply in the fossil-fuel-rich state. Especially after the oil bust a few years earlier, drilling was at a standstill and pipe got converted to pens and working chutes for cattle ranching. Ira's pens were to die for, especially for working bulls. They were six feet high with five rails of stout, four-inch pipe runners and six- or eight-inch corner posts for gate supports. The gates were built to operate in either direction for a mounted man. A cowboy could sort and pen cattle all day and never leave the back of his horse. He could even eat right there in the saddle. Big John Hughes did it right, no doubt.

Ira let horses behave like horses and get their bearings. Rather than drive them onto the pasture, we watched them mill around the corral while we had a bite and a long-awaited cold beer by the side of the truck. The mares and the younger stock ate and nursed and stood close to the water trough, accustomed now to sweet water from wells instead of the salty seep of their old home. One foal ram-bled around in his new digs and inadvertently wandered out the gate at the far end. He panicked when he found that he couldn't pass directly through the rails of pipe, thought he was lost, and began bawling like a scared calf. When his mama went through the gate to save him, she noticed the tender sprouts in the pasture and soon glued her head to the ground. A few other mares realized the unfairness of her eating lush grass while they were eating dried hay, and everybody followed in line out of the gate and into a new life in Oklahoma. Mares ate and looked around and watched birds and even snorted at the far-off coyotes baying. They looked like different horses out there, vibrant in the tall bluestem grass.

For the first time since I started the White Sands adventure, I relaxed. All of the hard work on this project had paid off in contented horses rummaging around in a green environment.

The wild horse bands originally had formed during the olden days when ranchers free-roamed their horses. Back then, a rancher only kept horses that would produce the kind of mounts he wanted, so any stallion crossed with any mare was fine with him. At gathering times the ranchers took the cream of the crop back to the ranch to work. Selective breeding today uses a different approach altogether.

On White Sands, each band of mares and juveniles had been ruled by a single dominant stallion. Now, with the horses moved off the range, the family structure would be just mares and foals. New hierarchies would begin to form with a dominant matriarch controlling the direction of feeding and the selection of members. In the wild, the mares encouraged their offspring to leave the band after about two to three years, an instinct that helped limit inbreeding. Most wild horses, if free to cover long distances, are more genetically diverse than any domestic breeds. At White Sands, new stallions had entered the gene pool up until about 1942, and were even said to have jumped the military fence from time to time to get to mares. Wild horses living on ample land are more able to deal with changing conditions and environments over time than are their domestic cousins.

Ira and I watched the horses adjust and centered our attention on the action of three mares, one that protected her foal by constantly stepping in between her new baby and any other horse. Another mare gently nuzzled her foal at the far end of the group a few yards from the nearest horse, and a third didn't seem to care where her foal went. That foal romped around like a sugared-up kid on a playground. He would find his mare and nurse, and then take off like a rabbit. Some of the foals walked the fences and the mares followed, annoyed at the interruption of their dinner.

Communication, like changing ear position and jostling, began among the juveniles. Each took a turn licking the red salt blocks put out in the pasture for them, and they seemed glad not to have to dig for salt. Other horses, newly full of green grass, meandered around and sniffed the new, humid air, the fence posts, and the persimmon trees. Some of them abruptly ran a few steps and then stopped, reared, and backed up to kick, behaving just as horses are supposed to. Sometimes they grouped with one another. New relationships would spring up, new alliances would grow. Each horse would find a place here in cattle country. With forage and water readily available, peace settled over the horses.

Ira had left the pastures intact from the previous year's heavy growth so that the horses would have an abundance of roughage. Usually he burned the fields to promote new growth, but too much green would have hurt the horses' digestion. I thanked Ira for his horse sensibilities, and we talked about equine nutrition. Neither of us used vitamin or protein supplements. We agreed that the wild, free-roaming horse had made it through tens of millions of years without concentrated formulas. In the near future, these animals didn't need anything that didn't arise from the good earth of Oklahoma.

Near dark, an old gray mare heavy with foal and full mammary glands wandered off to the far end of the pasture near a persimmon thicket and stood there neither eating nor adventuring. Ira said that the stress of the trip to Oklahoma would cause her to foal that night, but not until we'd left. "That mare will hold her foal in all night if we insist on helping or even watching," Ira said.

I felt responsible for that horse and her stress of a lifetime and had an oath to maintain that he didn't, so I returned to the pasture alone after midnight and drove the perimeter just inside the fence line to search for the old mare. I was concerned that if she foaled that close to a fence, something she never had to deal with in the desert, she'd lie down and the foal would pop out just under the fence and get up on the other side, unable to get back to his mare. I'd seen it happen twice in private practice, so I hunted for her like a worried father. I searched the persimmon thicket but she wasn't there, so I rambled over the hill and down to the dirt tank where trapped runoff collected as a water source for the horses. Nothing. I cruised back up the hill to another empty thicket.

I reminded myself that mares seemed to prefer to foal at night in privacy and apparently do have some control over their delivery time. I saw a dozen raccoons scurrying about and several opossum. Then I saw a gang of coyotes, which raised my hackles. They could take advantage of a stressed mare foaling on new turf in an unfamiliar range. I calmed when it occurred to me that she knew coyote and could handle them herself if a threat materialized. They might get the placenta, the afterbirth, but they had no chance with the foal. In the wild, horses like to foal and then move off from the birthing materials and liquids as they draw predators.

Just when I'd about given up, four eyes reflected in the halogen-beam of my pickup lights. There was the mare and her new colt, a solid black, healthy critter, nursing calmly on wobbly legs. When she had seen me enter the gates by the corrals, she had ushered her foal out of the persimmon thicket and headed elsewhere. She stood quietly and watched me. I guessed that she probably had trouble with the delivery—a bit premature and induced by stress on the foal—but she and the baby seemed just fine now, her placenta had passed, and the foal was getting the vital first milk. I relaxed at the sight. He head butted her a time or two as a way to encourage more milk, and I backed the truck away slowly, glad that the mare had made it out of the truck and into a clean pasture to foal in, and that the foal had enough space to rise and gain his grass-legs. I turned the noisy truck around and headed back to the Holiday Inn in Bartlesville, mumbling to myself. That colt looked like another Midnight, and I felt envy that someone else would have him.

We planned adoptions throughout the Midwest and as far west as California because the horses were basically owned by the American taxpayer. We figured that we could cover territory from Memphis to Los Angeles. The next adoption was scheduled for the good people of Oklahoma, at nearby Dewey, a few miles north of Bartlesville. We selected an old, unused, covered livestock auction barn there with plenty of space and life left in it. It was a perfect location because the area was populated by some of the best and brightest horse people anyone could find. I called Patrick Morrow, and we set off on a plan to adopt 370 head of prime, papered, famous horses from the Wild West who were currently knee-deep in the best grass in the world, five miles away from the livestock barn. This time, I would make sure the media reports and the press releases highlighted the need for adequate horse trailers, the covered four-horse variety with no center divider and a good, lockable back door. I was not about to get kicked by that mule a second time.

Les Gililland could sort horses in a cracker box, if he needed to, but the covered Dewey livestock yard was particularly spacious and safe. There were 140 stout pipe pens in the place for viewing horses, two or three per pen. There was an old-style amphitheater for the adoption raffle, and all of it under the comfort of a tornado-free Okie sky.

The horses selected for this adoption were carefully trucked in on Thursday from the nearby Tadpole pastures, and I was elated to see them safe and sound. That gave us two days to sort and settle and "train the horses," as Les called it, to course through the maze of alleys into the loading pen after adoption on Saturday. On Friday, the horses neatly sorted in pens, Les conducted a trial run for each pen. The horses were herded out of their new corral, driven along the same route they would take after they were adopted, and returned to their pen and fed. That way, on Saturday afternoon, the horses would already know the route, except then, a trailer would be inserted in the loading area and when the horses turned the corner thinking they were headed back to their pen, they would go freely into the waiting trailer. I would then close the trailer door and lock it.

When Ira Haughn showed up that afternoon, he introduced me to M. Scott Cornelius, an educated cowboy and soon-to-be friend and future travel companion. At five-foot-seven and 140 pounds, Scott would be Les's new assistant in the barn. That afternoon, Les and Scott and I sorted horses and trained them. Then we bedded them for the night, checked their water, and headed for supper. Afterward, I drove a slow three miles to the livestock barn, sat silently, and listened to the horses in the dark of the night. As I might have guessed, a glowing ember moved toward me in the dark and Les appeared, sighing and smoking. He flipped a five-gallon water bucket on its top and sat on it near me.

Holding a newspaper clipping from the *El Paso Times,* Les asked if I remembered the old green pickup at the Alamogordo adoption that had the cattle rack bolted to the bed behind the cab. I remembered it and had worried about the roadworthiness of the truck. Les knew the man who owned the truck was from just north of Las Vegas, New Mexico, near the enclave of Mora. Evidently the El Paso reporter had made friends with that adopter of four horses and followed them north to Peñasco and then on into the mountains just west of the Rincon area. The Pecos Wilderness area was attached to the man's property somewhere along the fence line, and if those horses ever got loose, there was a wild 250,000 acres of freedom up that way. Les read parts of the article to me. "A touch of kindness tamed the wildness in the four feral horses that J. D. Herrera adopted recently at the White Sands Missile Range adoption. For a mere $125, Herrera got what his heart desired." The desert horses would do fine as mountain stock.

I smiled, and Les pulled deeply on his cigarette, his head tilted away from the continuous white stream of smoke. His hat looked as if Georgia O'Keeffe had painted it on his sculpted skull. "He's now the proud owner of a black horse, a mare, with no name, but he hinted at Jeremiah Johnson, a character in a mountain man movie he said he watched a million times. But the skittish horse had a home now, for the first time in her life." Les chuckled. "The horse was fat, pregnant, I think," he mused, "It's like getting two for one." He read the last of the article, "Herrera said there was no white sand where he lived, just white snowstorms."

The article also mentioned a man named Witherspoon, who lived near a movie ranch outside Santa Fe, New Mexico. The horses he adopted from White Sands were appearing in thirty-second cameos for companies like Ford and Stetson. He said the White Sands horses were smart, strong, and trained fast, and that they respected them as survivors.

The article appeared to make Les happy and made me feel better, too. "Can you imagine your horses as movie stars?" I asked.

Les then began an explanation of why he was who he was. We talked about his life for more than two hours.

"I went and spent sixteen years on the East Coast after I got out of the Navy and then managed farms there. I got tired of being wet and came home," he said. A horse coughed off in the distance and Les was silent for a moment, listening, then continued. "I was working day-work for ranchers down in the basin and all around. I was roping one day, and a friend of mine said they were hiring range riders for the missile range and I'd been there a lot, out deer hunting. I probably had more experience with the place than the others. I started work there in 'eighty-seven."

Les essentially became a government cowboy for the White Sands Missile Range, a liaison charged with protecting the range and the ranchers adjacent to the range. The job wasn't easy, driving all over the two million acres. Ranchers hadn't cared to be told to leave when the missiles were tested. Les dealt with trespassing cattle and trespassing hunters and drove a truck to cover the ground, using a four-wheeler when he had to move cows off the missile range.

"I still make a better living on the same place I was supposed to grow up on," he said. "I don't have to work near as hard. I usually hit the area where my father's ranch was every other month. That house, the one where we went to release the Tumor Horse and you found that letter, once it was a great working place for the McDonald family."

Les listened to his guts and headed back to paved road if he thought something dangerous was out there. "You have to go by your instincts," he said. He nodded absently and pulled hard on his smoke. "Ninety-nine percent of the range's bad stuff falls into a fenced area. You see something that's metallic, you go around it. We still find stuff from World War Two and we map it and cross-check it with maps already made, so when we take hunters we know what's safe."

"Ever see someone step on a . . . ?" I started to ask.

"We had a guy get killed three years ago," he said. "He picked up a bomb and asked what it was and they told him put that shit down and he threw it down," Les said in a matter-of-fact tone.

I told him about the missile test that nearly blew me off of the lava flow. I described the stallions in the pasture in the middle of the lava field, the grass, and the whole of it. I told him I hadn't planned to tell anyone because I didn't want to cause trouble.

"They knew you were out there." Les said. "We stress safety and we check up on it."

"They knew I was out there?" I was surprised, and a little taken aback.

"Satellites," Les said as he sat back and flicked the ash on his cigarette. "They know everything, every day."

Les became quiet as we listened to the horses move and breathe in their pens. "I loved the horses," he said. "They were a traffic hazard—too many of them—and when they die the animal rights people throw a fit." Les cleared his throat and then continued. "If you don't maintain them, you're going to have them die. We've got old ones and young ones, but nothing to eat when the grass dries up and if the mama's going to die, the baby's going to die. These horses have to go a long way to eat and a long way back to water, and when it's dry, you'd find them ten miles from water." Les sighed and took another drag on his cigarette. "They made ditches, not just trails, going to their water, and they were ruining the environment and all the terrain around the water holes."

"Come again?" I asked. "About the babies?" Had I heard him right?

"There wasn't too many foals during the die-off. Most of them died before the mamas did."

"So you're telling me that baby horses did die?" I asked. "All I saw in the pictures were healthy foals running around dead mares."

"I didn't like the idea of getting rid of all of them," he said. "But when you're hauling water out to them and they're so weak you can push them out of your way, that's sickening. Hell, we'd have dead horses lying in the water troughs." Les finished his sentence and listened in the darkness. His ember glowed and it lit his face. His eyes had a glassy sheen.

What Les had just told me was that baby horses had, in fact, died and he had put down the unhealthy ones and gotten rid of the bodies before the media came. Hell, I would have done a cleanup, too, before I let troublemakers onsite, but if Les were right, for all this time I'd been following a bum lead. Baby horses *had* died along with the mares. The horrifying photos hadn't shown the whole picture. Les sensed my concern about putting down the foals and tried to smooth it out.

"When I could catch them, we gave a lot of them away and saved some more. I put one in the pickup and took it home to take care of it until I could find somebody who could take care of it for good. I'd even haul them inside the cab of the truck to get them to water."

"Les," I interrupted, "that's really going above and beyond."

"I just did it. I put them on a bottle until we taught them to drink out of a bucket, just like you'd done to little Sammy. I've done that twenty times." Les's voice cracked. "We got out of the summertime and the drought and first they were arguing over whose responsibility the horses were—then the senator got involved and everybody wanted them first. We took two truckloads to the sale barn and the crap hit the fan." Les was kind of shouting and then he just got up and left me sitting there listening to the horses stir and cough and move around in the barn.

I watched the man slide into the darkness of the livestock barn, the horses shifting the thick piles of hay that Les had fed them. He was a truly gifted and caring cowboy, "master of no man, servant to none," as Rhodes would have said. I respected Les for his passion and commitment more than ever. And right then, it seemed as if he was living out something Rhodes had written in *Good Men and True,* "It was predestined from the foundations of the earth that I was to come here at this very now to explain to you about cowboys . . . You've been led astray." I had some rethinking to do.

First thing the next morning I arrived at the livestock barn, just behind Les, and I exchanged niceties about the weather and sleeping and dinner the night before and whatever small talk took up the time walking from the trucks to the barn to check on the horses. Les stopped me with one long arm across my chest and I thought he was going to say something to add to the long discussion from the night before, but instead he signaled that I should listen closely, and he wondered if I was hearing the same thing he was hearing.

"Coughing," Les said.

We entered the barn to a chorus of coughing horses. After close examination, we saw that almost one hundred horses had runny noses and watery eyes. I looked at the dirt in the barn and might have started to blame the livestock yard for uncleanliness, but Les pointed to several horses whose noses dripped slightly with a pale-green mucus. That kind of snot took five days to develop, and it was bacterial. It was in the yearlings and the adult horses. It was not too serious, but I could not issue health certificates for travel as long as the horses showed those signs. If the horses went to adoption, the army would be blamed for every snotty nose within five hundred miles and earshot of ambulance chasers.

The public relations group in charge of the auction started calling the potential adopters and radio stations and television outlets trying to warn the 750 people from five hundred miles around not to expect the adoption to take place. With hundreds of sick wild horses on my hands and less than a day until these horses would have gone to new homes, I had to cancel the adoption, reload the horses on transports and take them back the five miles to Tadpole pastures where the good clean air, green grass, and fresh water would heal what ailed them. They'd be a heck of a lot better off there than in the dank, dark livestock barn. It would be a month or more before I felt comfortable enough to reschedule these wild horses for adoption.

Chapter 15

The Stallions

By late summer 1995, the White Sands wild horse team had captured, rescued, and moved eighteen hundred horses from the secret missile range. Originally our orders had been to rescue 1,125 wild horses in the first round, but the efficiency of the team and the ability of the Army staff and public relations department to mobilize for adoptions led General Laws to increase the number. Les Gililland's techniques made the difference. Adoptions had gone well in the New Mexico cities of Alamogordo and Albuquerque, and in Dewey, Oklahoma; Texarkana, Texas; and Memphis, Tennessee. The team had just wrapped up another successful adoption of nearly two hundred horses in the east Texas town of Marshall, when a call came to me that a truckload of our stallions bound for Los Angeles, California, was about to be barred from leaving the state of New Mexico. The state livestock inspector had notified the state veterinarian, who then notified the media that a nasty viral disease had been diagnosed in a county in New Mexico.

Vesicular stomatitis is an equine viral disease. An outbreak not anywhere near the clean White Sands of New Mexico was about to trap my last horses in red tape. VS affects cattle, horses, and pigs, and it has a wide range of other hosts, including many species of wild animals, including deer, bobcats, mountain goats, raccoons, and, on other continents, monkeys. Humans can also become infected with VS when handling infected animals. The disease is most likely to

217

occur during warm months in the Southwest, particularly along riverways and in valleys. The Tularosa Basin was a particularly hospitable area, but no cases had been reported there. Because vesicular stomatitis breaks out from time to time in the Southwest, it is essential that veterinarians and livestock owners be on the alert for animals displaying clinical signs of the disease, including blisterlike lesions in the mouth and on the dental pad, tongue, lips, nostrils, hooves, and teats. These lesions swell and break, leaving raw tissue that is so painful that infected animals generally refuse to eat or drink and show signs of lameness. VS is treatable, but severe weight loss usually follows because infected horses only consume about half of their normal intake, if they eat at all.

The potential pain for the horses, my horses, was one primary concern. If my horses were healthy, interstate transport restriction would cause a well-planned, expensive adoption set for Los Angeles to collapse. Yet, the biggest problem that I faced, the problem of governmental and international trade concerns, was that the outward signs of VS are similar to (although generally less severe than) those of foot-and-mouth disease (FMD), a foreign animal disease of cloven-hoofed animals that was eradicated from the United States in 1929.

I left Marshall, Texas, in despair, aiming to catch a plane with a destination anywhere near El Paso, whence I could drive to White Sands. My fears made the fifty-mile trip last forever; my adrenal glands swelled to the size of a fat hamster, and my throat began to feel scratchy. Luckily I found the last available seat on a turboprop flight out of Shreveport, Louisiana, that must have been on some kind of milk run. It stopped at every airport that had night lights, and I didn't know if it was my headache or just lack of sleep, but the nausea and the wind-shear whirling just outside the plane made reading that science book difficult. I needed a strong dose of Maynard telling me how a problem is nothing to worry about if a solution exists. Yet I didn't know where to begin. Besides the VS questions, I still had problems on a top-secret missile range, and the hell of it was that I couldn't talk to anyone about it.

Five hours later in the middle of the night, the puddle-jumper landed in El Paso, and I grabbed a rental car and screeched out of the parking lot at dark-thirty. I had at least ninety minutes to concentrate on the horses' current problem. In forty-eight hours, the borders to New Mexico would close and prohibit movement of any horses in and out of the state. Even though my horses, which by contract I owned, were as isolated as a herd can get, their proximity to Mexico and the wild game on the missile range forced me to consider that they could have the disease. I doubted it, but it was possible. First order of business was for me personally to assess the health of the stallions I intended to send to California. Two months earlier, I had given them an expensive upgrade in conditioning and nutrition in order to prepare them properly for the rigors of a long trip through Arizona to the City of Industry Equestrian Center in Los Angeles. If I failed to clear the border in time, they would be held up for weeks, probably months.

The hat trick required that I arrive at a top-secret missile range in the dead of night, find a way to travel onto the secret range, run the seventeen-hundred-pound stallions into the processing chutes, assess each for health, and then load them into a semi-lowboy transport and head west in hopes of passing the port of entry on I-10 before the state of New Mexico halted livestock movement in or out of the state.

I needed help. I hefted my heavy cell phone to my ear and called my new friend, M. Scott Cornelius. He cranked the engine of my brand-new Ford Powerstroke Diesel back in Bartlesville, Oklahoma, and started the thirteen-hour jaunt to Alamogordo. I told him to cut across country and I'd meet him at the Alamogordo Holiday Inn as soon as he got there.

When my head hit the pillow at the hotel in Alamogordo, I started having nightmares about horse diseases that were worse than being sleepless, so I sat up, poured too many coffee grounds into the little coffee pot, and cracked open my ever-present *Merck Veterinary Manual*. I needed to know everything Dr. Merck knew about VS, but since I had to wait to see the stallions to determine if they had overt clinical signs of VS, I started in on my anthrax reading.

The anthrax bacterium occurs naturally in the soil and needs only a nutrient-rich environment and water to thrive. Some scientists believe that a rainier-than-usual season followed by drought can make it more likely that animals will become infected—the spores develop in the moist soil and then blow into the air when the soil becomes dry and winds pick up.

Worldwide, there are twenty thousand to a hundred thousand cases of anthrax yearly, but the disease is very rare in the United States. In livestock, the clinical signs include staggering, trembling, difficult breathing, and severe respiratory or cardiac distress, collapse, convulsions, bloody diarrhea, and severe colic. I won't say that it didn't cross my mind that the sick group of horses in the first Oklahoma adoption might have had some serious infection, since I'd just buried little Sammy, but it was just a passing thought. The horses had faced cool nights and warm days in their new home, which had led to the horse version of the common cold. That respiratory condition had no relationship to the original die-off. All the horses recovered well from that "cold virus" in the stress-free environment Ira provided.

The photos of the Mound Springs herd die-off showed desperately sick horses. I still had a hard time believing that drought was the cause, even though it was likely. Having worked through Merck's anthrax section, I fed my fears for my horses and my paranoia for a little longer with information I had collected after the Oklahoma City bombing. According to the federal reports, an Ammonia Nitrate Fuel Oil (ANFO) truck bomb destroyed the Alfred P. Murrah building. A special agent employed by the Bureau of Alcohol, Tobacco and Firearms, who was experienced in such devices, had reported the details of the bombing to his superiors from the actual scene in front of the Murrah Building within minutes of the blast. This ATF agent was clearly qualified to make such an instant observation as part of a formidable group of bomb experts and arson investigators who handle major bombing crime scenes throughout the United States. He had also served in a top-secret government project in 1994 that conducted tests using ANFO and C-4 to blow up cars and vans in a classified U.S. government experiment known as "Project Dipole Might"—conducted at White Sands Missile Range.

Could the die-off at Mound Springs have been attributable to a fertilizer bomb test or to anthrax that had been kicked up out of the bacteria-laden soil and into the air by the regular ordnance tests on the range? Maybe anthrax or another poison had found its way into the herd's water supply. No, I had to recognize that the water tests had not indicated these problems.

One final tangent I indulged myself in was the idea of whether a secret, nighttime aerial vaccination program, say from a silent drone, could have been tested on the White Sands horses. Though it may seem far-fetched, now the GIs in 1994 were in an uproar over reported side effects from the Army anthrax vaccine. But if an aerosol vaccine had been tested, the blood from the horses would have shown a positive titer of antibodies against the anthrax bug in the vaccine. I also needed to check on the results of the tests I had ordered on the BA13-S vaccine bottles. In spite of all these feverish ideas, I had to admit that severe dehydration does cause many of the same clinical signs in horses as anthrax, so I simply might never know for sure what happened to them. Les Gililland seemed convinced it was dehydration and he had spent a lot of time trying to convince me that the die-off hadn't happened in just two days, but rather in a span of a whole dry summer. True, 122 horses were found dead, but actually horses had been dying for several weeks. Babies had died, as well, and their bodies weren't part of the count. My paranoid fears were really not amounting to much.

Nonetheless, when I checked into the Alamogordo Holiday Inn, my first call was to the lab in upstate New Mexico. Their report confirmed that the BA-13S that I had found in the root cellar at the old ranch was the common variety, 1942 Sterne strain anthrax vaccine for livestock. Ranchers kept their own stores of animal medicine, and millions of doses had been used all over in North America

back then. So, that vaccine, or a mutation from it, or a mad scientist running about the missile range had not killed the White Sands
horses. I would never know if an aerial vaccine had been tested, but
it was an unlikely candidate for killing so many adult horses while
leaving some foals standing around as healthy as the day they were
born.

It was time I accepted that the horses were emaciated from
long-term starvation and dehydration. The mares would not leave
the only water source they trusted because they needed to produce
milk for their nursing foals. The stallions and foals of the harem
would not leave the mares. In veterinary medicine we have a saying, "common things occur commonly." In other words, expect to
see what is common, most of the time. The agony at the time of the
die-off, the gore found by Patrick and his biologists, and the 122
dead horses at Mound Springs pointed to acute kidney failure due
to severe dehydration, a miserably painful end to a noble life. I could
finally close the White Sands wild horse rescue without worrying
that there had been a secret, nonobvious cause of death for the
horses to which the survivors might also succumb. Now, I just
needed to make sure the stallions would be safe.

The forty seventeen-hundred pound, monster-size stallions ready
for transport to Los Angeles were the only adult males that I had left
intact—able to breed. I wanted the White Sands genes to stay alive
in the general horse population. There were five Midnight grays
with yellow manes and tails, including one of the most dominant
stallions I'd ever seen; sixteen huge bays with black manes and tails;
seventeen sorrels with significant feathering on their fetlocks; and
two beautiful dark golden palominos with flaxen manes and tails. I
wanted to place these horses on the West Coast where I knew people would love and continue to revere their strong, turn-of-the-
century, big-hoofed genetics.

That morning, Scott Cornelius and I headed for the missile
range guard shack. Somehow, I needed to get Scott through the
screening process, quick time. I explained to the head of security

that Scott was my right- and left-hand wrangler and that without him, the dreaded equine disease sweeping the state might hit our precious White Sands horses. Scott passed his preliminary security check with flying colors, and I warned the guard that a large live-stock transport was behind me by a few hours. I also used the time to call a friend in Alamogordo to find out whether anyone had seen Maynard. Nobody knew where he'd been that last few weeks. Looked like I had to ride the river with Scott and forty monster-size stallions.

With Les in transit from the Marshall, Texas, adoption, Scott made a good hand at sorting big animals. He had worked wild horses with Ira Haughn for the last few years at Tadpole, and he knew the tricks of the trade. That made life workable where two men against three-dozen wild stallions in perfect bloom was bad odds. Les's system of dependable gates, good pens, and a great work-ing chute allowed me to examine each horse individually. I then wrote the health certificates. It helped considerably that Arizona did not require the blood test for equine infectious anemia as most other states did, but California did. I didn't have time to draw blood from forty stallions who preferred that I drop dead there and then, send it to the lab in Albuquerque, a five-hour jaunt to a lab closed for the weekend, wait for results, and then load on a transport that I called in earlier and beat the forty-eight-hour deadline at the Ari-zona–New Mexico border. Thankfully none of the stallions showed clinical signs of any disease—some bad attitudes—but no sickness. With twelve hours left to the drop-dead time at the border, I pointed to the loading chutes. If we hustled, we could make it. A flat tire on the transport, a down horse, a broken anything, and all of our work would be for naught.

We loaded those stallions on the waiting transport semi at break-neck speed, without incident, and the driver slid in behind the over-size wheel just as I signed the health papers and stuffed them in his pocket. We bid him farewell and watched the trailer groan under the weight. I did some mental math and I wondered what his weight restriction might be. My concentration was interrupted by the loud thud and the sight of a huge hole a stallion had just kicked through the wall of the brand-new trailer. Then I wondered if I could send Scott on alone to talk to the driver when they met up in Chandler, Arizona, and how much it would cost me to repair his trailer.

After a quick dinner of beef jerky, Scott and I loaded a goose-neck trailer with eighteen thousand pounds of WW Livestock panels and round-baled hay and drove west into Arizona. We were exhausted but pleased. Little did I know that when I left the Tularosa gates that evening, it would be the last time I was to set foot on White Sands Missile Range.

My truck was overloaded, but that Ford had guts and the torque we needed. I drove the steep hill west of Las Cruces and the weight slowed us down to five miles an hour. The truckers in front of us chattered on the CB radio and marveled at the ability of that candy-apple red Ford "back there" to pull that hill.

After several hours, Scott took a shift driving and I pulled a letter with an attached newspaper article out of my briefcase and began reading the story of a family who had adopted some of our horses. At the third adoption we'd held in Dewey, Oklahoma, Jimmy Brown, his beautiful wife Charlene, and his two well-behaved children, Chrystal, eleven years old, and young Weslie, seven, appeared to show off the great job he'd done with the two bay mares from an earlier adoption. They were likely Mound Springs, the darker one now a proud mother of a two-month-old filly. Jimmy had adopted the very horses most in need of rescue.

Jimmy Brown was a big gentle bear of a man, with an easy way around horses and kids. A former cowboy turned computer electronics serviceman, he didn't have a mean bone in his Oklahoma-bred body. Big Jim was an unbridled mustang advocate, always promoting the good stewardship of "critters," as he called them, and now, he had White Sands wild horses of his own and he had earned bragging rights. He had accepted the responsibility of gentling four wild horses, and he told any person who would listen, and some

In this corner of the orphan pen,
Little Midnight in the foreground, Belle on the right, and
Salt Creek Sam (Sammy) on the left.
Photo by Don Höglund.

who would not, that a wild horse "started out as wild deer." Like a proud new father, he displayed his mares and the new filly in the parking lot of the subsequent adoptions in Oklahoma. His horses stood quietly proving that he spoke the truth; he walked the talk. "If you're gentle with them, they'll be gentle with you." He told dozens of onlookers that he had taken his new horses home to a thirty-acre pasture near Mannford, Oklahoma, and everybody for miles around watched him unload the horses with "toothy smiles and filled hearts."

In two months, they were four for dinner at the barn. Young Weslie got the second mare adopted and named her Lady Dog. Her foal would be his lifelong horse. Chrystal had named her mare SillyGirl before the horse even put a foot in the trailer.

Jimmy had seen many BLM mustangs, but the White Sands herd had a powerful allure for him. I put Jimmy's letter on my lap and smiled when I told Scott, "I saw Weslie at the third Dewey adoption, and he told me that the mares and the new foal were the "gentlest animals anyone could ever hope for." The only problem was that they "loved to lick the paint on the vehicles and knocked the

Lady Dog and SillyGirl, Chrystal and her
brother Weslie's White Sands horses.
Courtesy of Chrystal January.

mirrors off the food truck getting to their feed." The young lad said
that wild horses had a bad reputation because "you could not cowboy these horses; we were going to treat them good and in one year
get title to them." His sister, Chrystal, had saddled her own mare and
would "go visit the neighbors." Jimmy liked to say that the White
Sands horses "had fifty years to breed out any weaknesses so that
they were a superior horse."

When I'd met red-headed Chrystal, she was smiling from earlobe to earlobe. She had big plans for her new friend, SillyGirl,
wanting to compete in the local barrel competitions, but she'd heard
the speech by my adoption assistants in which the word *rodeo*
seemed to be a bad thing. I explained that the only things I didn't
want—and every adopter agreed not to do—was to use their horse
as a professional bucking animal or to allow it to be killed for food.
Barrel racing was a great event from the backyard to the national
rodeo finals, and I hoped to see her there, in Las Vegas, one day.

Jimmy finished off his letter by writing that he wanted to form
an association of White Sands adopters. The horses' lives were protected by the honor of good people who cared, and he had not
heard of "any of those horses ending up as bucking horses or in

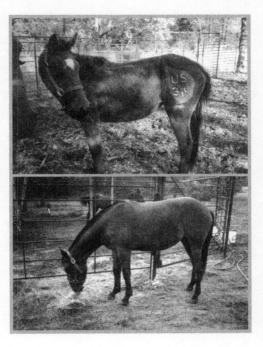

SillyGirl, before and after.
*Courtesy of
Chrystal January.*

meals for dogs." Somewhere east of Tucson, Arizona, cradled in the arms of Interstate 10 on a warm fall day, I put my head back, listened to the smooth drone of my diesel engine, and smiled as I dozed off.

We met the stallions and their driver in an empty livestock yard south of Chandler, Arizona. The driver justifiably puffed with pride as he gave me the papers I waited for, the weight station receipt from the Arizona border, port of entry. The net weight of the horses averaged 1,785 steaming pounds of horseflesh per heavily muscled stallion. I marveled at the numbers and at the amount of hay that must have gone through their systems, because they could not have weighed even thirteen hundred pounds when captured. With the Oklahoma hay that we had trucked in to White Sands, they had eaten fifty pounds per horse and gained three pounds per day in five months.

Now we had to capture each stallion again, this time in a makeshift chute constructed from the portable WW horse panels. I had to draw blood for the equine infectious anemia test that California required before moving the horses there. Happily, the laboratory I used for Coggins testing was located a few miles north of nearby Phoenix and had a marvelous turn-around time of four hours. Things were looking up for the Los Angeles wild horse adoption.

That afternoon, all of the horses tested negative on the bloodwork, so we reloaded them and took off toward Los Angeles and the City of Industry Equestrian Center, a beautiful fifteen-hundred-stall, ten-barn, five-arena paradise on top of a landfill in the heart of Los Angeles. I called a friend from my Disney days, the director the equestrian center, Dave Winn, and he rolled out the red carpet for me and our soon-to-arrive team of New Mexico and Oklahoma cowboys.

Scott and I were ahead of the transport, so we set the panels in place at the back door of a beautiful 120-stall barn where we could quarantine the tired stallions. Just opposite the front door of the barn was a small arena that would work perfectly for the adoption. When Les arrived the next morning with his crew of cowboys, Scott fell in under Les's leadership and the event began without a hitch. The stallions practiced their trial run to the arena and then settled nicely the night before the adoption, munching softly on their Oklahoma bluestem grass. The City of Industry Equestrian Center was a veritable paradise for horses and horse lovers.

On adoption day, the hillside was clustered with eager Californians, young and old alike, who just could not wait for a glimpse of real-life wild horses from the badlands of New Mexico. The California adoption was opened up to bidding, but every person there was given the strict Department of the Army documents forbidding the use of these fine animals in rodeos or for slaughter. I had no doubt that killer-horse buyers were on the ground at the Equestrian Center, but they lay low. I made it my job to scour the crowd for them, though I never saw anyone who even looked like a packing plant buyer among the hundreds of people from all walks of life.

When the big, dominant gray stallion turned from under the covered roof of the fancy show barn and strutted out, legs and tail high, and spun the sand high in the arena, the event hit its high point. His head reached seven feet high as he put it into the air to sense the damp air from the coast. He seemed to look each adopter in the eye. The crowd rose to their feet and backpedaled up the grass bank where they sat, mouths gaping. That stallion was more than eighteen hundred pounds of thrust and bone. He was magnificent, mighty, as if he could blaze a trail to heaven and back. With Dave Winn himself as auctioneer, and a fine one at that, it took more than an hour to complete the bidding for him. The palomino stallion took nearly as long as his cousin, the Midnight horse. By the end it was clear that many of the people in attendance believed that, as the old saying goes, "Paradise can be found on the backs of horses."

Chapter 16

A Wonderful Life
with Horses

I n *The Mustangs,* J. Frank Dobie wrote a story of the life and
times of the phantom white stallion of the Llano Estacado—the
staked plains of west Texas and eastern New Mexico. There, the
High Plains ends its southern limit and big cattle country begins. In
that wide-open range, the Western horse and his horseman thrived.
The first Hollywood films highlighted black horses, so black
became the coat color that most people think of when they imagine wild stallions. In many cases, however, the horses were black
when young and matured into white steeds.

The original Midnight, born in 1916, had the dominant gene
for the coat color gray. In contrast to true white (albino) horses,
who have no pigment in the skin, gray horses are born pigmented,
usually with gray skin. They go through lighter stages, but always
contain pigment in the skin and eyes at all stages of coloration.
Since gray is produced by a dominant gene, at least one parent of a
gray horse must be gray. If a gray horse does not have a gray parent, then it should be seriously considered that the purported
parentage is incorrect. Gray seems to beget gray.

At White Sands, I neutered dozens of gray horses with features
identical to those in photos of the original Midnight, including his
long-flowing yellow mane and tail. Yellow is a pigment that is a vari-

ation of red and cannot yet be explained by genetics. But all of the black younger horses on the northern part of the missile range and the adult mouse-gray horses had Midnight's features in their outward appearance as if planted in their DNA electronically. Several prominent ranchers in Tularosa and west Texas told me that the majority of gray horses in New Mexico prior to 1942 derived from west Texas ranches. So, from the middle 1920s until his passing in 1933, Midnight—the only son of the speed-horse Gray Badger and outstanding grandson of the great "bulldog" stallion, Peter McCue— was the preeminent west Texas sire for the ranch remuda, horses for the next day's work. The bulldogs or, as they were commonly called, the Steeldusts had a high degree of athletic ability, a quiet disposition, exceptional muscling with robust hindquarters, a low center of gravity, a deep "V" between the forelegs, and thick bone and foot tissues. The length of the legs did not exceed the heart-girth. All these characteristics distinguished the breed. Although the dark-bay coated Peter McCue was known to be 1,430 pounds and stood sixteen hands, he passed along his dominant genes for stout, smart, athletic, gray horses.

Aside from his predilection for passing on his sire's gray gene, fox-eared Midnight contributed a superior athleticism to contemporary quarter horses, which today have a catlike responsiveness and a perceptive intelligence that is not usually seen in horses, although they are all smart for one reason or another. Midnight was an ancestor to modern performance horses such as Easy Jet—one of the greatest quarter horse racers in history—and to Peppy San Badger— the "greatest cutting horse of all time"—according to his famous trainer and rider, Buster Welch.

I had ridden and trained a number of horses registered with a *Badger* or a *Midnight* in their pedigrees, but Little Midnight might have been one of the great foundation sire's closest direct links. In my mind, having the "wild" gene, as I called it, and the "domestic" gene, as I referred to the registered horses, I had the best of both worlds under saddle. Little Midnight was probably more closely related to the old guy than to the modern cutting horses I owned.

Of the other obvious descendents of Midnight in the midst of the White Sands horses slated for adoption, I also kept a young, tall blackish filly that I named Bell of Midnight, out of respect for a Midnight Jr. who spawned a filly known in the quarter horse world as Belle of Midnight. I took both of them with me to northeast Oklahoma, where I planned to train them to rope, cut, and perform tricks for the fun of it. Some trainers and horse enthusiasts don't ascribe to lying a horse down—they say it steals their spirit, but I find it simple, useful, and calming for the horse if done properly.

I also kept for myself Charlie—a Rhodes Canyon sorrel filly with a full blaze, and Snip—a Mound Springs bay mare with a black mane and tail. Both of these gentle horses were born on the Tadpole pastures. I did not have illusions of registration, or of creating a new breed, or of the re-evolution of known lines; I just wanted to enjoy the fruits of horses once used by the likes of Walter Merrick, Gene Rhodes, and Sheriff Pat Garrett—who aside from the companionship of his great horses might well have been the unluckiest lawman of the West.

Over the next year or so, I wrapped up the paperwork of the White Sands rescue and tied up the loose ends for the adoptions and bookkeeping. In the precious time that it took for my young equine recruits, Little Midnight, Charlie, Snip, and Bell, to mature and develop the needed strength and endurance for life and times with me, I tightened the lug bolts on my beloved Ford truck and some in my disjointed life and relaxed. I needed a break from the rescue, a journey that had threatened my life on a daily basis, and returned home to my life near Albuquerque to train horses. Some months later, I traveled to Paris to watch my son perform as a wrangler, campfire singer, cowboy, trick roper, and rider for Buffalo Bill's Wild West, now one of the world's largest-grossing live-entertainment shows. I marveled at how the show, which I had helped produce, had matured and become a world-class event and coveted stop-off for American cowboys and former rodeo talent.

But the lure of the real West once again drew me back to the States, this time to the green pastures of Oklahoma, and life in and around my good friends, Ira Haughn and the tough and durable M. Scott Cornelius. I wanted to see my Little Midnight colt and his fillies, and it was time to start their training in the round corral.

I moved into the sister-ranch house adjacent to Ira's main ranch house, just outside the thriving ranching community of Dewey, Oklahoma, and started training Little Midnight and his ladies. A muscular and sassy horse, he had a bit of an attitude and was not easy to train. His days as an indulged orphan at White Sands had given him a lack of respect often found in orphaned babies. I spent all of the late spring and summer months with the colt in the round corral working just as I had trained the prison inmates. I wanted Scott to be the first to ride Little Midnight. Even at nine hundred pounds, the colt, now seventeen months old, was too young to handle my upward-bound 210 pounds along with forty-five pounds of Circle-Y cutting saddle and accessories. I didn't want to risk a back injury to either of us, but he could definitely handle Scott's 140-pound frame. And Scott, the toughest middleweight I ever met, embraced the challenge.

On the outside of the pen, I watched Little Midnight race circles around Scott, who stood quietly in the middle, dusting his silver hat on his strong legs and watching the young colt's spirit. The colt had my saddle cinched to his back and he didn't like it. Twice already Scott had gone straight over the front of the colt's head the moment he had rested his pelvis in the saddle. The smart, overgrown colt pitched one time and then hit the brakes, and Scott failed to heed my reminder that if the last thing he saw after the jolt was ears, he was supposed to grab them. The young cowboy got fooled twice, at least, and I was willing to bet he didn't learn much more when he hit that hard pipe fence the second time. On the third try, Little Midnight flexed and sent him backward over the saddle toward the business end of the colt and completely into the adjoining corral. I eased a glace over the top rail, tipped my hat back, and checked for signs of human life. Scott didn't look at me, he just grimaced.

On the next try, Scott thought that this desert product was going to try to slam him to the ground one more time, same technique, so he sat back a bit. But this time the New Mexico–bred horse felt the change and continued to pitch forward. That miscalculation bought Scott a somersault into the Russian thistle in the corner of the hard-packed paddock. I thought about stopping the lesson and explaining that the horse could feel the shift in the rider's weight and that Scott needed to stay in the "well," the middle of the curve of the back and perhaps roll his shoulders a bit, but Scott waved my mouth shut. Evidently he wasn't done with the gymnastics. I shrugged; we said not a word.

Part of the challenge in Scott's lack of performance revolved around the fact that I had allowed a saddle only—no bridle—on the colt. Scott had little more than a couple of handfuls of saddle horn and a strand or two of black mane to hold on to, and that wasn't doing much for control of the horse. In theory, that was the main idea—to allow the horse to travel freely at first, to make his own decisions, and to decide to accept a rider, but I also didn't want the horse's head jerked around like a high school kid at a used car lot. I wanted to teach the horse that his options were limited, but still allow him to choose his path in a confined space. I was sure it would help Scott if he had a conversation with the colt, talked to the animal sort of man-to-horse. Scott hollered back that he was more concerned with trying to save his own life and he didn't think the horse could hear all the whispering.

Right then, Midnight seemed to enjoy the experiment, even if Scott didn't. Scott dusted off his Wrangler jeans again and rubbed the small of his back, just above the leather belt. He shook out the sting in his legs and stepped back to the fence to catch his breath and pulled out his can of Copenhagen. He tapped the can thoughtfully on the palm of his well-worked hand. I stayed quiet, not wanting to provoke a change in rider—I would be the one up next. But I thought of the Mexican proverb, "It is not enough for a man to learn how to ride; he must learn how to fall."

Scott stuffed an unhealthy quantity of the coffeelike tobacco into the gap between his perfect line of teeth and his lower lip and tongued it into place while he created a new strategy. He spit and wiped his swollen lips, noticing the blood on his fingers. I acted like I didn't see it. He pulled the humid air hard into his nostrils and lowered his chin, then stretched his sore neck sideways and gave the colt a long look. I could almost tell what both of them were thinking. I knew Scott wondered how that seventeen-month-old sucker could sunfish, flopping side to side and turning his belly up, so damn good. The colt probably wondered if the man would head back his direction. I was thinking that no matter how young the colt was, I was glad that I hadn't waited any longer to set a saddle on him. He was as tough as I wanted. I shot a hard glance at the colt when he lifted his upper lip and rolled it back. The fillies were a mile away. Could that be a smile?

I didn't give Scott any direction as he approached the colt again. I just allowed him to take another head-plant into the pipe, landing in the decades-old manure in the corral. I shook my head abruptly and cocked it in a "that horse sure can buck some" sort of look. I had to hand it to Scott, he bounced well.

The colt didn't kick at Scott, and I liked that. It meant that he wasn't vindictive. In the rodeo circuit, bucking horses often set the rider up like a tennis serve and swat the crap out of the ejected cowboy, causing substantial damage to body and pride. Little Midnight just didn't want to be ridden, or maybe he was just having a little fun. Scott limped over to the near corner and retrieved his well-worn silver-bellied Western hat, dusted it rudely on his leg again, and pulled it down on his ears. He grimaced and adjusted his worn leather gloves and pulled the drawstring closed at the wrist. He stuck his fingers to the end of it and pulled it all tight. Yanking his shirt sleeve back into position, he tightened his belt past the last loop and then started a slow, deliberate trek toward the colt standing at the other end of the small corral.

The horse didn't move a step. If a Polaroid had been snapped at Gililland horses in 1942, just before General MacArthur had the family escorted off that beautiful desert ranch, I could have been staring at a duplicate of that photo in flesh and bone. The colt was as good as any ranch horse from the 1940s. Watching Little Midnight back in the desert corral and later harassing the other youngsters in the pasture told me he had what we call "bottom"—he was fast, too. When that horse tucked his tail and hindquarters under him—"grabbing his ass" in cowboy terms—he could flat get the job gone.

Scott climbed slowly back in the saddle, and for the next hour or so I watched a classic Old West struggle play out like it had thousands of times before. In my experience, most horses would have grown tired of setting Scott down so hard so many times, and just stopped bucking. Scott landed hard again, but with a smile this time. To hear Scott tell it a few minutes after he got his wind back, he thought he'd been "stuck" in the saddle and had finally gotten the deed done. I thought that the horse kept ducking and diving back underneath him, so he kept landing back in the saddle by accident. He didn't love that theory.

We unsaddled the horse, and I told Scott that the next day I was going to give him an equalizer—reins. That made my sore friend plumb giddy; he could ride the way he knew he could. We cooled the colt, fed and watered him, and then headed across the road toward Ira's ranch house. I could smell the grass-fed beef and potatoes dinner that Ira had prepared for us. Scott looked back at the colt as the horse grabbed large mouthfuls of good, green Oklahoma bluestem, and their eyes seemed to engage.

"You know, Doc," Scott said, seeming to ponder his thought before he said it. "That colt must have bucked me off thirty times in the last few hours."

I hummed a bit and stalled until we'd crossed the road and started up the one step into the modest white ranch house. "It was thirty-one," I said. "I counted for you."

Scott stopped in his tracks and stared at me. "Was that the famous training method—no head gear?" he asked.

"Sort of, but mostly I just wanted to see if you could and would ride the horse without reins," I said, smiling at him. "It tells me if you have an independent seat, or not."

With one hand, Scott rubbed his sore head and with the other, he massaged his aching butt. "I was independent, all right," he said as he found the spot that hurt most. I pushed him on the shoulder. "Actually, it was only eighteen times." We laughed all the way through our first beer.

In many respects, Midnight was no different from many formerly free-roaming horses, gregarious—a social animal; horses like to be with other horses. He bucked poorly and once he found that bucking was work, he quit. In the beginning, I set the stage for Scott's experience as saddle-bronc rider. If confined, an untamed horse in a small pen will revert to his natural behavior if the rider appears as a saber-toothed predator, on his back and looking predatory. The horse will buck, pitch if he can, sunfish if he knows how, crow-hop if he doesn't, and if any of it unseats the rider, he will continue that behavior until it doesn't produce what he thinks he wants. Otherwise, the horse will run. Flight is a built-in behavior.

After several months, Midnight was approaching that time where he would become a fine horse and a good, trustworthy friend. He'd taken to the training experience and grown into a horse that could stand my two-hundred pounds on top of the tack. We were ready to ride.

One morning, Scott and I headed with the horses loaded in a truck to a gentle-sloping valley that the horses didn't know. We unloaded and tied them securely to the sides of the trailer. We saddled Midnight for me and the nice graying filly, Bell, for Scott. Though she had not been ridden before, I gave Scott a set of reins. Midnight stood as gentle as a sleeping cat and watched. We led Bell to an open space where three sides of the valley rose gently away for about a mile. After that, the pasture ran for miles, up simple inclines and down rolling grades. We pointed Bell uphill; the trailer blocked the only downhill avenue. Scott mounted and Bell stood for a moment. She surveyed Scott in the saddle. I stepped back and away. Bell vibrated a bit under the saddle and Scott shrugged. Little Midnight watched as if he knew what was up. And away she went. I

yelled to Scott just before the horse departed out of shouting distance, "The safest place you'll find is in the middle of that saddle.
Stay there." She ran full out and over the horizon.

That was the last I saw of Scott for a quiet hour. I mounted Little Midnight, no spurs, and for some reason, learned or unlearned,
he walked up that very same hill and never from that day offered
even to hump his back. I think he wanted to know where the hell
Bell had gone, just as bad as I did.

An hour later, Scott and Bell returned, the best of friends, she a
bit sweaty, he a better horseman for the experience. I slapped Scott
on the back and said, "Let 'em run if they want to run, it's their
nature," and then had to quote from *Lonesome Dove,* "Ain't nuthin
like ridin' a fine horse in new country."

The Department of the Army had allowed me to video most of the
historic events in the White Sands captures and had provided the
first crew of two cameramen and cameras, so I spent hours reviewing the films and enjoyed them as a high-tech, Old West adventure.
I also made daily exercise jogs along an old railroad crossing near the
small Oklahoma town of Lenapah. One hundred years earlier, and
up to the 1950s, Lenapah was a small bustling community and local
gathering point for cattlemen and their herds headed for the railroad lines in Kansas and on to processing plants east of Oklahoma.
Named after a tribe of Native Americans, Lenapah lay just east of
Osage country in northeastern Oklahoma, and on the eastern
boundary of the famous Chisholm cattle trail.

In 1865, the half-Indian trader, Jesse Chisholm, was given credit
for a cattle trail from Wichita, Texas, through Indian country in
western Oklahoma territory. Charles Goodnight verified this when
he said, "in conversation with me, he (John Chisum) said that one
Chisholm, in no way related to him, did pilot 600 steers from the
Texas frontier to old Fort Cobb, and he presumed that this was the
origin of the name of the Chisholm trail." Goodnight also verified
that, "I positively know that no trail north was laid out by John
Chisum." At the close of the Civil War, it became necessary to find

a market for the Texas cattle. The Kansas Pacific Railway had extended its lines westward to Abilene, Kansas. Joseph G. McCoy, recognizing the possibility of driving cattle to market, established shipping facilities in Abilene, and by a series of advertising activities, succeeded in persuading the cattlemen to drive their cattle there. McCoy extended the Chisholm trail north from Wichita to Abilene. Texas cattlemen extended the trail from Indian territory to southern Texas.

Many believe that the era of the cowboy ended in 1892, with the end of the last major cattle war in Wyoming. Some historians saw its demise as the advent of the barbed-wire fence that cut up the open range. The life of the Chisholm Trail, from 1867 to 1884, was fairly short. The trail and its many branches were finally closed by the barbed wire of livestock-raising farmers, and by the 1885 Kansas quarantine law. Texas fever, a lay term for babesiosis, created worries and multiple federal government regulations. Yet in its brief life, the Chisholm Trail saw more than five million cattle and a million mustangs driven from Texas to Kansas, the greatest migration of domesticated livestock known to man.

As I jogged along the railroad tracks, I felt a kinship to the place and to its past. Many of the White Sands forebears had come from this area and gone into productive walks of life as cattle drive horses, ranch horses, brood mares, and roping horses. And some of their offspring had returned here through adoptions. In fact, one young cowboy on a big horse was heading down the dirt road straight for me.

Smoking a hand-rolled cigarette as if he hadn't a care in the world, the young man and his mount approached me from about half a mile away. The colt was a mottled gray. The cowboy had a shock of strawberry-roan hair jutting out from beneath his tattered Western hat. They sauntered along the grassy bank beside the weathered, ancient remnants of once-active cattle pens, past a rail head that butted up to an old loading chute.

This solitary modern-day cowboy had on the full outfit; sleeping roll, duster, and camp gear were strapped on behind the saddle.

His boots were old as hell, but his face was full of brightness—as if totally unaware that civilization existed only a few miles away. The jingle-bobs on his spurs and their huge rowels glimmered. He pulled up with a howdy as if he'd never known another greeting, tipped his narrow skull, and rubbed his near-hairless face. I guessed him sixteen years tops, on the lam from school. We talked horses and cattle. I could smell his breath and it reminded me of old words, "as hard as kerosene," and his mount looked as fast as polished steel.

I stepped to the side of his horse but stood clear and spotted the big US brand on the left hip. I stood back and cocked a knee on the cedar post of the ramshackle livestock pen, and we started talking about White Sands and the Dewey adoption. Though I couldn't say I remembered that specific colt, the young man's eyes widened and his mouth broadened into an astonished smile at his horse's story. He told me that he was the one who was going to collect his horse the next day. He'd made arrangements with Les Gililland to leave the horse with water and grub and he would be back first thing in the next morning. Then I remembered the boy. I had 370 horses headed for parts known, some to old people and some to young cowboys like him. The dates and faces all kind of blended, but I remembered he needed to leave the horse for a few hours. He told me that he had counted out the $125 fee from paper and coins stuffed here and there, a second-party check for $35 with the note plastered on it calling it wages, and there in his shirt along his gaunt belly he held a handkerchief containing the last eight dollars in pennies. I remembered my office assistants telling me about it. He had returned later that night from somewhere across from the livestock pen, carrying his life with him: a saddle and bedroll and a leather sack of tobacco and fixings. He hustled that colt into a cattle working chute inside in the dark of night and saddled the graying colt and hopped aboard and green-broke that colt right there and then. He said the horse never even bucked a step. The colt was nervous, but "not counterfeit," he remarked. I figured the mother of invention had worked her miracles again, and he'd just done what was needed. This horse was this young man's transportation, working tool, and friend. It stood as calmly as if it had just filled its belly with warm mother's milk.

With the boy firmly planted in the old high-cantled saddle, I talked to him for more than an hour and got choked up because it looked like he was just in from the range and looking for all the cattle herds he should have been able to find and work in the rundown pens. He was a hundred years too late, but it didn't bother him and it sure didn't bother the game colt. Both were long-muscled and lean. The kid, as I would come to refer to him in later conversations, didn't seem to want to talk about his origins and I didn't force it, an Old West "leave the past alone" sort of logic that respected his silence about schooling and family. He was plenty talkative about his colt and friend, though, and recounted as how the adoption team had said the now four-year-old horse was straight out of Sheriff Pat Garrett's string.

I filled him in on the Midnight legacy and his offspring that I had adopted. He salivated at the thought of another horse, but he could only ride one at a time, and cattle work was slow that part of the year. His belly seemed to be sticking to his backbone, so I gave him the twenty I carried when running. I wished I had more to give him. Hell, I'd have given him a thousand bucks if I'd had it on me and hoped it wouldn't change his course in history and his re-creation of olden times. I shook his hand, noticed he was developing a good grip, and, as he started off down the road, I told him about a ranch that might need a good hand. I really didn't know but I felt that a dash of hope might brighten his life for the moment. I asked his name just as a flatbed truck ripped by, disrupting everything and scattering dust. The colt crow-hopped around the ditch a bit, but the kid rode out his mount's nervousness and headed on down the road. I watched the slow progress of that promising hand until he disappeared into a rising fog.

Another year passed, and in 1998 I hauled my four horses, now trained to take a rider and to rope and perform simple tricks like kneeling and sitting and prancing and lying down, to New Mexico. I'd rented a hundred-acre pasture forty miles southwest of Santa Fe, near an old ghost mining camp that had crumbled slowly into dust, and the services of Mark, a friend of a former inmate with whom I had worked in the prison program. An excellent horseman, patient and kind with animals, Mark was firm and intuitive as well. I had to travel and needed a good home for my colt and three fillies and someone who would exercise them and put them to good use. I didn't want them to be merely pasture or corral ornaments. So I hauled the horses to the rented pasture, gave Mark the reins, and showed him how I'd trained them to do tricks and to rope. I'd be back in a year or two, and I made him swear that those horses would never see a chopper or a town or be transported anywhere else.

For a farewell ride in the high country, I met up with Mark on a sunny fall afternoon and loaded the four horses in my stock trailer. Before I had to slip off to Peru on a consulting project, I wanted one last day with Little Midnight, Bell of Midnight, Charlie, the Rhodes Canyon sorrel filly with a full blaze, and Snip, the Mound Springs bay mare with a black mane and tail. That afternoon we rode high in the hills of Bandelier Wilderness. When we returned, I said a sad good-bye to my horses, stepped into my truck, and rolled the window down. I told Mark he could call them his if he took the best of care of them and never let harm come to them. But he needed to fix the fence in the back of the corral, because Little Midnight, no longer little anywhere, was an escapee in training. Mark nodded and slapped his fencing tool against his slim leg. I eased down the dirt road, through the foothills, past Cochiti Pueblo and looked over the hillside, wondering if I'd ever see those horses again. It about broke my heart.

Then I could have sworn that I saw four horses galloping off in the distance, a black one in the rear with his head low, herding a sorrel with a full blaze, a flea-bitten gray, and a tall bay with a black mane and tail. I rubbed my sad eyes a bit, pulled off the road, and grabbed my binoculars to scour the far-off elevations of the Bandelier. The heads of four horses drifted into the emerald green of the hillside and vanished. Could it be that these former ranch horses gone wild had slipped out through the downed fence in Mark's pasture and headed into the wilderness of New Mexico? I put my truck in neutral and let it roll down the five-mile slope toward Albuquerque. All of the past few years faded into the magnificent blue sky of the Land of Enchantment, a phrase coined by Eugene Manlove Rhodes, I reflected. I smiled, long and hard. I was happy. And the horses were safe. I never went back.

That was the last time any White Sands horses changed hands through me. I was done with the project and could credit myself with successfully helping to adopt out nearly two thousand formerly wild horses to good homes. Forced by animal rights groups, we had left about three hundred horses on White Sands for posterity or some other unsound reason, but I knew a follow-up environmental assessment was in the works and I'd bet all the horses would have to be removed soon. Tumor Horse was one of the horses left behind, and from what Les told me later, the big stud was the leader of his own small harem, something he never could have been with all of those tougher stallions ruling the range. Maybe he and his family would live out their lives on that rough land surviving as they have for about fifty-five million years—the oldest surviving land mammals.

To tell the truth, I felt wistful about the whole rescue, a little sad about moving those living legends off of the land that was their birthright. I was relieved that we had done it safely, which was my only real agenda in the whole operation.

One year later . . .
Les Gililland was as mad as he'd ever been. He hit the brakes and skidded to a stop feet before the rim of the Oscura Peak, stepped out into the brilliant day, slammed the door to his government-issue pickup, swearing to himself. Foam formed in the corners of his mouth as if he'd been screaming at someone. He stood two thousand feet above the Tularosa Basin, had a sixty-mile clear view of the

Les and foal, friends forever.
Courtesy of Tony O'Brien.

Jornada, and was forty miles from another human. He had a thick Environmental Assessment Supplement in his hand and, looking at it, he swore out loud, again. He read one line over and over and then threw the folder as hard as he could, out over the cliff, and watched red-eyed as the heavy packet tipped down and tumbled onto the wicked rocks below.

Les leaned back on the hood of his truck, pulled at his cigarette pack, and finding not a single smoke left, crumpled it and stuffed the package in his jean-jacket pocket. Then he buttoned up top to bottom and shivered. It was a cold, calm November afternoon. For almost two years Les had listened to people argue the fate of the remaining 375 horses on the White Sands Missile Range. He wondered if he should jump off after the folder.

Les had just been directed to capture the remaining 375 horses on his old ranch land. He had talked against the plan to Patrick, but in the end, he could quit or get to work. It was that simple.

Great, Les thought. *The horses were having an impact on sensitive habitats.* Who didn't know that? Did any of those horse lovers consider the adverse impact of the Gililland ranch taken by force and never returned to his family? Did they consider the adverse impacts of the regular bombings of White Sands? The horses could have had all the protection any good rancher gives his livestock. The property would have been protected by Smith & Wesson.

According to the new assessment, the only thing the horses brought to the taxpayer was aesthetic value. What other good were they to the Army except as missile range ornaments? Managing the remaining 375 horses was too costly. Compared to what? Les wondered. A three-thousand-dollar toilet seat? The cost of one surface-to-air missile that refused to take off, a missed target in Kuwait, or an M-1 tank that ran out of fuel somewhere in Iraq would pay to control these horses for . . . hell, forever. What about fertility control? From choppers, we could vaccinate the mares. Then they would have only one baby in three years. What was wrong with that? He didn't understand it, but now it didn't matter.

Les spotted movement at the bottom of the escarpment, in the thick mesquite just as it filtered out into the yucca and thorny brush. He eased the binoculars to his livid face, gritted his teeth, and stared at the stallion band. From his perspective, they looked like desert mice. There were the eight big males grazing under the mesquite trees. They were fat. The rains had come, and the fifteen-foot, fernlike mesquite trees, with taproots as much as 175 feet deep, had grown nutritious bean pods, legumes, a good source of protein. Eighty percent of the coyote sustenance in hard times was also from that beanpod, unless they found downed horseflesh to consume. Les couldn't predict the weather, but he could predict that the horses could be captured around water, so he slipped back in behind the steering wheel of his government-issue pickup to get ready for the next roundup. He thought about the stories he'd tell his son, Cory, to keep alive the legend of his family and the horses. Les hit the ignition, backed slowly from edge of the cliff, and started back to finish his mission as a cowboy and range rider.

On March 28, 1999, Les Gililland guided the last of the captured horses onto the floorboards of aluminum horse trailers and off White Sands Missile Range forever. He had lost his land and

his horses, yet he stayed on to see every last one of them saved. He
was the epitome of Rhodes's definition of good cowboy: "*A good
man* . . . meant a man who would do his damnedest every time,
who would help you out of trouble, sickness, danger, debt, disgrace,
or damnation." Jim Eckles of the public relations staff at White
Sands said these would be virtually the last feral horses on the range,
a sad thought when you think of Frank Dobie's view: "The most
beautiful, the most spirited, and the most inspiring creature ever to
print foot on the grasses of America."

Some of the horses left for Lakota Sioux territory and for other,
greener pastures, and most were treated well. Pictures on web sites,
in the quarter horse journal, show a predominance of fox-eared,
gray horses with heavy rumps and muscles. There might even be a
yellow tinge to their once-free flowing manes and tails. Perhaps the
United States Army has finally repaid the debt incurred at Palo
Duro and owed to the Spirit of the Horse.

EPILOGUE

"'Men work together,' I told him from the heart
'Whether they work together or apart.'"
—ROBERT FROST

I n 1995, the only legal option to help the White Sands' wild horses was to remove them. The military clearly stated then that they would not fund a sanctuary to maintain the horses in family groups in perpetuity. Adoptions to private citizens and kind-hearted, self-sufficient sanctuaries was the best alternative. I thanked the military for choosing life over predictable death for the horses.

But that was a military base. On public lands, management of our wild horses is governed by a 1971 law, passed unanimously by the U.S. Congress after an unprecedented public outcry. The Wild Free-Roaming Horse & Burro Act declared:

that wild free-roaming horses and burros are living symbols of the historic and pioneer spirit of the West; that they contribute to the diversity of life forms within the Nation and enrich the lives of the American people; and that these horses and burros are fast disappearing from the American scene. It is the policy of Congress that wild free-roaming horses and burros shall be protected from capture, branding, harassment, or death; and to accomplish this they are to be consid-

ered in the area where presently found, as an integral part of the nat-
ural system of the public lands.

By that original Act of Congress, forty-seven million acres of
public land were mandated to protect wild horses on three hundred
and three management areas. One hundred and two of those herd
areas consisting of twelve-point-five million acres have been
zeroed-out. And 70 percent of the remaining herds are at population levels that may not ensure long-term survival.

In the nineteenth century nearly two million wild horses graced
the western ranges. Those numbers dwindled, and since the early
1970s, two hundred thousand wild horses have been captured and
removed from public lands. Now fewer than twenty five thousand
wild horses eek out a living on the least desirable parts of public
lands in only ten western states.

In addition, nearly as many wild horses are penned in government holding facilities as survive in the wild. Due to a recent
change in the law—the 1971 Act—thousands of the captives are
likely headed for a cold meat-hook.

Regulatory protections for wild horses by the Bureau of Land
Management and its counterpart in the Department of Agriculture
were changed when Senators wrote into the 3,300-page federal
budget a mandate that the BLM sell wild horses deemed unadoptable to the highest bidder. The free-roaming horse was no longer
protected from commercial sale: This quiet legislation hid the commercial fate of publicly owned, wild, free-roaming horses.

Whether labeled wild, domestic, or feral (domestic gone loose),
the natural structure, physiology, and mental ability of all horses are
essentially the same today as they have been for eons. The definition and the state of being of the wild horse is best put by Profes-
sors Kirkpatrick and Fazio where, "The use of the word 'feral,' is
a human connotation . . . It is not scientific, rather descriptive of
association with man only." The free-roaming horse is a form of
wildlife, embedded with the wildness it has always had, and with
natural behavioral patterns as native as any wild animal's. The mor-

phology and biology of this prey species is as sensitive to its surroundings as is any plant, animal, or fish in any ecosystem. The wild horse should be released from the "livestock-gone-loose" designation and protected along with all of our wild species. The misnomer of the horse as a nonnative species has led to its mismanagement on public lands in spite of the good intentions of the wild horse act.

Many wildlife species have overpopulated rangelands in North America and in other parts of the the world. The public acceptance of traditional lethal methods for wildlife population control is changing, especially when the wild horse is considered as such a unique, environmental treasure. The answer is to make a permanent place on public lands for the American wild horse: An American wild horse preservation mandated and permanently funded by the taxpayer and ordered upon our public servants. To the extent where population control is needed, in-the-wild management can be mandated to include redistribution of entire family groups to suitable public lands originally governed under the Wild Free-Roaming Horses & Burros Act and the judicious implementation of continuously improved, independently studied, fertility control methods, with a much lower price tag than the current capture and removal policy. The Shackleford horses set just that precedent.

If the American wild horse is not the existing, original American native, then none of us ought to consider ourselves Americans. Should we allow the Spirit of the West to be eaten, because his existence is too costly or too annoying? These American Spirits should not be owned, they are Nobody's Horses.

ACKNOWLEDGMENTS

This book could not have been written without the inspiration of my son and best friend, Benett, the kind thoughts of my daughter, Alexandra, the love and support of Dr. Dana Lynn Broussard, and, in the beginning, the encouragement of the King of the Cowboys, Ty Murray, and the loving suggestions of my sister Elizabeth Ann. If Leslie Meredith, Senior Editor, Free Press, isn't the best editor ever, I'd be stunned. To each, happy trails.

About the Author

Don Höglund, DVM, is a doctor of veterinary medicine educated at Colorado State University. He is the owner of two companies: International Veterinary Consultants, a national and international animal healthcare and animal welfare consulting firm; Prion Technologies, a new firm providing consultation and technologies for the sanitation and decontamination of such maladies as Mad Cow Disease, Chronic Wasting Disease, and Sheep Scrapie.

Dr. Höglund has provided consultation and equine training services for the Department of Defense, United States Army, the Department of the Interior and Bureau of Land Management, the USDA, Intervet Pharmaceuticals, the Walt Disney Company, and Mr. Michael Eisner. He splits his time between Tulsa, Oklahoma, Fort Collins, Colorado, and Santa Fe, New Mexico.

Visit www.NobodysHorses.com.